DATE DUE

THE POPULIST CONTEXT

RECENT TITLES IN
CONTRIBUTIONS IN AMERICAN HISTORY

Labor Organizations in the United States and Mexico: A History of Their Relations
Harvey A. Levenstein

The Bonus March: An Episode of the Great Depression
Roger Daniels

The Meaning of Freedom of Speech: First Amendment Freedoms from Wilson to FDR
Paul Murphy

Family Law and the Poor: Essays by Jacobus tenBroek
Joel Handler

The Butterfly Caste: A Social History of Pellagra in the South
Elizabeth Etheridge

Bound with Them in Chains: A Biographical History of the Antislavery Movement
Jane H. Pease and William H. Pease

The Eleventh Amendment and Sovereign Immunity
Clyde E. Jacobs

First Freedom: Responses of Alabama's Blacks to Emancipation and Reconstruction
Peter Kolchin

California and the Dust Bowl Migration
Walter J. Stein

Purity Crusade: Sexual Morality and Social Control, 1868-1900
David Pivar

Victor Berger and the Promise of Constructive Socialism, 1910-1920
Sally M. Miller

THE POPULIST CONTEXT
RURAL VERSUS URBAN POWER
ON A GREAT PLAINS FRONTIER

STANLEY B. PARSONS

Contributions in American History Number 22

DISCARD

GREENWOOD PRESS, INC.
Westport, Connecticut • London, England

Library of Congress Cataloging in Publication Data

Parsons, Stanley B
    The Populist context.

    (Contributions in American history, no. 22)
    Bibliography: p.
    1. People's Party of the United States. Nebraska.
I. Title.
JK2374.N2 1877   329'.88'009782   72-824
ISBN 0-8371-6392-7

Library of Congress Catalog Card Number: 72-824
ISBN: 0-8371-6392-7
First published in 1973

Greenwood Press, Inc., Publishing Division
51 Riverside Avenue, Westport, Connecticut 06880
Manufactured in the United States of America
Designed by Vance Weaver Composition, Inc.

For Frances, Stanley, and May,
who reflected much that was good
of village America

CONTENTS

List of Tables ix
List of Figures xi
Acknowledgments xiii
Introduction xv

Part I
State Politics

1 The Politics of Economic Development 3
2 The Farmers' Complaint 22

Part II
The Structure of Power

3 The Village 35
4 The Political Leadership of the Village 48
5 The Populists and the Village 60
6 The Populists in County and State Politics 76

Part III
Cross Pressures

7 Cultural Conflict During the Populist Era 101
8 The Nebraska Populists: A Statistical Description 121

Part IV
Conclusions

9 The Agrarian Myth and Political Realities 145

Notes	149
Appendix	177
Bibliography	181
Index	195

List of Tables

1 Characteristics of the first quartile of Republican strength,   14
   1880–1888.

2 Characteristics of the first quartile of Democratic strength,   18
   1880–1888.

3 Iowa and Nebraska: Comparison of freight rates per 100   23
   pounds.

4 Chicago grain prices and Omaha-Chicago freight rates.   24

5 Commodity price differential between central Nebraska and   27
   Chicago markets.

6 Relationship between increasing mortgage debt and increas-   28
   ing number of mortgages, Hayes County, Nebraska.

7 Interest rates and commission rates, Nebraska, 1880–1892.   29

8 Farm equipment prices, 1880–1890.   30

9 Increase in Nebraska population, 1879–1889.   41

10 Occupational structure of the Nebraska legislature,   49
   1877–1899.

11 Residence of Democratic and Republican county leaders,   49
   1888–1893.

12 Membership in Nebraska House of Representatives by occu-   98
   pational group and political party.

13 Pierson product-moment correlation coefficients between   127
   Populist vote for governor, 1890, and selected economic,
   cultural and electoral variables.

14   Residential and ethnic voting patterns using sample precinct   129
     data: forty-six precincts, Nebraska, 1888-1900.

15   Voting and income data by precinct: Hamilton county,   131
     Nebraska (Presidential election of 1892).

16   Selected issue areas and the number of roll calls considered   133
     in each area.

17   Occupational groups in the Nebraska legislature.   133

18   Mean disagreement scores for all categoric groups: major   134
     issue areas.

19   Disagreement scores by categorical groups: railroad issues,   134
     1891 house.

20   Railroad issues: distribution of categorical groupings by   135
     scale position.

21   Cultural issues: distribution of categorical groupings by   136
     scale position.

22   1891 Nebraska house disagreement scores: twelve education   137
     issues.

23   Interest roll calls: distribution of categorical groupings by   138
     scale position.

24   1891 Sugar roll calls: distribution of categorical groupings   138
     by scale position.

25   1891 State institution: distribution of categorical groupings   138
     by scale position.

26   1891 Medical care roll calls: distribution of categorical   139
     groupings by scale position.

27   1891 Militia roll calls: distribution of categorical groupings   139
     by scale position.

28   1883 Railroad issues: distribution of categorical groupings   140
     by scale position.

List of Figures

1	Republican tendencies, 1880-1888.	13
2	Democratic tendencies, 1880-1888.	19
3	German, Irish and Bohemian county percentages, by quartiles.	20
4	Sample counties, Nebraska, 1890.	36
5	Commodity prices and the Republican vote.	61
6	Independent vote, 1890, by quartile.	86
7	Hamilton county: percentage of vote for governor (a sample Populist county).	87
8	Decrease in Republican voting strength, 1888-1890.	88
9	Cuming county: percentage of vote for governor (a sample Democratic county).	89
10	Nebraska: percentage of vote received by major political parties in gubernatorial elections.	92
11	Fusion tendencies, 1894-1900.	94
12	Howard county: percentage of vote for governor (a sample Populist county).	95
13	Douglas county (Omaha): percentage of vote for governor.	96
14	Scotts Bluff county: percentage of vote for governor (a sample Republican county).	97

Acknowledgments

A major influence on this monograph has been that of Allan G. Bogue, whose interdisciplinary interests and scholarly example greatly influenced my approach and method. Lewis Atherton offered suggestions that helped expand the scope of my original dissertation, and Samuel P. Hays added new dimensions to my understanding of politics. My colleagues at the University of Missouri, Kansas City, Lawrence Larsen, Robert Branyan, and Herman Hattaway, offered stylistic advice during departmental seminars. James C. Olson drew from his knowledge of Nebraska to make important factual and organizational suggestions, while Richard Jensen, Robert Zemsky, and James Hilty acquainted me with the values and dangers of legislative roll-call analysis. Specific criticism of the content of the work was generously extended by two fellow students of Nebraska populism, David S. Trask, whose dissertation emphasizes the cultural elements in Nebraska politics during the 1880s and 1890s, and Robert Cherny, whose work relates to populism and progressivism. Ross Stephens and Dale Neuman of the UMKC Political Science Department made significant contributions to the conceptual and methodological aspects of the work.

Financial aid has been generously extended at critical times by Mr. and Mrs. H. S. Black of Deadwood, South Dakota. Dean Wesley Dale of the UMKC Graduate College obtained several important grants, and a grant secured by Dean Edwin Westermann of the College of Arts and Science made possible a summer fellowship at the Inter-University Consortium for Political Research at the University of Michigan.

The courteous and informed cooperation of the staff at the Nebraska State Historical Society greatly facilitated the research on the project. Other libraries that made their research facilities available include the State Historical Society of Missouri, the Wisconsin State Historical Society, the Kansas State Historical Society, the University of Missouri Libraries, and the British Museum. Mr. Robert Newlin and the staff of the UMKC computer center were helpful and generous of their time. A decade of faithful research assistants, including Tom Daily, Stephen Herman, and Stanley Black Parsons, did much of the leg work for the statistical parts of the study.

Mrs. Sharon Steiner and Mrs. Clair Hildebrand typed the manuscript in several of its forms, and finally my wife, Shirley Black Parsons, gave encouragement and consolation during the years of research and writing. I am greatly indebted to them all.

Introduction

Throughout the waning decades of the nineteenth century, the western farmer seemed a chronic revolutionary. From the Grangers and the Greenbackers of the 1870s to the Populists of the 1890s, many fervently believed that they were not getting their fair share of the rewards of the new industrialism. Just as so many passionate orators claimed, the rapid settlement of the frontier had not brought affluence to all of its inhabitants, and the farmers, together with later generations of historians, attempted to determine some of the multitude of factors responsible for this dilemma. The western farmer's golden age, if it had ever existed, seemed to be ebbing away in the 1890s when many midwestern and southern farmers mounted their most determined effort to maintain a parity with more successful groups in American society. This great effort, populism, brought vivid drama to the plains and prairies of the western Midwest; there was an endless parade of farm wagons down "O" Street in Lincoln, Nebraska, on a hot Fourth of July in 1890; the "raise less corn and more hell" type of rhetoric of Mary Elizabeth Lease; and the emotional "cross of gold" speech of that sympathetic Democrat, William Jennings Bryan. Damned by some for their irrelevant attempt to maintain an agrarian America, praised by others for being in the vanguard of the reform movement, populism has become one of the most controversial movements in American political history.

For many years, most historians held that populism constituted a part of the great stream of liberal, anti-big business reform which culminated in the New Deal. Populist platform statements in favor of the Australian ballot, the direct election of Senators, the income tax, and railroad regulation were cited to prove that Populists stood as the predecessors of the Progressives and the New Dealers. Generally, the Populist reforms that failed to become laws were forgotten, as were their numerous socialistic and nativistic tendencies.[1] After the publication of Richard Hofstadter's *Age of Reform* in 1955, some of the earlier enthusiasms concerning the Populist movement subsided. No longer did Populists stand as unsullied visionaries, who, fifty years ahead of their time, anticipated the reforms of the 1930s. Many critics pointed to the less admirable aspects of the movement, and some even went to the extreme of branding them native American fascists. By the 1960s, the word "populist" itself came into popular usage as a pejorative term connoting an irrational mass movement.[2]

In contrast to the enthusiasms of some popular commentators and ideologues, most professional historians have taken a more thoughtful position between the liberal and revisionist interpretations. From Walter T. K. Nugent's *The Tolerant Populists* (1963) to Sheldon Hackney's *Populism to Progressivism in Alabama* (1969), historians, with few exceptions, have avoided the extremes of popular writers and have clarified many of the positions of both liberals and revisionists. Nugent demonstrated that revisionist arguments of Populist racism were largely overdrawn, while Hackney illustrated the weaknesses inherent in the liberal Populist to Progressive reform continuum. Through such valuable studies, the earlier, more one-dimensional explanations of populism have been significantly modified. The basic concerns, however, have remained largely the same. Were the Populists really liberal, or were they really the predecessors of the New Deal?[3]

Contemporary liberal and revisionist attempts to evaluate populism from the reform perspective have added to the richness and diversity of the interpretation of American history. A reform-oriented synthesis, however, need not be the only concern of historians. Social scientists of many persuasions, from Frederick Jackson Turner to Robert A. Dahl, have posed questions which can take populism out of the reform synthesis and place it in other analytical perspectives. One of the most fruitful of these is the contemporary concern about the nature and structure of power. Although John D. Hicks' *Populist Revolt* represents the classic liberal synthesis concerning the nature of populism, he includes an important reference to the frontier theory of Frederick Jackson Turner. Hicks' concern, however, is the relationship between the closing in of the frontier and the genesis of populism, not that between the structure of society in newly settled areas and the protest movement itself. Turnerian interest with frontier democracy can become helpful as a point of departure for a study of populism when it is used in conjunction with the current literature dealing with power relationships in many different environments.

Diverging from the liberal concept that power in the late nineteenth century rested with an industrial elite, contemporary students of politics often see power as held by a fluctuating number of conflicting interest groups. Robert Dahl in *Who Governs?* emphasizes this fluid, pluralistic structure of American politics. Dahl and his followers, however, use twentieth-century subject matter for their political model. Few would insist that twentieth-century models would necessarily fit nineteenth-century reality.[4]

Although historians have never methodically attempted to describe the political structure in the late nineteenth century at the state and local levels, several have treated the subject in conjunction with broader studies. Robert Dykstra in *The Cattle Towns* dealt with the structure of politics at the town and county level in Kansas, while Merle Curti in *Making of an American Community* carefully analyzed the political structure of a single Wisconsin county. Both leave the impression of a more pluralistic politics being practiced during the period than do many of the earlier liberal historians.[5]

A study of the structure of politics depends on many elements and different levels of abstraction and activity. Not the least important of these are the personal and group interactions at the state, county, and even the precinct level. The farmer's complaints and ideology have been widely explained and evaluated, but his relationship with other groups at a grass-roots level have only been casually observed. Analysis of the political structure in the late nineteenth century, then, can delineate those groups which joined or fought the Populist movement. Most historians are familiar with the Populists' descriptions of their enemies, but the epithets "plutocrat" and "corporation" are vague terms for one's opponents, just as are the terms "wild-eyed radical" and "anarchist."[6] The structure of political conflict during the Populist era needs to be more rigorously drawn. Who were the Populists and who were their enemies? What were the local interests and ambitions that helped influence political loyalties of the time? These questions can be answered only by grass-roots political studies; their answers will reveal the farmers as they existed in society next to other social and economic groups—the businessmen, railroaders, speculators, and industrialists of the era.[7]

The structure power of the Populist era has been neglected for several reasons. First, most historians find analysis of politics at the state and national level more suited to their methodological techniques. Metropolitan newspapers, letters, or memoirs of nationally known figures offer solid ground on which to base research. On the other hand, grass-roots political activity during the last decades of the nineteenth century is difficult to investigate because of the scarcity and unevenness of available material. Public records are missing or have been destroyed. County editors either omitted important political information from their columns, or reported it in the most haphazard manner. Many Populists referred to the conspiracy of silence practiced by the Republican and Democratic editors of Nebraska, who hoped that populism would fade away if they ignored it. A similar practice apparently applied to the Farmers Alliances themselves. On some occasions, the editors of the county papers would report county conventions in great detail and print a complete list of precinct delegates. Then, for the following two or three years, they might relegate similar conventions to a short paragraph. The county editor's need for time and advertising space serve to limit the contemporary historians' systematic study of local politics in the late nineteenth century. Because of these factors, anyone attempting to reconstruct a local political situation is on less sure ground, methodologically speaking, than the student of modern political behavior. Some sources and techniques, however, are available for a contemporary study of local politics during the Populist era. Power relationships can be reconstructed from the social, political, and economic items in the county newspaper. Voting statistics to the precinct level are available in some counties. Census manuscripts supply a cultural and economic description of most citizens. When used and analyzed, these sources show important aspects of political life as it existed in the villages and rural areas of the plains during the last decades of the nineteenth century.[8]

The state of Nebraska was chosen as representative of the behavior of the people in the Populist states of the Great Plains. This decision was taken knowing full well that variations in political behavior will undoubtedly occur from state to state and that conclusions based on Nebraska can serve as only tentative models of other plains states that embraced the Populist cause.

Populism has been effectively studied in terms of the complaints and platforms of the farmers, the pronouncements of the elite, and the programs and accomplishments of the movement. This study is primarily concerned with the political context of populism, with the political structure of the era, and with the power relationships between competing groups at the state and local level. Other aspects of the movement, such as its economic or cultural origins, will receive somewhat less attention, not because they are less important but because they have previously received more scholarly interest. In some respects, though, this is more than a study of populism. Hopefully, it explains something about the American farmer's failure to exercise effectively his political and economic power during the last half of the nineteenth century and to make this failure more understandable to us who live in the more pluralistic and democratic society of the late twentieth century.

PART I
STATE POLITICS

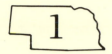

The Politics of
Economic Development

During the thirty-five years following the Civil War, the United States emerged as the greatest economic power in the world. The estimated property value increased from $16 billion in 1860 to $89 billion in 1900, while the population nearly tripled.[1] The difficulties inherent in such rapid industrialization were magnified by a change in the structure of the country, a change from a nation of farmers to a nation of city-dwelling industrial workers and businessmen. Because the East was the cradle of industrialism, it frequently provides the focal point of the history of the nation, while the West and South are often labeled agrarian or colonial areas and sometimes are depicted as leading a holding action against a surging, eastern-dominated industrialism. Although there is little doubt about the East's economic dominance, it must be recognized that both the West and South participated in the amazing growth of the era. Business, industrial, and speculative interests in these sections adopted the methods and goals of their eastern mentors and very often enjoyed as spectacular rewards as did their eastern brethren. The West, to vast numbers of business and commercial groups, was much more than a haven for the yeoman farmer. It offered vast opportunities for speculative growth, as well as opportunities arising from a dynamic industrialism. Somewhere, though, in the thought of many Americans, the West became synonymous with "farmer," and the lives, interests, and aspirations of other groups existed only as a foil for the supposedly dominant agrarian interest. Although this assumption has sometimes reached a

3

level of an "agrarian myth," farmers actually played only a minor role in the political affairs in the state of Nebraska. Before the farmers' revolt swept the state, Nebraska politics usually revolved around the competing interests of semi-isolated communities, ambitious groups of men, or cultural antagonisms between the many different ethnic and religious groups that had settled in the state. No significant differences in economic philosophy divided the Republican and Democratic parties; both actively engaged in providing an economic climate for maximum growth and speculative possibilities rather than designing programs to meet the needs of the farmer. The significant bills introduced into the legislature in the 1880s, with the exception of those associated with prohibition and other cultural issues, deal almost entirely with providing a climate for economic expansion.

The most effective leadership in providing for the economic growth of Nebraska during these years was found in the Republican party, which had dominated Nebraska politics since the Civil War and had brought about a massive change in American voting power. Since most of Nebraska's population of native birth came from states that fought with the Union, they voted overwhelmingly Republican, and waving the bloody shirt proved the best argument a politician could use in appealing to them. The strength of the Grand Army of the Republic, the linking of the old veterans with the Republican party, and the obsession of the population to continually relive the war gave the Republicans a lead in any political contest.

The northern, Republican, native born settlers were also overwhelmingly Protestant and pietistic in their religious convictions. For many, these connections were nominal, but for others their religious beliefs carried a stern pietistic commitment to spread their own moral code to other groups in the society. Their utopian concern for the righteousness of others added a moralistic fringe to the Republican party, antagonized Nebraskans of a Catholic-ritualistic persuasion, and proved perplexing to the more economically oriented political leaders of the party.[2] Originally the Nebraska Territory had been Democratically inclined, but the new waves of pioneers who settled the central and southwestern counties were overwhelmingly Republican. It was these sections of the state, not the more politically balanced eastern counties, that made Nebraska so overwhelmingly Republican after the Civil War. General John Thayer, Republican governor of Nebraska from 1887 to 1891, became a political force in the state primarily because of his war record and his long association with the GAR. Significantly, Thayer gave added strength to the already high Republican vote in the newly settled southwestern counties when he first ran for governor in 1886.[3]

Aside from the tariff issue, and a somewhat greater emphasis on federal power, the Republican party had little to distinguish its economic program from that of the Democrats. Economic development and capital procurement were the major concerns of the leaders of both parties during the 1880s. Inevitably, their interest in agrarian reform programs such as the regulation of freight rates or the enactment of usury laws was tempered by the feeling that the beneficial effects of agrarian reforms must be weighed against possible losses of eastern capital. During the booming 1880s, this was a particularly difficult situation since all of Nebraska's leaders were heavily committed to economic expansion, but, at the same time, had real sympathy for the farm population.

Although there was unanimity among Nebraska Republicans over the primacy of economic development, there were different degrees of emphasis. Individual ambitions and local interests played an important role in these differences and make it difficult to delineate factional disputes among Republicans. There was, however, some continuity of factionalism within the Republican party; within certain limits, it is possible to delineate three fairly consistent factions. First, there were those Republicans who emphasized the beneficial role of the railroads. Among this group were employees of the great railroad companies in the state, inhabitants of cities and villages closely dependent upon a particular railroad company, and many citizens who felt that transportation was the key to further economic expansion. John M. Thurston, counsel for the Union Pacific, was the outstanding example from among this group. Second, some Republicans, such as Edward Rosewater, editor of the *Omaha Bee,* felt that railroads had acquired a disproportionate share of political and economic power in the state. Rosewater and his faction tended to view Nebraska politics in terms of a struggle against railroad control. The third and largest group within the Republican party, often village or urban business and professional men, were those leaders who directed their primary allegiance toward their own interests and to the party itself. They did not discount inordinate railroad power, but they also realized the vital role railroads played in Nebraska's economic development. Caught in this dilemma, they constantly hedged and shifted their position, and on specific occasions threw their decisive power to either wing of the party. They were the cautious reformers who delayed effective railroad regulation in the 1880s.[4]

Of the factions in Nebraska Republicanism, the "railroaders" attracted by far the most attention. Thurston consistently occupied positions of leadership in this wing of the party. He had arrived in Omaha as a struggling young attorney in the early 1870s, and his ability and political interests soon won him a seat in the state legislature, where he became closely associated with another rising young Republican, Church Howe of Otoe County. Howe had considerable influence over Thurston's early career and was instrumental in his rise to prominence in the party. Howe was then a lobbyist for the Missouri Pacific and he helped Thurston secure his position as assistant attorney for the Union Pacific.[5]

Thurston soon became the leader of the railroad faction in the Republican party. Although many contemporaries viewed this group as a monolithic force within the party, the railroaders remained far from cohesive because they divided their loyalties among the various railroads in the state. Essentially, Thurston represented the economic and political interests of the Union Pacific Railroad Company and the city of Omaha. Because of his association with Omaha, he gave up his early prohibitionist sentiments and joined those partisans of Omaha who felt that prohibition would ruin their retail trade.[6]

Being a partisan of Omaha and a champion of the Union Pacific were synonymous in Thurston's mind, just as they were to Omaha's Democratic politicians. As assistant to the Union Pacific's chief counsel, Andrew Jackson Poppleton, a Democrat, he became an active lobbyist for the railroad. By 1889 Edward Rosewater accurately pointed out that Thurston had so effectively carried out the legislative policies of his superior that he was promoted to chief counsel of the railroad. Although upon succeeding Poppleton he swore to abandon his role in "oil room" politics and devote himself to the legal business of the company, Thurston soon became the most active politician in Nebraska. Through the use of passes, political and economic allies, corporate patronage and his great organizing ability, Thurston headed the best organized political group in the state. His superior in the Union Pacific hierarchy, Charles Francis Adams, had vigorously condemned railroad politics in Massachusetts, but condoned Union Pacific politics in Nebraska.[7]

Although Nebraska politics of the 1800s did not revolve around ideological differences between the contending political parties or factions, Thurston held to the few dogmas that distinguished Republicans from Democrats. He defended the protective tariff and the GAR just as did most other Republicans,[8] but the railroad received his greatest loyalty. At the same time when insurgent Republicans were blaming many of the farmers' problems on excessive railroad rates, Thurston claimed that rates represented bedrock figures. He attributed the farmers' hardships to the fact that the steamship companies charged high rates from New York to European ports.[9]

Personalities and ambitions played a great part in the politics of the period, and Thurston became allied with Omaha, the Union Pacific, and railroad Republicans for other than economic reasons. Chief among these was his personal feud with the colorful, antimonopolist editor of the *Omaha Bee*, Edward Rosewater. In 1882 Rosewater's journalistic competitor in Omaha, *The Republican,* attempted to win an Omaha circulation war by claiming that Rosewater had been a rebel and a spy during the Civil War. Rosewater immediately sued for libel and Thurston defended the editors of *The Republican*. After a colorful trial Thurston won the editor's acquittal, but he also won the undying animosity of the usually vindictive Rosewater.[10]

Despite the bitter attacks of his factional antagonists, Thurston became the most important Republican politician in Nebraska after the mid-1880s. His great organizing abilities were used with success at the state level as chairman of the Republican League. In 1888 he served as temporary chairman of the Republican National Convention where he gave a seconding speech for Benjamin Harrison.[11] Although Thurston identified closely with the interests of the Union Pacific, he did see the crisis of the western farmer and of western Republicanism, and he pleaded for recognition of their condition before the eastern Republican leaders in the spring of 1892.[12] Because he consistently supported James G. Blaine at Republican national conventions, Thurston never received a cabinet post similar to that of his Democratic counterpart, the Bourbon leader, J. Sterling Morton.[13]

Similar to Thurston in outlook, but emphasizing the needs and aspirations of Lincoln and the Burlington Railroad rather than Omaha and the Union Pacific Railroad was Charles H. Gere, editor of the powerful *State Journal*. Gere had gone to Lincoln as private secretary to Governor David Butler and remained to become the city's most effective champion. For years competing towns tried to wrest the state capital from Lincoln, and Gere, together with other city fathers, successfully stalled these attempts. They acquired railroads by generous bond offerings, promoted factories, and defended the university. The Republican party in Lancaster County became the major instrument for Gere's plans, plans which were approved and aided by the Burlington Railroad Company.[14] Most of Gere's programs for Lincoln met with astounding success, and, by the end of the century, Lincoln was one of the few state capitals which could boast that it was the home of both the state university and the state prison.

The most important group within the Republican party was comprised of those leaders who thought of the party as a vehicle for winning elections, governing the state, and, in this course, advancing their own local and personal interests. Most of these men had little direct interest in promoting railroads. They accepted passes and fees for legal work, lobbying, or their goodwill, but they were not basically railroad men. When the time came when the railroads proved to be unpopular with the electorate and thus hindered the fortunes of the party, these men became cautious reformers. Their position was not particularly cynical or hypocritical, for they, more than many of the more dedicated reformers, realized the almost magical role the railroads played in the development of the state. Contrary to the belief that poor farmers were the most rebellious, some of the most avid pro-railway sentiment came from sections of the state which were poor, but desperately in need of railroads.[15]

The career of Church Howe provides the best illustration of the professional Republican leader. Howe lived on a farm near Peru in Nemaha County where he had moved shortly after the Civil War. He entered politics through the Grange and in 1872 became the Granger candidate for the state legislature. In 1876 he became a Granger state senator, but shortly afterward joined the Republicans because, pragmatically, "he was tired of setting up with a corpse."[16] Similar successes marked his political career with the Republicans, as he was reelected state senator in 1882 and 1884, and in the latter year became a member of the Republican National Committee. Howe was in and out of the legislature thereafter and showed a remarkable flexibility in his political convictions.[17]

Early in his career, Howe had associated with the reform elements in the state. In 1881 he introduced a bill into the legislature to prohibit legislators from using railroad passes,[18] but shortly after he changed his whole attitude and opposed the most significant bill for railroad regulation introduced in the early 1880s. Just as most other village leaders, Howe associated the welfare of Nebraska with the welfare of the railroads. When speaking against a railroad regulatory bill in 1881, he remarked:

> During the whole of this session of the legislature, the position which I have taken in the railroad question has been that the interests of the people and the interests of the railroads have been identical. . . . Regulations made by these corporations under the necessities of commercial law are lower and better than the house has the right or power to make, for they give to us the aid of the lines east of us, which we cannot otherwise obtain. . . . I believe this bill to be useless, inoperative, and unconstitutional. . . .[19]

Some of Howe's opposition to railroad regulation sprang from sources other than subservience to the railroads. A case in point is a bill introduced in 1883, which would have required railroads to build a depot at any point at which two railroads crossed. Howe led the opposition to the bill because such a crossing existed but a few miles from his home town, Auburn. If a depot were to be built at the crossing, business would be taken away from his village.

The Auburn town fathers had previously foreseen the problem and contracted with the railroad that no depot should be built at the crossing. Howe received the stigma for the defeat of the "reform" bill, but the motive behind his opposition was the promotion of village interests and not railroad dictation.[20]

During the mid-1880s, Howe moved closer to the railroads and in the process became the chief target of Edward Rosewater and his *Omaha Bee.* Rosewater, a master of invective, kept up a steady stream of accusations against Howe throughout the decade, and it was primarily his influence that caused Howe to lose his race for Congress in 1886. According to Rosewater, Howe was the chief distributor of Union Pacific passes in Southeastern Nebraska and the chief force behind the defeat of railway regulatory legislation during the 1885 session of the legislature.[21]

During the period of promise and growth that characterized the great Nebraska boom of the 1880s, Howe remained closely allied with the railroads. As president pro-tem of the state senate, he opposed the election of the railway commission by stating that the cost of the change would be too great for Nebraska's meager resources. Most observers felt that an elected commission would be more difficult for the railroads to control.[22] He opposed a liberalization of railroad employer liability benefits and finally displayed a poor bit of political timing when he accepted the position of vice president of the Missouri Pacific Railroad.[23]

Despite his railroad sympathies, Church Howe was first and foremost a professional politician in the Republican party. When the boom collapsed and the storm of populism broke upon the state in 1890, Howe became one of the first of the Republican politicians to appreciate the need for a change in party policy. After reaching a long-sought goal of being the chairman of the state convention, he shocked the assembly by vividly pointing out the dangers of the Populist movement to his party. His use of the phrase "the old ship is leaking" in referring to the state GOP became the watchword of those within the party who cried for reform.[24] Howe then helped draft the "progressive" Republican platform in Nemaha County, a platform which many contemporaries called hypocritical, but illustrated that in order to preserve their power Howe and the party were willing to turn on many of their former supporters. The Nemaha platform endorsed the Australian ballot, a more stringent usury law, equal taxes, railroad regulation, unlimited coinage of silver, and protective tariff.[25]

Howe's reaction to the events of 1890 was more positive than popular clichés spoken to avoid political oblivion. He resigned his vice presidency of the Missouri Pacific Railway Company and said in a very timely statement:

> Again I am tired of being part of a machine. A western rail-
> road official is like a chessman and is moved about at the
> pleasure of the players who reside east of the Allegheny
> mountains. He is part of a machine operated from Boston
> and New York and loses all his individuality in his efforts
> to do the bidding of the eastern managers. If the entire
> management of the railroad property in the West was left
> with local officials much of the friction would be obvi-
> ated. . . . most of the western managers are men of broad
> views, but their hands are tied and they can't do anything.
> The eastern owners reserve for themselves the right to dic-
> tate rates. . . .[26]

Although Howe's political enemies were skeptical of his spectacular conversion, Howe put the success of the party before any allegiance to the railroads and became a true reformer. In 1891 he publicly tore up his railroad
pass and later became "the most able and prominent champion of reform in
either branch of the 1893 legislature."[27] The *Omaha World Herald*'s political
columnist, "Al Fairbrother," in commenting on Howe's about-face during
1890, still thought of Howe as a Missouri Pacific man but noted that Howe
had served the people well by voting for bills which required a two-thirds
vote on railway bonds, Nebraska citizenship for all detectives operating
within the state, an 8 percent maximum interest charge, and, a bill to ease
the requirements for securing a liquor license in Omaha.[28]

Howe's perambulations can be extended to many of Nebraska's leading
Republicans. They were interested in the electoral success of the party, but,
unlike Thurston, they did not maintain allegiance to the railroads after it
became impolitic to do so. They had never been simply bribed as the Rose-
waterites constantly asserted: rather they, as Howe, felt that the best interests of the state were being served by the expansion and prosperity of the
railroads.

Edward Rosewater inherited the remains of the old Anti-Monopoly party
of the early 1880s and with Charles H. Van Wyck led the "reform" wing of
Nebraska Republicanism during the last two decades of the nineteenth century. A Bohemian Jew, Rosewater arrived in the United States in time to
serve as a telegrapher during the Civil War. After the war, he emigrated to
Omaha and shortly afterward became the editor of the *Omaha Bee,* which he
soon built into the dominant newspaper in the state. As editor of this dominant paper, Rosewater demanded a major role in the Republican party, a
role which both the railwaymen and many of the small-town editors and

businessmen were not ready to grant him.[29] Nebraska politics, as described by Rosewater, was a battle between the representative of the "people" (himself) and those who had sold out to the "corporate" or railroad interests (anyone who opposed him). Rosewater seldom attacked the railroads directly; he concentrated instead on those Republican politicians whom he felt were in league with the railroads. Some of Rosewater's analysis corresponded to the reality of the situation, for leaders like Thurston were inextricably tied to railroad interests, but others felt that, for all their vices, the railroads were contributing to the best interests of the state. Some of the division within Republican ranks resulted from Rosewater's combative disposition. As one writer put it, he possessed a "native tendency to ascribe either unworthy motives or downright stupidity to [his] opponents," and once he made an enemy he could seldom be reconciled to him again.[30]

Rosewater did not join in some of the other aspects of reform associated with the era. In 1889, for example, he crankily engaged in baiting the state legislatures on the grounds that it had spent too much of the taxpayer's money:

> The reckless extravagence [sic] of the legislature knows no
> bounds. There is no limit to the avarice of the members, no
> restraint to their plundering passions. Every movement indi-
> cates a close conspiracy, a boodle combine to throw open
> the treasury and squander the contents. The boldest and
> most shameless raid on the state treasury is that of the
> Lincoln insane asylum. This institution with proper man-
> agement should be self-sustaining. Every county is obliged
> to care for the inmates; there is no escape from it.

After establishing the fact that boodlers conspired to rob the people simply because the institution was not self-supporting, he launched his attack in all directions at once:

> In all other directions the raid on the taxpayers is equally
> terrific and appalling. Over one hundred thousand dollars
> has been recommended for building a wing to the Nebraska
> asylum, a job which can be deferred for two years without
> any injury to the state or its unfortunates. The Peru normal
> school comes in for fifty-seven thousand nine hundred dol-
> lars. If one half dozen or more normal school bills now pend-
> ing should pass, it is impossible to estimate the burdens
> which will be heaped upon the taxpayer in the coming years.[31]

Rosewater's concern for frugality in public office, and his attack on public expenditures in general, illustrated that the reformer also played politics. He also found it expedient for several years to keep from any direct attacks on the nativistic American Protective Association. Only when the APA's objectives directly came into conflict with his own did he condemn nativism in Omaha.[32] As is often the case the reformer contained some of the crank.

Although Rosewater occasionally let personal animosities and ambitions determine his political position, he and Van Wyck represented the reform wing of Nebraska Republicanism. His strength was comparatively independent of any organized group, for county editors as a whole resented the power of his paper and worked against his building an organized following.[33] When political and economic conditions became unstable, however, the *Bee* was able to unite with temporary reform groups to influence great numbers of dissident voters to vote for the candidate who won Rosewater's approval.[34]

Although Rosewater led in the pre-Populist reform movement, he was far removed from the pure agrarian orientation of the farmers. He usually found it expedient to unite with regular village and urban Republicans in their desire to promote the economic growth of the state. In most cases, he directed his antagonism only toward the Thurston wing of the party or against his personal enemies. Like most other Republican and Democratic leaders prior to the Populist revolt, he was too involved in the development of the state to question seriously the validity of the status quo. His crusades were usually directed at his personal enemies, and his goal was often no more revolutionary than a plea for honesty.[35]

Throughout the 1880s the Republican party provided the only political leadership for the state of Nebraska. Although the Republicans represented a wide range of interest groups and often became embroiled in the cultural antagonisms of the era, the party and its leadership were primarily interested in rapid economic development. Figure 1 and Table 1 illustrate the strength of the party in the central and western portions of the state, areas which were experiencing rapid growth and needed the technology and capital of the East. In relation to the Democrats, the strongly Republican counties were somewhat more rural, somewhat less affluent, and considerably more Protestant than their political rivals. By the end of the decade, many farmers in these counties were the most vulnerable in the state to the tides of fortune on the frontier.

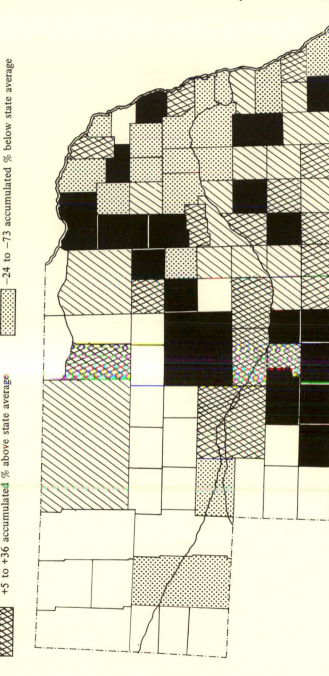

+37 to +66 accumulated % above state average

+5 to +36 accumulated % above state average

+4 to −23 accumulated % below state average

−24 to −73 accumulated % below state average

SOURCE: *The Nebraska Blue Book and Historical Register, 1918* (Lincoln, 1918). Political tendencies were computed for each county by determining that county's deviation from the state average percent of each party in gubernatorial elections. Deviations were then summed and divided into quartiles.

Figure 1: Republican Tendencies, 1880-1888

Table 1: CHARACTERISTICS OF THE FIRST QUARTILE OF
REPUBLICAN STRENGTH, 1880-1888

County	Rural Population per County	Catholic Population per County	Value of Farm Products per Farm	Arable Land in Wheat per County
Antelope	80.2%	5.5%	$621	4.60%
Boone	80.4	4.5	433	5.90
Burt	68.7	4.1	845	3.03
Clay	65.8	6.4	791	2.22
Custer	91.2	3.9	436	6.30
Frontier	62.5	6.1	396	7.48
Furnas	75.2	4.1	450	8.40
Harlan	73.7	4.9	502	10.90
Hitchcock	76.4	7.8	283	7.49
Knox	80.6	14.9	339	5.73
Lancaster	24.8	7.4	546	0.67
Pawnee	72.9	7.1	746	0.62
Phelps	71.0	2.2	679	15.18
Red Willow	64.4	6.3	317	9.49
Sherman	89.5	11.2	387	9.53
Valley	71.5	9.3	445	8.96
Republican average	73.91	6.93	523.33	6.46
(Democratic average)	(60.40)	(15.42)	(701.00)	(5.65)

Source: U.S., Department of Interior, Bureau of the Census, *Eleventh Decennial Census of the United States, 1890.* Statistics were taken from vol. 16 (population) and vol. 18 (economic statistics).

The internal structure of the Democratic party prior to the Populist era was less complex than that of the Republican. There was no consistent economic reform group in the Democracy, and Democratic politics usually revolved around the personalities and ambitions of two men, J. Sterling Morton and Dr. George S. Miller. Despite a marked lack of concern for the farmer, the Democrats gained significant strength during the 1880s. This was not because they faced issues which were important to Nebraska's farm population, but because they were the happy beneficiaries of German defections from Republicanism resulting from cultural antagonisms, such as prohibition, woman's suffrage, and the use of the English language in parochial schools.

Nebraska's Democrats were even more village- and city-oriented than their Republican antagonists. Their great gains in strength during the 1880s came in Omaha and from the more prosperous areas in the state, while the areas of farm discontent were heavily Republican. Consequently, the Bourbon leaders were even less inclined toward economic reform than were the Republicans.[36] Besides an environmental situation which did not demand great concern for reform, Nebraska Democracy followed two contented leaders.

The most influential of the two leaders was J. Sterling Morton, Nebraska's "Sage of Arbor Lodge," who had emigrated to Nebraska before the Civil War. He soon became a successful promoter and businessman and engaged in Democratic politics for nearly forty years. During most of his career in Nebraska, Morton was the embodiment of the Bourbon Democratic leader who tried to make tariff reform and a strict laissez-faire policy the ideological basis of his party. Early in his career, he became a Burlington railroad propagandist in booming the state and in attacking the regulatory schemes of the Grange. When the state constitutional convention met in 1875 and adopted a constitution giving the legislature power to set maximum freight rates, Morton wrote in a letter to the *Chicago Times* that the regulatory provision was:

> An absolute prohibition of the railroad development of that state by corporations having money of their own. . . . A red flag and a sign [saying] small pox would not more effectively prevent intrusive calls at a private residence than will this red flag of communism, hung out by Nebraska, prevent the development of that state by a general investment in its railroad system.[37]

Just as many of the other leaders in village and urban Nebraska, Morton felt that progress meant economic growth, and, to implement growth, he engaged in a lifetime of promotional activity. He was, for example, a leader of the State Agricultural Society, a village-dominated organization which attempted to promote better agricultural techniques among Nebraska's farmers, and he became the father of Arbor Day through his efforts to grow trees on the Nebraskan prairies.[38]

By giving the Democrats a much more rigid laissez-faire position than the Republicans, Morton succeeded in weakening Democratic strength in many rural areas. Throughout his period of leadership, the party consistently lost strength in the newly settled counties in central and western Nebraska. Morton's rigidity also included an idealistic and mugwump attitude toward politics, which led him to ignore patronage and other problems of the practicing politician. When he served as Secretary of Agriculture in the Cleveland administration, *The Atlantic* magazine noted:

> He has acquired the habit of mind of one always in opposition, which for a man of courage readily takes the form of recklessness of speech. He has worked out the greater problems in a somewhat theoretical fashion, so that his convictions are not always based upon large information and

experience; and once possessed of a conviction, he is unde-
terred by possible consequence from delivering it with an
uncompromising earnestness. Uncalled upon during a long
career to put his political principles into practice, he has
had small need to adjust them to existing conditions. . . .
Mr. Morton is not an astute politician, and he never will
manage conventions or intrigue for power. . . .[39]

Dr. George L. Miller, an Omaha physician and the editor of the Omaha
Herald, was second only to Morton in the Nebraska Democracy. Like
Morton, he advocated a laissez-faire point of view, which had little appeal to
the embattled farmers of the state. When he appeared as a witness before the
Commerce Committee of the United States Senate in 1865, he stated that he

had come to the conclusion that legislation is a hindrance;
that commerce will assert itself over statutes and that gov-
ernmental interference for or against the railroads would
bankrupt them; and that anything that tends to cripple any
part of trade is wrong.[40]

The only ideological difference between Morton and Miller was their approach to the tariff problem. While Morton consistently advocated free trade,
Miller was more amenable to compromise and took a "tariff for revenue
only" position.[41]

Although Nebraska Democrats were more homogenous than the Republicans in ideology and economic groupings, they tirelessly engaged in factional
disputes. Two elements were largely responsible for this. First, Miller, as a
citizen and protagonist of Omaha, was inextricably tied to the interests of
the Union Pacific railroad. Morton, on the other hand, was a publicist for the
Burlington Railroad Company and therefore closely associated with its fortunes. When the two transportation giants collided, as they often did, the
hostility engendered affected Democratic unity adversely.[42] Second, the
rigidity inherent in their ideological position carried over to their concept of
party organization: both men found it difficult to compromise on party issues, such as patronage or candidates. Consequently, during the 1880s, the
Democrats were even more divided than the Republicans. Only when the
Bryan Democrats won control of the party after 1892 did the Nebraska
Democracy differ significantly from the Republican regulars on most economic issues. When this happened, Morton and many of the leaders at the
village level deserted the Democracy for a more conservative Republicanism.[43]

Despite their factional disputes and ideological rigidity, the Democratic party greatly increased its strength during the 1880s. Although the Miller and Morton leadership seldom mentioned it directly, the party vote increased dramatically in the German, Irish, and Bohemian counties in the eastern third of the state. Native American beliefs and antagonisms, expressed through prohibition legislation, agitation for women's suffrage, and Sabbatarianism, violated the religious and cultural beliefs of the Catholic and other ritualistic Christian groups and propelled them into the Democratic party. In many ways this was an easy coalition, for the Bourbon leaders' philosophy of laissez-faire and small government fit neatly with the immigrant's demand for "personal liberty" and the protection of his traditions from a Protestant-dominated government. German, Bohemian, and Irish sympathy for the Democracy increased in proportion to the Republicans' acceptance of their militantly pietistic, prohibitionist wing. In the late 1870s these antagonisms hardly existed, but the 1880s saw a series of measures proposed to the state legislature, which established cultural antagonisms as a most important factor in Nebraska politics.[44]

Morton realized the importance of the prohibition issue in the early 1880s and encouraged Mayor James Boyd of Omaha to hold the first antiprohibition rally ever held in the state in the fall of 1882.[45] Boyd and other Democratic leaders made it clear to the liquor dealers that the Democratic party defended their interests and that it would be politic for them to return the favor.[46] Consequently, the Democrats included an antiprohibition plank in their 1882 platform, a plank which became one of the most important issues in the gubernatorial campaign of that year.[47] Predictably, the Democrats' antitemperance stand arrayed the Protestant ministers against them, and Morton had to admit to Dr. Miller:

> There is not a single Prohibitionist in the state of Nebraska who will vote for the Democratic Ticket because the platform upon which that ticket stands is squarely, fairly and unmistakenly against the whole theory of Prohibition Legislation. But show me a radical pulpit-hanger of any denomination or sect—one who preaches politics every Sunday mixed with the Puritan Doctrine of prohibition and I will show you always, without exception an individual who is voting for Dawes and the Republican ticket throughout.[48]

The tariff was the second major issue which the Democrats attempted to use in the 1880s. Morton in particular advocated this peculiarly mugwump solution to Nebraska's economic misfortunes. He realized that the issue had little appeal to Nebraskans, so he usually referred to his campaigns in 1882 and 1884 as a means of "educating" the populace to the real nature of their difficulties, a transparent device of unsuccessful politicians.[49] Unfortunately for Morton, Nebraskans never reacted to his educational campaigns concerning the tariff; most preferred other explanations of their difficulties. On economic issues which were more relevant to the farmers, both Democratic factions were too committed to village leaders and to their visions of economic growth to attack the railroads, middlemen, or bankers.

Figures 2 and 3 illustrate the areas of Democratic strength in the state and afford a visual correlation between Democratic voting strength and the German, Bohemian and Irish population. Table 2 illustrates this material statistically. In Table 2, both the income and wheat variables describe the fortunate geographical position of Democratic groups—in the more prosperous corn- and hog-producing area of the state.

Table 2: CHARACTERISTICS OF THE FIRST QUARTILE OF DEMOCRATIC STRENGTH, 1880-1888

County	Rural Population per County	Catholic Population per County	Value of Farm Products per Farm	Arable Land in Wheat per County
Cass	52.3%	11.0%	$851	5.20%
Cedar	87.5	15.3	530	5.03
Cheyenne	76.0	11.8	116	1.82
Colfax	73.7	25.6	717	5.05
Dakota	71.7	11.1	1040	3.26
Dodge	56.3	18.6	846	5.02
Douglas	5.2	11.8	928	1.38
Greeley	81.3	12.8	564	5.87
Keith	80.7	9.2	223	9.20
Otoe	49.4	12.6	847	3.40
Pierce	88.7	18.8	800	15.57
Platte	70.0	17.1	680	5.16
Richardson	69.8	9.1	690	3.67
Sarpy	87.6	15.6	868	2.89
Stanton	77.9	18.6	848	8.21
Democratic average	68.40	15.42	701.00	5.65
(Republican average)	(73.91)	(6.93)	(523.33)	(6.46)

Source: Eleventh Decennial Census of the United States, 1890.

Democratic voting behavior in Nebraska during the 1880s reflects two basic interests. Primarily, it illustrates the relationship between Democratic

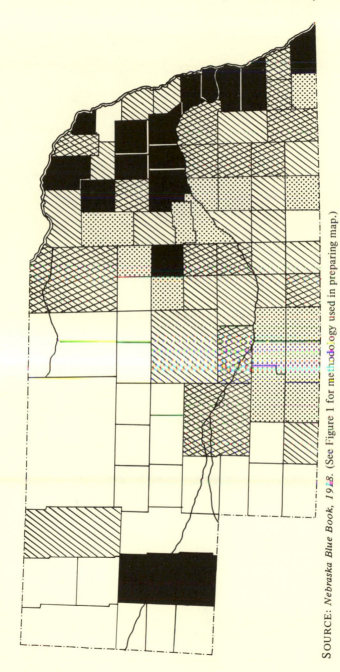

1st Q. ■ +30 to 90 accumulated % above state average

2nd Q. ▨ +29 to −19 accumulated % above/below state average

2rd Q. ▨ −24 to −38 accumulated % below state average

4th Q. ▨ −39 to −122 accumulated % below state average

Figure 2: Democratic Tendencies, 1880–1888

SOURCE: *Nebraska Blue Book, 1928.* (See Figure 1 for methodology used in preparing map.)

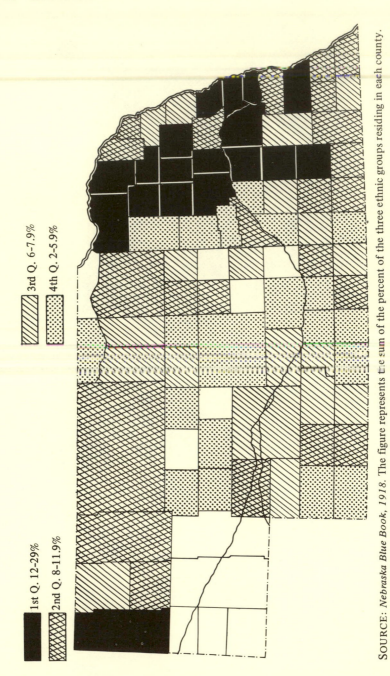

SOURCE: *Nebraska Blue Book, 1918.* The figure represents the sum of the percent of the three ethnic groups residing in each county.

Figure 3: German, Irish and Bohemian County Percentages, by Quartiles

1st Q. 12-29%

2nd Q. 8-11.9%

3rd Q. 6-7.9%

4th Q. 2-5.9%

voting and groups with a Catholic cultural background. The upper quartile of Democratic counties shows 15.42 percent of the population of counties with a Catholic or ritualistic cultural background, while the Republican counties show 6.93 percent. This is the most significant item that differentiates the followers of the two political parties. The rural variable illustrates that, during the 1880s, Democratic strength came from two sources, Omaha and the older German counties north of the Platte. For these two reasons, the average percentage of population living on the farm in Democratic counties was lower than in the first quartile of Republican counties.

The structure of the major parties in Nebraska illustrates the ethnic, rather than the class, nature of much of nineteenth-century politics.[50] To a large extent, political loyalties revolved around the cultural characteristics, which could be ethnic or sectional residues of the Civil War. The parties divided far less on economic, occupational, or class lines than is common in the twentieth century. Indeed, a great consensus on economic policy and goals existed between the Republican and Democratic leaders: all eagerly sought to maintain the booming economic conditions of the 1870s and 1880s. In their enthusiasm, they often neglected the interests of the farm population, a group blessed with overwhelming numbers but seemingly unable to achieve their goals related to economic success. Urban, business or professional men were the real leaders in Nebraska state politics; the farmers were often left to complain.

2

The Farmers' Complaint

The farmers' interests were not effectively represented in Nebraska politics during the 1880s. During the middle part of the decade, most Nebraska farmers shared in the profits from the land boom and reaped the rewards of the boomer psychology of the state's village leaders. During these years, the farmers accepted the point of view and leadership of the older political parties and usually registered this approval at the ballot box. In some ways, however, the farmer's approval of his leaders' policies was doomed to be short-lived, for the farmer and the business leader often had divergent interests. Notwithstanding his substantial profits from land speculation, the farmer was still a producer of commodities, and such items as low freight and material costs were of the utmost concern. He was a petty capitalist vitally interested in lowering his costs of production. When hard times struck, especially in the newly settled portions of the state, the farmer modified his approval of the old economic practices and attacked those institutions that represented the most significant elements of his production costs. The farmers' attacks on railroads, mortgage lenders, and middlemen characterized one part of the farmers' program during the 1880s, just as it did later.

The most common complaint of Nebraska farmers concerned what they thought were excessive and unfair freight rates. When they felt particularly antagonistic toward the railroads, they explained excessive rates in terms of greed and monopoly.[1] At other itmes, more dispassionate farm leaders presented their arguments in more sophisticated economic terms, such as the obvious overcapitalization of many of the railroads. In actuality, the spirit of the real-estate boom had permeated all groups on the frontier, and the railroader, no more or less than the farmer or villager, had succumbed to it. In Nebraska in the 1880s, track mileage had been greatly overextended, and the railroads were usually overcapitalized. Traffic was so sparse in many areas that it could not produce the revenue needed for operational costs and debt retirement. The Burlington, generally considered to be the best-run railroad in the state, reported that in the fiscal year 1886-1887 it earned 7.7 percent on a capital investment of $53,453,100. In 1887-1888, the road earned 3.1 percent, while in 1889-1890 it earned 4.6 percent.[2] Even when considering the watered stock, profits after 1887 were hardly exorbitant. The Union Pacific did not pay a dividend to its stockholders after 1885 and sank into bankruptcy in 1893.[3] The blame for the overexpansion of track mileage rests on the railway promoters, but they were subjected to such pressure from other groups participating in the booming economy that more conservative expansion would probably have cost them the confidence of their financial backers.[4]

Even the validity of the farmer's charge of high freight rates is hard to evaluate. While railroad leaders such as the Burlington's C. M. Holdredge bemoaned the low return on capital investment, farmers and shippers pointed to lower rates in neighboring states. The Iowa rate schedule furnished the most common comparison. In the spring of 1890 when agitation for lower rates reached one of its periodic peaks, the *Omaha World Herald* printed the comparison of Nebraska and Iowa rates shown in Table 3.

Table 3: IOWA AND NEBRASKA: COMPARISON OF FREIGHT RATES PER 100 POUNDS

Distance	1st Class	2d Class
25 miles		
Iowa	17¢	5.95¢
Nebraska	22¢	10¢
100 miles		
Iowa	24¢	8¢
Nebraska	52¢	30¢
400 miles		
Iowa	61¢	25¢
Nebraska	110¢	71¢

Source: *Omaha World Herald,* April 5, 1890. See also Ralph A. Knudsen "Regulations of Railroad Rates in Nebraska" (Master's thesis, University of Nebraska, 1937), 49, 101.

The railroads countered the farmers' and shippers' arguments with several facts of their own, pointing out that railroad rates had decreased steadily since the first settlement of Nebraska.[5] Table 4 illustrates the steady decreases in freight costs in comparison with the declining prices of corn and wheat and shows how the rapid decline in freight rates actually maintained price stability in Nebraska.[6]

Table 4: CHICAGO GRAIN PRICES AND OMAHA–CHICAGO FREIGHT RATES

Year	#2 Corn (cents per bushel)	Omaha–Chicago (rate per bushel)	Gross Income from Omaha
1883	54¢	10¢	40¢
1885	43¢	11¢	32¢
1887	40¢	6¢	34¢
1889	34¢	6¢	28¢
1890	39¢	5¢	34¢

Year	#2 Wheat (cents per bushel)	Omaha–Chicago (rate per bushel)	Gross Income from Omaha
1883	102¢	12¢	90¢
1885	84¢	12¢	72¢
1887	76¢	9¢	67¢
1889	86¢	9¢	77¢
1890	90¢	9¢	81¢

Source: Compiled from statistics in Arthur R. Bentley, *The Condition of the Western Farmer as Illustrated by the Economic History of a Nebraska Township,* Johns Hopkins University Studies in Historical and Political Science (July–August 1893), 51. Bentley obtained the marketing information from Howard Bartels and Co., Chicago. I defined gross income as the Omaha–Chicago freight expense subtracted from the Chicago selling price of the commodity. Freight costs from interior points in Nebraska, other marketing costs, and production costs would enter into the final, and very difficult, determination of the farmer's net profit. The figure was included in the table to illustrate that some of the edge was taken off falling commodity prices by declining railroad rates and to illustrate that the railroads did not take all of the farmer's money.

Lower freight schedules during the 1880s did not stop the farmers' and shippers' demands for railroad rate regulation. The farmers' part of the struggle for regulation often has been noted, but urban and village shippers also played a significant part in the regulatory movement. The protests of urban shippers took several forms. For example, urban editors frequently suggested that river transportation be developed to compete with the railroads and force lower rates.[7] Omaha shippers and wholesalers complained that the railroads discriminated against Omaha by offering lower freight rates to other Missouri and Mississippi River cities, by excessive switching rates and tolls across the Missouri River, or by railroad favoritism for the long hauls to the Chicago stockyards rather than to those of South Omaha.[8] On the other hand, shippers and wholesalers in the interior of Nebraska felt that Omaha enjoyed a significant advantage over them. Omaha, a favored "pet town" in Nebraska and the West, paid $56.25 for a carload of merchandise from Chicago; Grand Island (in the central part of the state) paid nearly twice the shipping charges, or $104.40 for the same service.[9]

Part of the difficulty of setting fair rates in Nebraska arose because some of the states lying to the east had passed pro-rata intrastate rates, which compelled the railroads to increase their rates on long hauls. Although the laws reduced rates within these states, they raised rates between Nebraska and the markets of the East.[10] Reform groups continually complained about the influence of railroad lobbying in forestalling rate regulation, but it is evident that conflicting interests among those who wanted to regulate was a major factor in delaying rate control. A case in point involved a railroad rate bill proposed in the 1891 Nebraska legislature. There was comparatively little organized opposition to the bill, and it easily passed the House. In the Senate, the bill was not opposed by any party organization, but business groups in Beatrice, Hastings, and Kearney petitioned for its defeat. The interior cities feared that the railroads would again make up for intrastate losses by raising through rates.[11]

Much of the history of Nebraska politics in the early 1880s focuses around railroad rate regulation. In the early 1870s, when Grangerism swept the Midwest, there were 594 local Granges in Nebraska. The proposed state constitution of 1871, written under Granger influence, gave the legislature the power to regulate the railroads, but a controversy over taxing church lands resulted in the defeat of the entire constitution and its regulatory provisions. Effective railroad regulation was thereby delayed until the early 1880s with the enactment of the Doane Law, which prohibited "unjust discrimination" against shippers and places and prohibited the railroads from charging more for a short haul than for a longer one over the same line.[12] But it did not establish the farmers' major goal, the regulation of all rates in the state.[13]

The next effort to regulate railroad rates occurred after the Anti-Monopoly party showed great strength in the election of 1882. Their candidate for governor, E. P. Ingersoll, received 16,992 votes, while the fusion Anti-Monopoly-Democratic candidate for state treasurer won the election and became the first non-Republican to hold state office in Nebraska's history. Farmers were jubilant, and most observers felt that 1883 would be a banner year for the forces of reform in the state. The reformers almost held the balance of power in the state legislature. In the House, they and their Democratic allies came within four seats of the Republicans. In the Senate, there were seven Anti-

Monopolists, seven Independents, eleven Democrats, and fifteen Republicans. The reformers, however, were badly split. Although the Democrats welcomed the opportunity to defeat their political rivals, they could not join whole-heartedly in any coalition that threatened the economic interests of village Nebraska. Consequently, the Democratic leaders would not join with the Anti-Monopolists in the balloting for United States Senator, and both parties went down to defeat before Charles F. Manderson, an organization Republican.[14]

After defeating the Anti-Monopolists in their hopes for the Senatorship, the Republican-controlled House of Representatives reported that it found no evidence of favoritism or unjust discrimination toward persons or places by the railroad companies in the state.[15] The Senate, which was controlled by Democrats and Anti-Monopolists, felt differently, so the two houses compromised on a proposal to present to the voters a constitutional amendment providing for a Board of Railway Commissioners. Although legislators intended only an advisory function for the board, the electorate defeated the amendment by an overwhelming vote of 44,448 to 22,297 in the November election, an indication that most of Nebraska's citizens did not consider railroad regulation as desirable as did some farm leaders.[16]

Regulation of railroads became the dominant campaign issue in the 1884 election, and the next legislature passed the most comprehensive regulatory legislation proposed up to that time. The law resembled the Iowa Maximum Rate Law of 1874.[17] It established a railroad commission comprised of three state executive officers and fixed maximum rates for passenger fares, but it failed to give the commission the power to fix other rates. Disputed freight rates still had to be handled through the state courts.[18]

Criticism of the commission brought a further change in the laws in 1887. The legislature changed the name of the body to the State Board of Transportation, named two new state officers as members, and hired three permanent secretaries. Its regulatory powers, however, remained the same. Although passenger rates were lowered to three cents per mile for the state as a whole, the courts still retained the final power in making decisions on unfair rates.[19] Critics hurriedly pointed out that the board remained basically "a railroad commission whose chief end is to draw their own salary, freights going up and down at the will of the railroad companies."[20] The legislature remained the only body clearly possessing the power to fix rates, and, with the exception of passenger rates, it had failed to act.

The determination of railroad rate schedules proved particularly difficult in Nebraska during the 1880s. Because of increased efficiency and a larger volume of traffic, railroad rates declined throughout the whole period. When the first rate bill passed in 1881, it froze rates at the 1881 level. In modern more inflationary times, this would indeed be rate fixing, but in the late nineteenth century, under deflationary circumstances, it became difficult for the rate adjusters to keep even with the downward trend of rates. Even without successful regulatory commissions, the freight rates for Nebraska fell over 50 percent in the 1880s, a significantly greater drop than the general price level.[21] When all the various factors are considered, it is difficult to see how freight rates could have been significantly lower. This is not the whole story however. The fact that railroads were continually lowering rates and not making exhorbitant profits does not mean that farmers on the plains, far from major markets, could afford even the rates which were charged. Table 5 compares the prices for corn and wheat in Chicago with the prices received in central Nebraska. Whether rates were fair or unfair is beside the point, for it is evident that when prices were low, as in 1890, the nearly 50 percent higher price received for corn by farmers closer to the major markets could have been the difference between hard times or bankruptcy.

Table 5: COMMODITY PRICE DIFFERENTIAL BETWEEN CENTRAL
NEBRASKA AND CHICAGO MARKETS, 1884-1900

| | CORN | | | WHEAT | | |
| | Central Nebraska Price | Chicago Price | Difference | Central Nebraska Price | Chicago Price | Difference |
Year						
1884	25¢	57¢	32¢	60¢	95¢	35¢
1888	40	50	10	65	81	16
1889	30	35	5	75	98	23
1890	22	34	12	60	87	27
1900	29	42	13	47	67	20

Source: Newspaper quotations from county newspapers in central Nebraska. All quotations except that for wheat in 1889 were taken from the first July issue of the paper. The 1889 quotation was taken in April.

Second only to the railroads as antagonists of many farmers were the mortgage lenders. Contrary to Jeffersonian ideology, the Homestead Act had not provided free land for those who engaged in commercial agriculture. The move west required capital, and, even when secure on a homestead, the farmer found it necessary to invest in more land or mechanical equipment in order to remain competitive in a commercial market. From 1880 to 1887, the amount of money loaned for farm mortgages in Nebraska rose from $7,583,582 to $26,213,154.[22] Although the total mortgage debt in most Nebraska counties increased greatly during the 1880s, historians have failed to point out that the population of these counties increased also. Hayes

County, which was settled between 1885 and 1890, is a good example of the simple relationship between rising mortgage debt and rising population. (See Table 6.)

Evidently a farmer obtained a mortgage shortly after he settled in Nebraska; but the vast increase in mortgage debt reflected an increase in population rather than second or third mortgages on the same property. A large

Table 6: RELATIONSHIP BETWEEN INCREASING MORTGAGE DEBT
          AND INCREASING NUMBER OF MORTGAGES, HAYES
          COUNTY, NEBRASKA

Year	Number of Mortgages	Total Mortgage Debt	Average Mortgage Debt per Farm
1885	34	$ 13,932	$409
1886	337	137,440	409
1887	685	297,518	434
1888	818	397,477	485
1889	800	346,513	433

Source: See Floyd M. Farmer, "The Land Boom in South West Nebraska" (Master's thesis, University of Nebraska, 1936), 60.

portion of the farmers' debt came from his first mortgage borrowing for more land, machinery, or other items associated with farmer-businessmen operating in an expanding commercial market.[23] Most farms were purchased outright, but the money used in purchasing machinery and capital improvements came from local bankers and moneylenders. A Hamilton County editor explained some of the reasons for mortgage indebtedness in the following manner:

> We think the farmers in Hamilton County whose farms are
> embellished by the things that make up the conveniences
> and comforts of life, are mortgaged almost without excep-
> tion, unless the capital that created the comforts were im-
> ported. . . the man who invests money improving his place
> has raised that money by mortgaging his farm.[24]

Interest rates on the rapidly increasing mortgage indebtedness have been a point of confusion for those attempting to evaluate the farmers' complaints. Omar M. Kem, the Populist Congressman from Broken Bow, states in his memoirs that, in the late 1880s, he was paying 24 percent interest on a loan. Similar reports were often found in the farm journals and repeated in text-books to illustrate the usurious nature of the loan companies.[25] These claims, however, are not substantiated in the United States census reports. The 1890 census reports that the average mortgage rate in Nebraska in 1890 was 8.3 percent, a rate which county newspapers generally confirm.[26]

Table 7: INTEREST RATES AND COMMISSION RATES, NEBRASKA,
1880-1892

Year	Rate	Commission
1880	8%	2%
1883-1886	7	2
1887-1889	7	1
1892	6	1
1892[a]	6	0

[a]Loans over $2,000 by some companies.

Source: Arthur F. Bentley, *The Condition of the Western Farmer as Illustrated by the Economic History of a Nebraska Township,* Johns Hopkins University Studies in Historical and Political Science (Baltimore, 1893), 45.

Table 7 shows the average interest rates, plus service charges, for the years between 1880 and 1892.[27] Scores of advertisements in the county papers throughout the state confirm the census bureau's statistics. Generally advertised rates, exclusive of commission, ran from 7 to 8.5 percent between 1885 and 1895. For example, the First National Bank of Aurora advertised loans at 7 percent and paid 5 percent on time deposits.[28] This figure represents a differential of 2 percent between the prices paid and recieved for money, an amount which would return only a modest profit after taking into account handling costs and the relatively small volume of such institutions. When the Hayes County Alliance entered the loan business in competition with the private firms, it could do little better, for it borrowed at 6 percent and loaned at 6 percent plus costs.[29]

The point of confusion between the farmers' claims and the real situation is the chattel mortgage. Populist orators and propagandists quoted the rates they were paying on their chattel mortgages. These mortgages involved a vastly higher rate than did the real estate first mortgage. Rates up to 36 percent were probably common, as they are common on this type of agreement today. There is some disagreement among historians over the importance of the chattel mortgage,[30] but the fact remains that the chattel mortgage existed in addition to the real-estate mortgage, and it was the high rates of interest on the chattel mortgage that were so frequently quoted in agrarian polemics. In Keith County, for example, the actual value of stock, vehicles, and farming implements totaled $257,000, while the total chattels were $183,000.[31] Obviously, the chattel was a critical factor which contributed to the farmers' desperation in the last decade of the century.

Although the farmer did suffer from high interest charges, the extent of the injustice was considerably less than the farmers would have had their fellow citizens believe. Interest rates were higher than in the East, but the risks were undeniably greater and the rewards sweeter in the West. As one contemporary put it: "The farmers may often have suffered from excessive interest and grasping creditors; but it was less frequently the avarice of the lender that got him [the farmer] into trouble than the fact that he was too sanguine and too prone to believe that he could safely go in debt, on the assumption that crops and prices in the future would equal those in the present."[32]

When the speculative bubble burst in Nebraska in the late 1880s, many farmers found themselves financially overextended and fell victim to the high interest rates of the chattel mortgage lenders or to the increased payments on principal and accumulated interest on their real-estate first mortgage. The *Omaha World Herald* claimed that one-third of the debt in the county was interest on money already borrowed.[33] By the time of the Populist uprising in Nebraska, the burden of real estate and chattel mortgages constituted another factor which projected the farmer into political action.

Closely related to the agrarian belief that bankers extracted usurious interest rates was the feeling that bankers and the wealthy in general shared the responsibility for the marked increase in the value of the dollar. For debtor farmers, the appreciation of the dollar meant greater difficulty in meeting mortgage and other fixed costs incurred in more prosperous times. Appreciation after the Civil War was a fact, but it affected what the farmer bought just as it did what he sold. For example, the Chicago price of number two wheat declined about 20 percent from the early 1870s to the early 1890s, but freight rates and many items of machinery declined even more.[34] A comparative price list printed in the *Omaha World Herald* (Table 8) illustrates the dramatic decline in the prices of farm necessities.

Table 8: FARM EQUIPMENT PRICES, 1880-1890

Article	1880	1890
Self binder	$315.00	$130.00
14" steel beam plow	28.00	14.00
Mowing machine	85.00	50.00
Plain wire	00.065	00.035
Riding cultivator	45.00	25.00

Source: Omaha World Herald, September 21, 1890.

Although deflation did not seriously weaken the farmers' position vis-à-vis what he bought and sold, it did weaken his ability to meet his fixed costs.[35] When deflation combined with the collapse of the real-estate market after 1888, the Nebraska farmer found himself in real trouble. Taxes, high tariff, and other agrarian woes could be borne if land prices continued to rise. When they did not, Nebraska's farmers were ready for another political revolt.[36]

Other groups in Nebraska emphasized different factors as the cause for the farmers' troubles. Businessmen and railroaders often cited the overproduction of farm products as the basic cause of the farm depression. These men, more often than the farmers, recognized that vast new competitive areas were opening in South America and Australia. Consequently, some of them turned their attention to making Nebraska farmers more competitive by emphasizing the production of perishable crops like pork or sugar beets.[37] Much of the program of the businessman-dominated State Agricultural Society revolved around overcoming the handicaps of Nebraska's agriculture and in lowering the high transportation costs resulting from the state's geographical position.[38]

Populism in Nebraska resulted from a complex of events. The farmer emphasized the economic causes: the effect of railroad rates, the evil of usury, taxes, or the appreciation of the dollar. Businessmen emphasized the overproduction of farm products and the competition from world commodity markets. Nearly overlooked because of the promotional atmosphere of the era was perhaps the simplest explanation of them all—the difficulties the undercapitalized farmers experienced adjusting their crops and farming methods to the new environment. A combination of all of these gives us an idea of the important causes of populism. There is, however, more to populism than the farmers' violent reaction to deteriorating economic conditions. There was a vague political and cultural discontent evident in the movement, which has led some historians to see latent nativism and even fascism behind the Populists' analysis of their social and economic position.[39]

After 1888, the economic position of many Nebraska farmers became desperate, but cultural and political factors combined with the economic to produce the fervor of populism. Political alienation and revolt are born of more than economic distress, and in the Nebraska revolt it partially resulted from feelings of political frustration and alienation which existed in the farmers' environment. The government of the pre-Populist era did not respond to the farmer, nor was it the exclusive property of the railroads. The village dominated much of the political and economic life of late nineteenth-century Nebraska, and it was in the farmers' conflict with the village that some of the frustrations which produced the Populist revolt arose.

PART II
THE STRUCTURE
OF POWER

3

The Village

Although small farmers made up the bulk of Nebraska's population, they were not the dominant figures in the economic or political life of late nineteenth-century Nebraska. Outside of the metropolitan centers of Lincoln and Omaha, the centers of economic and political power in the state were the scores of small villages that dotted the Nebraska prairies. Village inhabitants reflected the optimism and the speculative interests of the farm population, but they had unique economic and cultural opportunities of their own. Although villagers often sympathized with agrarian problems, the farmer's specific solutions to his problems often resulted in economic and social effects detrimental to the continued growth of the village. Consequently, political and economic conflict resulted from the differences of interests between the two groups.[1]

In Part II of this study, an attempt will be made to sketch the ambitions and interests of the dominant groups in the village. Since it is impossible to study every village and surrounding countryside in Nebraska, six county-seat villages with their respective counties serve as a sample (see Figure 4). These counties are used in Part II of this study, and they represent 6 percent of the counties in the state in 1890. Two factors determined selection of the counties: the availability of source materials, chiefly newspapers, for the late 1880s and early 1890s, and the political climate of the county. Of the six counties, two were Republican, one was Democratic, and three were Populist. The Republican counties, Hayes and Scotts Bluff, are located in the arid,

35

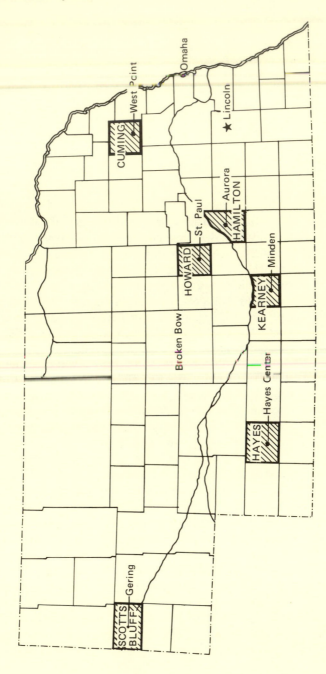

Figure 4: Sample Counties, Nebraska, 1890

western section of the state. The Populist counties, Hamilton, Howard, and Kearney, lie in the central third of the state, while the Democratic county, Cuming, is located in the prosperous northeastern section.

The village quickly became a center of political and economic power in post–Civil War Nebraska. With the exception of the earlier settled eastern and river areas, Nebraska filled with immigrants during the two decades following the Civil War. In all of the counties studied, the settlement process proceeded in essentially the same manner. At the same time that the agricultural areas of the counties first came under the plow, young tradesmen moved into the hamlets, which soon became the trading centers of rural Nebraska. These pioneer businessmen believed that opportunity lay in moving west and establishing a stake in a growing community. Many of them became phenomenally successful in their ventures, and some lived on in their communities to become known as "town fathers." In most of the villages of this study, there were some individuals who had come to the village early, been active in its promotion and its projects, and later exercised great influence because of nearly universal recognition of their promotional contributions to the community. Nebraskans were obsessed with economic growth, and, in the 1880s, they looked forward to seemingly endless progress. Omaha, Kearney, West Point, Aurora, and hundreds of other cities, villages, and hamlets had visions of metropolitan grandeur if the previous decade's rate of growth could be maintained. Consequently, the town fathers of the soon-to-thrive villages were the objects of special veneration.[2]

Of the villages in this study, West Point, settled in the late 1850s, offers the best example of how the promotional abilities of village leaders influenced the building of pioneer communities. The universally respected father of West Point, John D. Neligh, migrated to Nebraska from Pennsylvania shortly before the Civil War. Using Omaha capital and the salary he received from his postmastership, Neligh launched into nearly a half-century of promotional activity in West Point. He became president of the first bank. In the mid-1870s, he allied himself with other leading citizens in an effort to utilize the waters of the Elkhorn River to bring manufacturing to West Point. The company, to be capitalized at $500,000, sent Neligh to New York City to sell stock at $25 per share. Although the company failed, the building it had constructed was used for a succession of business enterprises, which added to the economic base of the community. In addition to being engaged in banking and manufacturing ventures, Neligh became president of the County Agricultural Society and mayor of West Point. When he died in 1896, the *West Point Republican* wreathed its pages in mourning for the "father of West Point."[3]

Scotts Bluff County, one of the last counties in Nebraska to be settled, also had a first citizen. Martin Gering, who gave his name to the county seat, was also typical of the entrepreneurial leadership of village Nebraska during this period. Gering led many of the projects vitally needed for an isolated frontier community. He expended some of his own capital for a road from his new community to the first county-seat town, Sidney. He erected the first brick building on the main street of Gering, and he led the movement in which several leading citizens of the community donated a bridge to the village so that it could tap the trading area north of the North Platte River. Finally, he was one of the early promoters of irrigation in Scotts Bluff County. Gering, like most other town leaders, invested heavily in town and rural real estate.[4]

A similar community leader lived in Hamilton County. General Delevan Bates, an early settler in the county, served at various times as county superintendent of schools, member of the city council, member of the school board, and mayor. He was instrumental in obtaining the county seat for Aurora, building the court house, and securing the Republican Valley Railroad. When he served on the school board, he personally advanced the money needed to pay for the land on which the town built its first high school.[5]

Other villages in Nebraska had their town fathers. Some matched the vigor of a Neligh or Gering; others won the title with less arduous effort. M. J. Abbott of Hayes County was honored by Republicans, but because his editorship of the *Hayes County Republican* became stridently partisan, he received little admiration or affection from the Democrats or the rural folk. But Abbott, too, took part in various village-promotion ventures and became active in town and county politics.[6] On the other hand, the Paul brothers of Howard County, though acknowledged to be the founders and leaders of St. Paul, the county seat, did not engage actively in political leadership or controversy.[7]

Joel Hull was the recognized "Father of Minden," the county seat of Kearney County. He surveyed and plotted the town, erected some of the first buildings, sired the town's first son, and led in the victorious county-seat struggle and the successful attempt to secure a railroad. Inevitably he was president of the old Settlers Association, but like the Paul brothers who founded, rather immodestly, St. Paul, the county seat of Howard County, Hull did not play as noticeable a political and economic role as did some of the other town fathers.[8]

The amount of leadership supplied by the town fathers varied considerably in the different counties in the study, much of which can be attributed to personal differences. James Neligh's entrepreneurial visions surpassed those of the Paul brothers in Howard County. Circumstances also influenced development. Some villages such as West Point or Gering provided better locations or resources for entrepreneurial success than Minden or St. Paul. Successful leadership inevitably revolved around the potentialities and personalities in a given area.

Sharing the leadership and entrepreneurial activities of the town fathers was a wider group of citizens generally referred to in the county press as the "old settlers." The time of settlement in the county often played a significant part in defining leadership roles and served as a major criterion of community prestige. Scarcely a decade elapsed after the founding of a frontier village before an "old settlers association" sprang up, with the most respected old settler or town father as its president.

The old settlers of the county or village generally followed nonpartisan paths in their efforts to promote their village. Their basic interests were the immediate problems of village development and, except in the counties where prohibition became a bitter partisan issue, party politics did not overtly color economic or social relationships. Consequently, a great deal of social cohesion existed between the Republican and Democratic old settlers in most communities.[9]

The old settlers as a group displayed great vitality and power in the villages of late nineteenth-century Nebraska. Very often they rallied around a town father such as Neligh in Cuming County. In Cuming, other early settlers included Uriah and John Bruner and J. C. Crawford, the only Democrat of the group. With Neligh, these other early settlers assumed leading roles in the development of the community. They established or managed leading mercantile and manufacturing establishments, played an active part in local politics, and eventually became significant political figures at the state level. Although they belonged to different political parties, they maintained friendly relations with each other in both social and economic activity. For example, Neligh and Crawford became partners in a sawmill venture, while Neligh and the Bruners organized the first bank in West Point.[10] Crawford even married a Bruner daughter. Neligh became the first president of the Agricultural Society and Crawford became its second. Thus, in the early years of West Point and Cuming County, a fairly recognizable group of citizens, most of whom had been among the original settlers, participated in and to a great extent directed the activities of the community. These men all lived in the county seat, and their interests were closely tied to village prosperity and growth. Although succeeding years brought new business and professional leaders to the community, these men held their influential positions. When businessmen organized the West Point Board of Trade in 1890, J. C. Crawford drafted the bylaws while, in the same year, Neligh became the almost unanimous choice for mayor of the village.[11]

In Hamilton County, a similar pattern existed, differing only in the fact that General Delevan Bates did not achieve the preeminent position of John D. Neligh in Cuming County. Again the town leaders to a large extent were synonymous with the leading old settlers of village residence; and, as in Cuming County, the elements of political and economic power were more closely related than is usual today. After Bates, the most influential man in Hamilton County and Aurora was L. W. Hastings, the editor of the *Hamilton County Republican*. A group of influential lawyers and businessmen gathered around Hastings. Although they were an informal group, they had enough cohesion to be recognized and labeled as the "old-timers."[12] The group consisted of A. W. Agee, lawyer, state senator, sheriff, and an influential GAR and temperance worker; Edward J. Hainer, lawyer, banker, and later a Congressman; J. J. Farley, banker and state representative during the 1880s; and A. J. Spanogle, merchant and also a state representative during the 1880s. All of these men were Republicans. The Democrats produced village leaders in three brothers, A. N., William, and C. R. Glover, and in D. S. Woodward. The Glovers were merchants and bankers; Woodward was a physician.[13]

The power structure of Kearney County was less clearly defined than in some of the other counties. Joel Hull, the most respected citizen, played a less decisive economic role than did his counterparts in other villages; however, a group of old settlers existed, which, typically, combined economic and political leadership. Lewis A. Kent, banker and city councilman, Otto Abrahamson, banker, and James A. Cline, president of the Agricultural Society, were all business leaders who often mixed in local politics.[14] Despite the activities of the Minden businessmen, Kearney County did not show the same degree of homogeneity between economic and political leadership existing in some of the other counties. More than an average number of political leaders were farmers who came from areas outside the county seat. The county also produced fewer state political leaders than did most of the other counties studied. Evidently participation in politics at the state level lent enough prestige to the participants to enable them to maintain leadership for a considerable length of time. In Kearney County, where no leaders of statewide importance developed, there was a greater diffusion of leadership.[15]

In Scotts Bluff and Hayes counties, the same pattern prevailed as in Kearney and Hamilton counties. The town fathers and the old settlers, who had settled in the town and entered banking, mercantile, or speculative occupations, were and continued to be the most important leaders in both the economic and political life of the county. Many of these leaders easily moved on to active participation in politics at the state level, and a surprising number achieved some kind of national recognition. Many served a term or two as Congressmen, became national committeemen, or performed some task for a national committee. Any belief that the small-town leaders had only parochial views probably reflects a great deal of the twentieth-century urban bias.[16]

The town fathers, old settlers, or town clique enjoyed the respect and rewards of leadership because they filled a vital function in pioneer communities. The Nebraska village of the late nineteenth century depended to a large degree on the activity, optimism, and speculative ability of its early promoters. These men made and maintained their position and fortunes by promoting the economic expansion of their communities. The most noticeable feature of any Nebraska newspaper during this period was the unrestrained feeling of optimism and growth, a feeling which pervaded nearly every local news item. Community after community became imbued with an exhilaration born of a combination of hardship, common purpose, and an unquenchable optimism, which tended to unify it around its leadership.

The feelings of optimism and growth were bound to subside in most communities, but while they existed, frontier Nebraska was a heady place. Throughout the 1880s, land values boomed as the state grew in population. Table 9 illustrates the surge of population growth between 1880 and 1890.

Table 9: INCREASE IN NEBRASKA POPULATION, 1879-1889

Section	Population (in thousands)		Increase
	1879	1889	
Eastern	283	605	322
Central	159	353	194
Western	10	100	90
TOTAL	452	1,058	606

Source: U.S. Department of Interior, Bureau of the Census, *Eleventh Decennial Census of the United States, 1890.*

The boom was both rural and urban. The increase in rural land values continued from the Civil War period, but the urban boom was largely confined to the middle and later 1880s. Twenty towns wanted to become the state capital. Kearney hoped it would replace Washington, D.C., as the national capital,[17] while, according to the *Omaha Bee,* "Additions were laid out for miles around the county seat, McCook."[18] The banner years for the real-estate boom in southeast Nebraska were from 1886 to 1888, while in the western counties it continued into 1889.[19]

The older settlers of Nebraska villages were the chief beneficiaries of the real-estate boom. In Gering, the officers of the Gering Building and Loan Association announced on April 11, 1890, that their association would return fourteen dollars and fifty cents per share. The shares had originally cost twenty-four dollars, so the stockholders received over 50 percent for their initial investment. Martin Gering was vice president of the association, and its other officers, James Westervelt, Peter McFarlane, Asa B. Wood, O. W. Gardner, and Edward W. Sayre, were the old settlers in Scotts Bluff County. In the same year, the West Point Building and Loan declared a ten dollar and thirty-three cent dividend on stock worth thirty-six dollars and thirty-three cents for a profit of 40 percent.[20] In addition to their interests in building and loan, banking institutions, or mortgage companies, village leaders personally held a great deal of land for speculative purposes both in their village and the surrounding countryside. As a group, their prosperity clearly depended upon the continued growth and prosperity of their county.[21]

In order to insure the expansion of their communities, village leaders in nineteenth-century Nebraska fit into the general stereotype of the aggressive village boomer. County (and Omaha) newspapers carried yearly lists of new buildings, giving even the precise cost of the "grand" new "mansions" of the village elite. Newspapers frankly admitted competition among citizens for the most splendid dwelling.[22] Leading citizens traveled East to attract settlers, while railroads provided cheap rates for easterners to travel to the West to look things over. Even in Hamilton County, which was well settled by the 1890s, the city council took an active part in attracting settlers from the East.[23] In Lincoln, farmer politicians often complained that "the 'Boomers,' bankers, beet sugar men, etc., are overrunning the legislature. They sing a great song about 'development,' 'home industry' and 'don't drive capital out.'"[24]

The initial objective of the town fathers, old settlers, and other promoters in Nebraska's small villages was to secure a railroad for their village. Without a railroad few villages could hope to grow and prosper, and, by the late 1880s, most counties in Nebraska had such a railroad. Only the western section of the state still thought of railroads as the major solution to economic growth. In the western counties, as in those of the eastern section, businessmen usually led the fight to obtain rail transportation. City fathers Bates and Neligh led the fight in Hamilton and Cuming counties, respectively. In Hayes Center, which never obtained railroad transportation, the town fathers began to agitate for a railroad shortly after settlement. A committee composed of the village leaders promoted a countywide mass meeting and managed to get themselves instructed by the assembled citizens to negotiate with and offer "incentives" to the Northwestern Railroad.[25] Scotts Bluff County also slumbered without a railroad until the mid-1890s, a fact which necessitated the transporting of heavy canal building equipment from Alliance by wagon.[26]

The farmers were not alone in agitating for lower railroad rates. Once they obtained rail transportation, village inhabitants became increasingly interested in lowering existing rate structures and in other railroad "abuses." The *Kearney County Gazette,* a paper which never approved of the various farmers' movements, agitated for decreased rates continually throughout the 1880s. Its editor, W. D. Hart, protested, as did later Populist agitators, that it took one bushel of wheat to get another to market. Other village editors pointed out that the rate from the interior of the state to the Missouri River was twice as great as that from the river to Chicago.[27] Some village leaders did more than protest. In Kearney, the town father Joel Hull and old-timer James McPheeley sponsored a convention of village citizens, which passed a resolution asking the state government to construct and operate a railway to the Gulf of Mexico. Both men spoke for the project.[28]

Although the Democratic and Republican county editors generally did not follow the farmers in their various agrarian protest movements, they often criticized railroads, bankers, and the existing order in general. M. J. Abbott, the combative and later anti-Populist editor of the *Hayes County Republican,* often sympathized with the plight of the farmer:

> High freight rates and low values catch the farmer as be-
> tween two large millstones, and if he turns to escape he
> falls into the fire and is rendered out by the money lender
> at the rate of two to five percent a month.[29]

After securing rail transportation for their community and county, most village leaders turned to developing further the local economy. The prevailing hope was that they might lure some sort of manufacturing plant to their community. This was no easy task for there were more ambitious speculators than plants in this era, and much ambitious talk ended in vain.

The village most successful in acquiring industry was West Point. This community proved especially suited to industry since it was located on the Elkhorn River, had an especially vigorous group of promoters, and was close to Omaha capital markets. Since beer-drinking Germans inhabited the area around the town, brewing became the most important activity in the village. In 1869, some unidentified capitalists erected a ten thousand dollar frame brewery, which, by 1892, produced 5,000 barrels of beer a year for northeastern Nebraska. The brewery continued in operation until prohibition.[30]

During the 1870s, community leaders in West Point made repeated attempts to establish additional manufacturing establishments in the village. James Neligh, J. S. Crawford, the Bruners, and E. K. Valentine tried to establish a company to manufacture flour, paper, and woolen goods, but they achieved only temporary success.[31] In Hamilton County, E. T. Hainer opened several new creameries, a fact which brought a typical note of commendation from the editor of the *Hamilton County Register* because creameries brought in money from "outside sources."[32]

In western Nebraska, where village leaders showed considerably more interest in agriculture than did their eastern counterparts, citizens of Gering and Hayes Center thought of improvement in the more basic terms of obtaining railroad transportation and of improving the efficiency of agricultural production. In Scotts Bluff County, improvement interests centered around irrigation and the culture of the sugar beet. Gering leaders early recognized the importance of irrigation in the North Platte Valley. Even before the settlement of Gering in 1885, over five hundred acres in the area came under irrigation.[33] The influential editor of the *Gering Courier,* Asa B. Wood, promoted irrigation from the first settlement of the community. In 1889, Wood reported that irrigation worked well on the lowlands to the north of the river and that it should work equally well on the southern side near Gering. Shortly thereafter, the south side farmers met to plan an irrigation program but technical difficulties held back the development of the south side of the river until 1895 when Wood organized the Gering Irrigation District.[34]

W. P. Akers, an attorney in Gering, became the president of the first canal company, the Farmer's Canal Company, and by 1890 there were 2,700 acres under irrigation in the county. A year later, there were 143 miles of canal in the county. Direction of later irrigation work passed to Judge William H. Wright, a New York promoter who moved to Gering and led the enterprise until 1903, when he lost it to a New Jersey concern.[35]

Leaders in western Nebraska suffered no illusions concerning the attitudes of the other parts of the state toward their problems. They recognized that eastern and southern sections of the state were either indifferent or hostile toward irrigation. Promotion of irrigation legislation soon became a virtue demanded by westerners of their representatives at Lincoln. In 1889, Henry St. Raynor of Sidney pushed through the legislature the first comprehensive irrigation law. Southern and eastern Nebraskans, however, felt that western appeals for irrigation would harm the agricultural reputation of the state and endanger further settlement. The Democrats, whose power was concentrated in Omaha and the better agricultural areas of the state, did little to aid their party in the western part of the state when they resolved in their 1889 convention that "there was already enough available land to glut the home market for nearly all farm products."[36]

After the drought of 1891, in which irrigation proved a boon in areas of marginal rainfall, the westerners held periodic meetings, conferences, and rallies at Sidney, McCook, and Lincoln and petitioned the state and national governments for various types of aid.[37] Their agitation finally resulted in state administration and irrigation district legislation.[38]

Closely associated with irrigation, particularly in the minds of westerners, was the promotion of beet sugar production in Nebraska. In order to encourage beet production, the legislature of 1889 had passed an act giving the sugar producers a bounty of two cents a pound.[39] Many business groups and community boards of trade in the state promoted the sugar-bounty bill because they felt sugar production might prove to be a major manufacturing interest in Nebraska. Nebraska's Senator, Charles F. Manderson introduced a bill into the United States Congress providing for a bounty on every ton of sugar beets raised, in addition to a payment of eighty-five cents on every one hundred pounds of sugar made from beets.[40]

In 1890, Henry T. Oxnard, an eastern entrepreneur, erected the state's first sugar beet refinery, and the initial reports of success drew other towns into a scramble for the industry.[41] Norfolk was second to build a refinery, and, despite the hard times after 1890, the *Omaha World Herald* reported in 1891 that the towns were booming and that everyone was talking about sugar beets: "Merchants have pictures of beets on their letterheads and real estate values are soaring. Six months ago, there were between seventy-five to one hundred empty houses in Norfolk. In May, 1891, four hundred new houses are planned to house the factory employees."[42] There were 2,300 acres of beets in the vicinity of Norfolk which, it was believed, would return about $60 an acre. The factory management planned to buy $138,000 worth of beets annually from farmers and provide a substantial factory payroll for the community.[43]

Beet sugar production proved particularly appealing to the citizens and promoters of Scotts Bluff County. *The Gering Courier* foresaw the practicability of beet production in the North Platte Valley before the factory was constructed at Grand Island. In April 1889, editor Asa B. Wood of *The Courier* reported that a professor at the University of Nebraska was investigating the possibility of raising beets in western Nebraska, and that if the amount of saccharin proved satisfactory a factory would probably be located in the area, thus supplying the valley with a profitable industry.[44] Eventually the combination of irrigation and sugar beets made this area one of the richest agricultural areas in the nation.[45]

Village leaders also attempted to attract state institutions, utilities, and public construction, so that they, too, could provide business for their towns.

The promotional and entrepreneurial qualities of the village leaders became the standard for judging success in late nineteenth-century Nebraska. They were the qualities emphasized by the village editors in their evaluation of potential political candidates. Of these qualities, the first prerequisite for the majority of the Democratic and Republican county editors was success in business; making money was a virtue admired by most village editors.[46] The editor of the *Hayes County Republican*, M. J. Abbott, supported the Republican gubernatorial candidate in 1890, L. D. Richards, as "a member of the strong, conservative business element which has given Nebraska its good name."[47]

Despite local accolades concerning his conservative business practices, the typical village leader of this study became deeply involved in speculative and promotional activity, and, just as in the case of the farmer, much of the capital that he used for promotional activity came from rising real-estate values. When this source of capital dried up, the prairie village lost its dynamic qualities and became the sleepy Main Street of the twentieth century. Without the prospects for dynamic growth, the role of community economic leaders declined, and other groups preempted much of their political power.

Although village leaders generally thought in terms of the promotion of their town, they were not unalterably opposed to agrarian reform proposals. Republican and Democratic village newspapers in the 1880s abound with references to the injustices of the railroads, moneylenders, and trusts. The well-known agrarian analysis of American society in the late nineteenth century was not the only voice raised against the injustices of the time. The Democratic *Cuming County Advertiser,* edited by a man later to be a McKinley backer in 1896, observed: "That the producing classes are being deprived of a proper portion of the proceeds of their toil, is a fact that needs no argument. . . . The farmers are becoming alive to the fact that they are not having a fair chance in the race."[48]

Despite some similarities in approach, the farmers and villagers parted company when they began analyzing the particular causes of the farmer's troubles. While the farmers blamed village businessmen for some of their discomfiture, the villagers found many things to criticize about the farmers, especially their business habits. They felt that many of the farmers' difficulties resulted from poor management, from buying unnecessarily large amounts of goods on credit, and particularly from the haphazard way in which the farmers took care of their new, expensive machinery.[49] Some county editors failed to recognize the economic implications of commercial agriculture and counseled the farmers to return to subsistence agriculture:

> What has happened to the old fashioned farmer who used to salt down his meat, raise all his own vegetables and take corn to town? The other day a farmer came into town with corn which he had sold for 15¢ a bushel and took home with him a bushel of apples at $1.50 and a bushel of potatoes at 25 cents. . . . All of these could be produced on the farm for 75 percent less money.[50]

Besides attributing farm difficulties to poor business practices and a departure from the practices of subsistence agriculture, village editors also adopted the partisan explanations offered by their political parties. The Democratic *Hayes County Herald* took the position that a lower tariff would solve most of the farmers' problems, while the Republican *Hamilton County News* blamed the demands of labor for high wages.[51] In most cases, the village editors offered their comments in helpful goodwill. They accepted many of the agrarian criticisms of the social order and saw a great deal of validity in others, but they modified them to fit their own needs and points of view.

Although the villager sympathized with the farmer, he had many interests which he did not share with his agrarian neighbor. The farmer, it is true, had speculative interests just as the villager, but the farmer was less actively involved in direct speculation. The value of his land closely reflected the net profit he could show after paying freight rates, interest charges, and taxes. Hence, the very nature of commercial farming made him look at the situation not as a speculator but as a producer interested in cutting costs. The villager, on the other hand, realized that opportunity lay in maximum growth. Although the two had a common interest in securing prosperity for the farmer by lowering freight rates and the use of other agrarian programs, the villager could pursue such activity only if it did not interfere with his promotional schemes. Any interference with the status quo in terms of financial structure, leadership, or the flow of capital from the East would interfere more significantly with plans for factories, railroads, irrigation, or sugar-beet production than would hard times for the farmers. In this fundamental difference rested the variations between the agrarian and village acceptance of populism.

4

The Political Leadership of the Village

State political leadership like economic leadership during the 1890s rested to a disproportionate degree in the small towns and villages of Nebraska. Not until 1890 did Omaha produce a governor, while Lincoln had to wait until well into the twentieth century to place one of its citizens in the governor's chair. More important for this study, few farmers became leaders at the state level. Prior to 1890, no governor, senator, or congressman had been a practicing farmer when elected to office.[1] Inhabitants of villages and cities consistently dominated the state legislature both in numerical strength and political influence. Table 10 illustrates the occupational and residential background of the leaders and members of the Nebraska legislature during the last two decades of the century. Village leaders also dominated party leadership at the county level to an even greater degree than they did at the state level. Table 11 shows the domination of county political positions by village residents.[2]

Just as leadership in promotional ventures fell to a relatively few inhabitants of the county seat, so did these same village leaders greatly influence state and county politics. The old-timers formed a recognizable group in county politics, as well as in social and economic affairs. The pattern of village domination of political leadership in each county was roughly similar, but significant variations between counties in this study require that each county be described separately.

In Hamilton County, the Republican party rallied around the official county paper, the *Hamilton County*

Table 10: OCCUPATIONAL STRUCTURE OF THE NEBRASKA LEGISLATURE, 1877-1899

Year	Farmers in Senate	Farmers in House	House Committees Chaired by Farmers
1876-1877	20%	47%	35%
1878-1879	33	58	35
1883	32	50	29
1885	30	45	38
1889	n.a.	47	n.a.
1891	75	77	94
1892-1893	44	66	n.a.
1895	43	53	33
1897	39	61	n.a.
1899	n.a.	57	42

Source: The data used in this table were secured from house and senate journals or legislative manuals for the years in which data are entered in the table. Lists of committee membership were obtained from the same sources. Data on senate committee leadership were not included because so few farmers held such positions during the 1880s.

Dual-occupation individuals, i.e., those who listed themselves as farmer and banker, were classified as nonfarmers. This reflects the fact that many village businessmen either practiced some gentleman farming or held farms for speculative purposes and/or the political desirability of identifying as closely as possible with the mass of the electorate.

Table 11: RESIDENCE OF DEMOCRATIC AND REPUBLICAN COUNTY LEADERS, 1888-1893
(In percent of sample)

Office/Position	Number	County Seat	Other Village	Farm	Unknown
County chairman	23	56%	21%	5%	17%
County officers (clerk, treasurer, sheriff, county attorney)	51	49	14	4	35

Source: Compiled from the political items in the county newspapers used in the study. Many office holders served more than one term in office; these were counted only once.

Republican. Founded in 1874 by L. W. Hastings, the *Republican* soon became a power in county politics. By the late 1880s, editor Hastings usually occupied a key office in the county Republican organization. In reward for its editor's political orthodoxy, the *Republican* enjoyed the advertising of a greater number of the county's businessmen than did the Democratic *Aurora Sun.* Hastings' paper served as the voice of Hamilton County Republicanism, and around its editorial leadership gathered a group of influential lawyers and businessmen of the community. Although this was an informal group, it had enough cohesion to be labeled and recognized as the old-timers.[3] Included in the group's membership were community leaders General Delevan Bates, A. W. Agee, D. A. Schoville, John J. Farley, N. F. Stanley, and Edward J. Hainer.[4]

All of these men, with the exception of Bates, had held public office at the state level, all lived in the county seat, Aurora, and all were active in county Republican organization. Most of them had begun their political careers in Hamilton County by holding one of the county offices.[5]

In addition to the inner circle from Aurora, there was a second group of Republicans from other towns in the county who shared political leadership. Although these men were not mentioned as prominently in the Aurora papers, they held more seats in the legislature than did the Aurora men. Most of them came from the smaller villages in the county, Hampton and Phillips, and, like the Aurora clique, they did not represent primarily agrarian interests.[6]

In Hamilton County, village residents as a group supplied a disproportionate number of the political leaders. The villages of Aurora, Phillips, Marquette, and Hampton, with about 15 percent of the county's population, supplied nearly 75 percent of the county's representation in the lower house of the Nebraska legislature. Of the ten representatives who served between 1880 and 1889, three came from Aurora, three from Phillips, and two from Hampton; only one came from a farm (leaving one whose residence cannot be determined).[7]

The lack of agrarian representation embarrassed Hamilton County leaders and elicited defensive statements from them concerning their guardianship of agrarian interests. On one occasion, the *Hamilton County Republican* assured the citizens of the county that although O. P. Duncan, a legislative candidate and businessman from the village of Phillips, was not a farmer, "He is personally interested in agriculture and is therefore identical with the farming class."[8] However, an opposing paper put it another way, suggesting that the Aurora "shysters 'used'" the Republicans from the other parts of the county.[9]

The villagers' domination of political leadership was even greater than the distribution of representatives indicates because the residents of the villages, especially Aurora, dominated the county conventions. This gave them control of the nominations for county offices and the power to elect delegates to the congressional, senatorial (state), and state conventions.[10]

Political life in Kearney County was somewhat less structured and leadership was less well defined than in Hamilton County. The town father of Minden, Joel Hull, resided in the county for over ten years before he became active in Republican politics. Republicans also lacked an influential and partisan newspaper editor to rally the party followers. The *Kearney County Gazette* was a solidly Republican journal throughout the period under study, but, because of a rapid succession of different owners, its editors lacked the influence in local politics that established old-timers could wield.[11] With the city father and Republican editors refraining from effective political participation, leadership in Kearney County Republicanism often fell to a group of Minden lawyers, James L. McPheeley, George B. Godfrey, and A. H. Burnett. These men were old settlers in the county, but they remained practicing lawyers and did not enter widely into other forms of economic activity as did many lawyers at that time. All of these men had run for public office and served on the county central committee, with McPheeley and Burnett as county chairmen. [12]

In addition to the lawyers, two leading businessmen represented Minden in county politics. Lewis A. Kent, president of the First Minden Bank during the 1880s, began his political career in the county as county clerk in the previous decade. In 1887, he won a seat in the state senate for one term and afterward served as county commissioner and as a "dry" city councilman. Kent's successor as president at the First Minden Bank, Otto Abrahamson, also participated actively in local politics and served from 1887 to 1891 in the state legislature. Kent and Abrahamson, together with the lawyers and other Minden residents, were often referred to as the Minden "ring" by the Farmer's Alliance and Democratic writers.[13]

The Minden Republicans were closely tied to the economic interests of the village, but they showed a wide range of approaches to economic problems. While Otto Abrahamson was known as a "Burlington Man," James McPheeley and Joel Hull actively opposed the Burlington's interests by proposing a state-owned railroad through central Nebraska to the Gulf of Mexico.

Although Kearney Republicanism received significant support from the county seat, there were fewer Minden men associated with either leadership or county officeholding than there were in some of the other counties studied. A list of officeholders compiled from the *Minden Register* in March 1890 shows that the only business and professional men active in politics were the lawyers and bankers previously mentioned.[14] More rural and unknown names appear on these lists compiled in Kearney County than in any other county in the study.[15]

In Howard County, the Republicans barely managed to control the county during the 1880s. Large numbers of Polish and Danish settlers had moved into the southern and western parts of the county and gave several precincts there overwhelming Democratic pluralities.[16] However, the county seat, St. Paul, consistently voted heavily Republican, and its vote gave a slim margin in the county to the Republicans. Republican leaders in St. Paul apparently felt that little could be done to win the Polish and Danish precincts; they made few overtures to these voters and took the lead in county politics and office holding themselves.

Preeminent among Republican village leaders was the founder of St. Paul, J. N. Paul. Paul, a lawyer and president of the St. Paul State Bank, supplied his name and prestige to the party and served in the state senate in the latter part of the 1880s.[17] Other influential Republican leaders from St. Paul were A. E. Cady, the president of the First State Bank and state representative from 1887 to 1889; Charles Chinn, cashier of J. N. Paul's Bank and county chairman in 1890; Alfred W. Gumaer, lumber dealer and state representative in 1889; Robert Harvey, long-time county clerk and publisher of the *Republican Advocate*; and Charles Chaflin, editor of the *Saint Paul Phonograph*.[18] In the latter half of the 1880s, these residents of St. Paul wielded great influence in the county organization and dominated the highest level of public officeholding. Inevitably, they were referred to as the "St. Paul Ring."[19]

Village politicians outside of St. Paul won the lesser political offices in the county. Rasmus Hannibal, son of the founder of the village of Dannebrog, played a prominent part in Republican politics and served as county treasurer from 1887 to 1891. With the exception of Hannibal, Republicans made little effort to appeal to the newer immigrant groups and left the Danes and Poles to the Democrats.[20]

Far-western, newly settled counties showed a greater equality of officeholding between village and rural precincts than Nebraska's older, central counties. Scotts Bluff County was organized in 1889, and the five major county offices (clerk, treasurer, sheriff, county judge, county attorney) were distributed among the inhabitants of five different precincts. The county commissioners also resided outside the county seat, and the offices rotated quite freely among people seldom mentioned in the local newspaper. As the county grew, however, the number of officeholders from the villages increased. By 1893, two of the five county officers lived in Gering, and, in 1895, three came from that city. Although the sample of officeholding is small, county officers tended to come increasingly from the village, and they tended to be recognizable civic leaders.[21] The residence of county officers in Scotts Bluff County for 1889–1895 follows:

Gering	6	(village precinct)
Highland	2	(no village in precinct)
Mengo	2	(no village in precinct)
Mitchell	1	(no village in precinct)
Roubadeau	2	(no village in precinct)
Unknown	3	(no village in precinct)

The village precincts supplied nearly 40 percent of county officeholders. The only citizen of the county to hold state office also lived in the village of

Gering. In Scotts Bluff County, the increasing population, together with the advantages resulting from proximity to government and the media of communications, gave village residents increasing political power.[22]

The Republican politics of Hayes County revolved around the interests of the county seat, Hayes Center, and the personality of one man, M. J. Abbott, the combative editor of the *Hayes County Republican*. In the county election held soon after the founding of the county in 1887, residents of Hayes Center won three of the four major county offices. Abbott won the most important of these, the position of county judge. For both Democrats and farmers, editor Abbott personified all the forces that antagonized them. A staunch prohibitionist, he referred to the Democrats as the "sour mash ticket" who "always stand with the cattlemen against homesteaders."[23] Alliancemen suffered equally under his vitriolic pen, when he wrote: "The independent ring—the only real ring—started out with a bold front and with a confidence born of an assurance of success. The forces of secret organization. . . the conglomerate mass of calamity howlers, disgruntled cranks and boodle politicians."[24] Abbott served throughout the era as secretary of the County Central Committee and set the style of Hayes County Republicanism during the late 1880s. In the short time the county was settled, businessmen and other village residents provided much of the political leadership. After 1890, though, other areas in the county were more equitably represented, a condition which probably reflected the Republican desire to offset the growing power of the Populists.

Republican leadership proved remarkably homogeneous in the two Republican and three Populist counties examined in this study. Although many farmers participated in Republican politics even to the state level, a great majority of the working leaders of the party came from the business elite in the county seat. Moreover, there was a great deal of overlapping between political and economic leadership in these communities. This partially accounts for the hesitancy of the village-oriented state legislature to pass reform legislation which would upset the prevalent boom psychology of the 1880s.

Village leaders dominated most Republican county organizations in Nebraska, and they paid little attention to farm or reform groups. Even many older Republicans who had participated in earlier anti-monopoly movements remained outside the official party organization. In most of the counties studied, a real hostility existed toward the reform wing of the party and its sometime leader, Edward Rosewater of the *Omaha Bee*. Much of the villagers' hostility grew from basic economic differences, but some arose from Rosewater's flamboyant journalism and the competition which the *Weekly Bee* offered county newspapers. Whatever the source of the hostility, the fact remains that reform-minded Republicans found little welcome in the regular County Republican organization. Unfortunately, when the banner of reform became a political necessity, the Republican party had been so cleansed of reform elements that it took a great struggle to rid the party of its conservative leadership.[25]

In small towns in Nebraska, a significant minority of citizens voted Democratic, and many central and eastern counties of the state gave the Democrats a respectable percentage of the total vote. Democrats in central Nebraska counties, such as Hamilton and Kearney, were usually included among the founder's group, and in many counties they had their own struggling newspaper. In most areas of village life, Democrats differed little from their Republican counterparts in ideology or economic status.

In Hamilton County, the Democratic party had its newspaper, the *Aurora Sun,* and on several occasions in the county's history the Democrats even showed marked strength at the polls. The most influential Democrats in the county included E. W. Hurlbut, editor of the *Sun,* and the three Glover brothers, who were merchants and bankers. In 1885, Hurlbut, as the new editor of the *Sun,* led a movement which ended a period of fusion between the Democrats and the farmer-based Anti-Monopoly party. The Glovers participated in state politics, as well as in county politics, and were associated with the Bourbon leadership of the party, which staunchly opposed fusion with the farmers after the mid-1880s. None of the Democratic leaders were extreme partisans, and they mingled socially with the more numerous Republican leaders.[26]

The major national issue between Democrats and the Republicans in pre-Populist Nebraska was the protective tariff. Democrats, as well as Republicans, saw injustices in certain railroad practices and in the operation of eastern trusts; but to an even greater extent than the Republicans or the farmers, the Democrats had a single solution: cut tariffs. But despite all their indignation and oratory directed against the tariff, the Democrats made little impression on the electorate. Farmers in Nebraska did not respond to the tariff issue either before or during the Populist era.[27]

The only success that Hamilton County Democrats won during the five years prior to the Populist era occurred in the election of a county treasurer in 1889 when they briefly merged with the Alliance. The victory was not so much a victory of superior organization or basic political strength as a successful attack on a system obviously in need of reform. Prior to 1889, the county treasurer personally received the interest credited to the county accounts in local banks. The state treasurer had done this for years, and the custom had spread to the county level. It was a generally recognized evil, and the Democrats used the issue effectively; with the Alliance's help, they elected a Democrat to the county treasurer's office.[28]

In addition to the tariff and occasional political opportunities, such as the issue of the treasurer's retention of interest, the Democrats attempted to make political capital out of the farmers' dissatisfaction with the railroads. Typical of the rhetoric of both parties was the *Sun*'s comment on a Republican candidate in 1889: "Now will the people, the taxpayers of the district support the railroad nominee or will they vote for Charles D. Casper, who has no railroad backing or sympathy behind him?"[29] Although this example is from the Democratic newspaper, there is no evidence in Hamilton County to show that Democrats proved to be greater enemies of the railroads than were the Republicans. In terms of the farmers' goals, the major differences existed between Democratic leaders in Aurora and their own followers in rural precincts.

The relative fluidity of Republican politics in Kearney County was accompanied by greater activity and success by Democrats and third-party advocates. The Democrats showed strength in the Danish and in the poorer precincts in the county, and on some occasions they won county offices.[30] The fact that much Democratic strength lay outside the county seat apparently worked for a greater dispersion of Democratic leadership than was the case in Hamilton County. Both Pat A. Hines and I. W. Hawes, who served as county chairmen during the late 1880s, lived outside of the county seat. Minden, the county seat, produced only two leading Democrats, R. P. Stein, the editor of the *Kearney County Democrat,* and Robert St. Clair, an old settler and attorney. Neither man had the influence over this county's politics that Hurlbut or the Glover brothers exerted in Hamilton County.

The influence of rural precincts and their leaders caused the entire Democratic organization in the county to sympathize with agrarian demands. Throughout the mid-1880s, Kearney County served as a proving ground for Democratic and agrarian fusion attempts. Unlike their counterparts in Hamilton County, Minden Democrats eagerly participated in this movement. R. P. Stein, for example, ran for the state senate on an Alliance-Democratic ticket. Pat Hines, the most dynamic Democratic leader in the county, consistently advocated fusion with agrarian groups throughout the decade. The Kearney County Democrats showed the most consistent agrarian orientation of any county in this study.[31]

Howard County Democrats based their strength on Polish and Danish immigrants in the southern and western parts of the county. Nevertheless, the two dominant leaders in Democratic politics, X. Piasecki and J. O. P. Hildebrand, came from the county seat, St. Paul. Piasecki and Hildebrand were often mentioned as the virtual rulers of the Howard County Democracy.[32] During the 1890 county convention, Edward Steel, a delegate from the Warsaw precinct, told the convention that "St. Paul ring had everything its own way, and the county delegates danced to the music without a murmur."[33]

In the western counties included in the study, the prohibition issue dominated the energies of the Democratic party. The issue in these counties polarized itself more around the old parties than it did in the more populous and ethnically diverse counties to the east where it was frequently settled under local party labels. The Hayes County Democracy, for example, divided over the prohibition issue. The Hayes Center faction, led by John M. Hughes and Cal Wilson, wanted saloons in the village, a fact which made the Democratic farmers within the party uneasy. The wet orientation of village Democratic leaders alienated rural leaders and tended to align them with the Alliance and against the Democrats, a melancholy situation usually avoided in central Nebraska where the local labels often relieved pressure on party leaders.[34]

Democratic leaders in Gering, the county seat of Scotts Bluff County, were similarly handicapped by the prohibition issue. Union labor, Alliance, and Republican organizations all waited to recruit farmers alienated by the wet position taken by the Democratic party.

Democratic leaders throughout central and western Nebraska were usually recruited from the same residential and occupational groups as their Republican counterparts. In most instances, this resulted in a close and friendly cooperation with village Republicans. The basic differences between the two groups were the rhetoric of the tariff debate and the vital local issue of prohibition. Village Democrats formed the core of the opposition to prohibition but, at least in central Nebraska, they were able to enlist considerable Republican support in most villages.

There were significant exceptions, however, to the picture of Republican and Democratic harmony described in Hamilton County. Some Democratic leaders in Kearney, Hayes, and Howard counties showed a marked inclination to cooperate with agrarian reformers throughout the period studied, which resulted in Democratic–farmer fusion tickets at the county level during the last half of the decade. This tendency was particularly noticeable in Kearney and Hayes counties, which had a significant number of Democratic leaders recruited from rural areas. Although the Democratic party followed the urban-oriented Bourbon leaders, Miller and Morton, during the late 1880s, the party contained a significant number of recognized and established leaders who would cooperate with agrarian demands. Structurally, the Democratic party in the counties covered in this study was better prepared throughout the 1880s to take up the banner of reform than its Republican opponents.

In Cuming County, the usual political pattern of party domination was reversed, and the Democrats reigned as the dominant political group. But here more than in some of the Republican counties, leaders from the county seat dominated the party. "Judge" J. C. Crawford was the leading Democrat in the county, as well as one of the community leaders in West Point, the county seat. A lawyer, banker, and businessman of varied interests, he was closely associated with John D. Neligh, the town father and leading Republican. Crawford became a perpetual and unsuccessful candidate for circuit judge, but his numerous political defeats did not hinder him from becoming a Democratic leader with a statewide reputation. In addition to Crawford, West Point produced a large number of eminent Democratic leaders: Otto Bauman, president of the First National Bank and candidate for state auditor in 1894; P. F. O'Sullivan, lawyer and candidate for state auditor in 1892; and M. J. Hughes, banker and candidate for Congress in 1896.[35]

Cuming County received greater than average recognition from the Democrats because of its consistent Democratic majorities and because its Democratic leaders proved to be loyal followers of the urban leaders, Morton and Miller. Like other leading Democrats in Nebraska villages, J. C. Crawford and Otto Bauman supported McKinley in 1896.

Although the Democrats dominated Cuming County, several local Republicans received state and national recognition. E. K. Valentine of West Point served first in Congress and then as sergeant-at-arms of the United States Senate. Uriah Bruner, Crawford's father-in-law, was a candidate for governor in 1878, while Neligh was a candidate for the Republican nomination for Congress.[36]

Both statistical data and subjective evaluation of power relationships have indicated that Nebraska politics was dominated to a great extent by entrenched village and urban interests. Furthermore, in most of the counties included in this study, it made little practical difference if village Republicans or Democrats controlled the political machinery of the county, for the goals of both parties, with the exception of the prohibition–cultural question, were essentially the same. The truth of the situation was not lost to the farmers, for the letters columns of county newspapers abound with references to domination of county politics by village cliques. A Hamilton County farmer expressed his frustration and revealed the methods of village domination of county politics in the following letter to the *Aurora Sun:*

> Mr. Editor: We wish through the columns of your paper to
> say a few words concerning the Republican convention held

in Aurora, Oct. 5th. We attended the convention expecting
to see the farmers, who composed nine-tenths of the delegation, do something to lessen the burden of taxation, which
is increasing every year in this county. But we saw them
led blindly as in the past, and the result shows that not one
farmer is represented on the ticket of the five principal offices. It is true that most of them own land, but none of
them have done any farm labor for years. When Mr. Koster
told the people that we wished to see a man in the treasurer's office do the work for $2,000 and turn over the inter-
est on the surplus to the treasury of the county to help pay
the expenses, he was hissed and called a queer stalwart Republican.

> We saw a few of the so-called leaders of the Republican
Party control the entire convention. The bankers and attorneys of Aurora did the business of the convention, and
the delegates from the county shut their eyes and said yes.

> We heard one official remark just after his nomination
that not one farmer in fifty was capable of performing the
duties of any of the county officers.[37]

Another contemporary account pictures the county decision-making process
from the viewpoint of the farmers:

> Bankers and lawyers were presumed to be endowed with
superior wisdom and acumen which particularly fitted
them to be the especial advisors and guardians of the
people in all matters political. . . . When it came to the
more important legislatures and congresses that they
alone were qualified to fill these big positions. . . . Convention nominations were usually made on the day preceding the conventions in the back room of the "bell
weather" Shylock of the county.[38]

The power of the villages is also obvious in the personnel of the delegations sent to the state conventions of the major parties. Here again, the villagers used their domination of the county convention to select delegates to
the state conventions. A Nance County correspondent reported this situation
and its results:

> Let us look at a few facts. In a great many counties of our
state it was a very easy matter to get to the state convention;

at the county convention there were many hundred precincts which were not represented. Counties as far east as
Nance and Cass proved no exception to the rule. . . . Brad
Slaughter could promise him [Richards] the Nance County
delegation but he could not give him [Richards] a majority
of the Nance County votes.[39]

Statistical data, a study of community power structures, and the testi-
mony of contemporaries have all indicated that the fortunes of Nebraska's
farm population rested in the hands of men not directly interested in agriculture. Undeniably, many village leaders concerned themselves with agrarian
problems, but the difficulties of the farmer were not their primary interests.
The farmers of Nebraska realized this fact and verbalized it on many occasions. Because of the difficulties of communication and organization in rural
areas, the agrarian population seemed content to follow the leadership of
business and professional men as long as economic conditions remained prosperous. However, when the economy collapsed in the late 1880s, the farmers
organized the Farmers' Alliance and the Independent party and challenged
the political and economic leadership of the village and urban groups.[40]

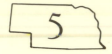

The Populists and the Village

The reasons for the dramatic rise in agrarian political and economic activity in the late 1880s are described in the Populist press and have been discussed in previous chapters. The western farmer blamed railroad rates, high interest charges, and high taxes, along with the appreciation of the currency, for most of his troubles.[1] The Nebraska farmer had endured these difficulties throughout the 1880s, but two new factors, which became important in the late 1880s, served as the immediate causes of the farmers' revolt. These factors were the collapse of the real-estate boom in 1888,[2] and the wide fluctuations of commodity prices between 1888 and 1890. (See Figure 5.)

The years 1889 and 1890 were critical for the Nebraska farmer. Corn prices were comparatively low during the middle years of the 1880s, but they plummeted to less than twenty cents per bushel during 1888. This was at least partially responsible for a substantial increase in Alliance political activity during the latter part of 1888 and in early 1889. In 1890, a great drought struck the state and caused nearly a 300 percent increase in corn and wheat prices. Many farmers who had gambled on putting cheap corn into larger numbers of cattle now found corn priced far above their reach. The combination of excellent crop years with low prices, and poor crop years with high prices and short supply, had devastating economic and psychological effects on the farmer. Commodity price fluctuations, together with the prospective loss of his capital because of declining real-estate values, combined with general agrarian complaints to produce the fervor of 1890.

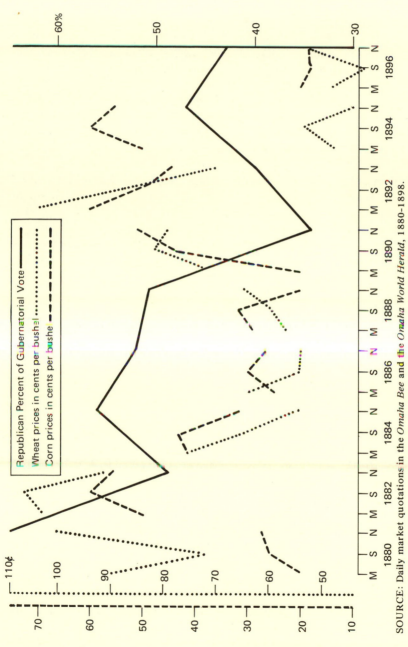

SOURCE: Daily market quotations in the *Omaha Bee* and the *Omaha World Herald*, 1880–1898.

Figure 5: Commodity Prices and the Republican Vote (Omaha Commodity Prices in March, September, November)

The great growth in agrarian economic and political activity that preceded the Populist revolt began in 1889 and became significant in early 1890. By the summer of 1890, the number of local Alliances had grown from two hundred to fifteen hundred, a state Alliance newspaper had been organized, and the farmers had embarked on a political movement, which their contemporaries labeled a "revolution."[3]

There is little material concerning the organization and growth of local and county Alliances in most of the counties in Nebraska. This is particularly true of the years prior to 1889 when there were few newspapers dedicated to the Alliance point of view. In some counties, however, it is possible to piece together some of the facts concerning the origin of the movement. The six sample counties in this study were selected primarily because they contained comprehensive county newspapers whose issues for the late 1880s are still in existence.

Hamilton County became one of the most important Populist counties in the state. It consistently returned great numbers of Populist votes after 1889, and it was the home of one of the most noted Populist legislators, Fred Newberry. Newberry served two terms in the Nebraska House of Representatives and was the author of the Maximum Freight Act, the most important act passed during the Populist era in Nebraska.[4]

The Hamilton County Alliance had existed since the early 1880s, but it did not become truly significant until 1889. At that time, a revived organizational drive began and was carried out by three hired organizers. One of these men, L. C. Floyd, remains obscure, but the other two were prominent residents of the county. W. H. Fall was a Democratic politician, and James A. Wilson was one of the most successful farmers in the county. Wilson reportedly received three dollars for every convert he made, a sum which he turned over to the newly established Alliance library fund. Although Wilson was one of the largest landholders in the county, his name had never appeared in conjunction with either the Republican or Democratic leaders in Aurora.[5] By early 1890 the Alliance membership in Hamilton County reached nearly a thousand and by midyear, Valentine Horn, an old Anti-Monopoly politician, headed the newly formed county organization.[6]

Wilson, Fall, and other early Alliance organizers in Hamilton County proclaimed that their organization would establish "business" organizations to secure better prices for farm products.[7] These associations soon sprang up in the villages of Phillips, Bromfield, Aurora, and Hampton, and they bought and sold basic commodities such as grain, coal, and flour. Initial enthusiasm in the county ran high; the Democratic *Aurora Sun* reported that farmer enthusiasm reminded them of that of the old Free-Soilers.[8]

Unlike the Hamilton County Alliance which became dormant between 1885 and 1888, the Kearney County Alliance remained active politically and economically during the 1880s. An Alliance ticket for county officers polled seventy-six votes in the county election of 1886, and a resident of the county served on the Alliance State Committee during the middle years of the decade. Throughout the 1880s and 1890s, this Alliance, Anti-Monopoly, and later Populist group, remained intact and kept much the same leadership. Three men, Edward Krick, Pat H. Driscoll, and J. T. Kellie, led the Alliance during these years and became influential Populist leaders after 1890. They led the Alliance into continual forays in county politics, and, on some occasions, they ran fusion tickets with the Democrats.[9] The continuity of farmer leadership led one of the opposition papers to accuse the Alliance-Populists of letting a clique dominate their conventions in much the same way that the conventions of the older parties were dominated by a small group.[10]

In Hayes and Scotts Bluff counties, the two western counties used in this study, organization of the Alliance only shortly preceded the election of 1890. These counties were sparsely populated and had been settled for only a few years. During the spring of 1889, farmers' clubs were organized in nearly all of the precincts in Hayes County. As in Hamilton County, the first wave of organization followed the drop in commodity prices. Farmers showed such fervent interest during these early months that the club in Government Precinct numbered forty members by the first part of March 1889.[11]

During the fall of 1889 many of the newly organized clubs officially sponsored debates concerning the possibility of joining the Farmers' Alliance. By the following spring, most of them had decided to affiliate, and soon they attracted some state Alliance leaders to the county to speak to them. The organizers of the farmers' clubs included two businessmen from the county seat, E. L. Evans and J. W. Ivey, but dirt farmers dominated the Alliance organization. Jasper Koontz, a prominent Republican farmer with no previous reform activities, became the first president of the county Alliance, and later became a Populist state senator. The Alliance in Hayes County immediately became a formidable political organization, but it did not engage in any of the economic activity characteristic of the Alliance in other counties.[12]

The Alliance had a late and inauspicious beginning in Scotts Bluff County. It was not until the spring of 1890 that the farmers began to organize in the valley south of the county seat, Gering. By May, the farmers felt strong enough to consider the question of political action, a question which the editor of the Republican newspaper believed to be unnecessary because of the "sympathetic" nature of Scotts Bluff County Republicanism.[13]

In the northeastern counties of the state, the economic issues which pre-
cipitated the rapid growth of the Alliance in the other sections of the state
were largely eclipsed by the increasing urgency of the prohibition issue. For
example, in heavily German Cuming County, prohibition overshadowed eco
nomic concerns; the county press, consequently, contained fewer notices of
Alliance activities than that of any other section of the state.[14]

As a general rule, the rapid growth of the Farmers' Alliance received the
approval of county editors as long as the members stressed issues that were
not antagonistic to the regular Republican and Democratic interests in the
village. Most groups in rural Nebraska could at least unite rhetorically against
the railroads, plutocrats, and trusts, which they all seemed to believe worked
against western interests; however, the village and agrarian Nebraskans divided on specific programs for remedying these inequities. In this respect, the
Alliance changed the nature of farm protest from a vague tirade against dis-
tant "interests" to specific programs, which often countered the interests of
local leaders.[15]

The complaints usually attributed only to the Populists were actually indigenous to the whole plains state environment; the Populists did not have a
monopoly on monopoly-baiting. The staunchly Republican *Hayes County
Republican,* for example, anticipated Populist complaints before the Alliance
moved into politics: "The old story of trusts, pools and usurers is known to
us all and we have suffered accordingly, and how long we continue to suffer
such bondage remains only for us to say. . . . We can build our own railroad
and govern the same."[16] Not only were Republican and Democratic papers
sympathetic with the broad and vague outline of the farmers' complaints, but
they had almost universally applauded the organization of farmers' clubs and
Alliances: "Our grange is prospering finely. It seems that the people are awakening to a full understanding of their positions for never before has the determined disposition to organize been so manifest."[17]

The original feelings of goodwill held by many village groups toward the
Alliances also are illustrated by the following item from the *St. Paul Phonograph,* then a Republican paper: "Whether the Alliance ever elects a candidate
or not the movement will have done lots of good. It has set the people think-
ing on the political questions of the day and they will study it [*sic*] intel-
ligently too."[18]

The motives for village approval of farmer organizations stemmed partly
from real sympathy for the farmers' difficulties and partly from a desire to
mollify and hence keep the farmers under control in the old parties. The Republican editor of the *Hayes County Republican* reasoned that since it would
take years to train new men to act in the state legislature, the farmers would

be better off if they relied on the experience of previously elected village legislators.[19]

As the Alliance became increasingly powerful, it developed explicit programs to solve the farmers' problems at every level of political and economic activity. The radical nature of the Alliance rationale in the eyes of the nonagrarian segments of Nebraska's population grew because of the farmers' vigor in pushing into areas from which they had heretofore been excluded. This political awakening of the farmer, together with his cooperative and socialistic schemes, his distrust of the old leadership, and the sheer power of the movement, increasingly disturbed many of the old leaders and dominant groups in the state.

By the early summer of 1890 the initial, though qualified, approval of the revived Alliance by village leaders turned to outright hostility. The reasons behind the villagers' attack on the Alliance fell into two categories: the radical and noisy attack on the status quo, and direct agrarian attack on the economic and political leadership of the village entrepreneurs themselves.

The farmers' attack on the status quo partially arose from a sense of economic desperation and political alienation. Omar M. Kem, the two-term Congressman from Broken Bow, expressed the feelings of the farmer in the following manner. Kem "had worked hard but remained a very poor man, despite frugal habits," until at last he wrote, "I feel like crying out. My God, my God, why hast thou forsaken me?" Kem, like other Nebraska farmers, "talked with his neighbors" and found that they felt that forces outside themselves were responsible for their plight. Kem wrote in his memoirs:

> In my investigations I found that the laws of our country
> were made and were executed by one class of our people,
> namely, the monied class, that they either sat in the halls of
> Congress and our state legislature in person, or they con-
> troled absolutely the fellow who did sit there. . . . This
> monied class was composed of those who loaned money,
> those who built and ran the railroads and the great manu-
> facturing industries.[20]

Kem's belief was a variation on the theme that many Republican and Democratic editors had used throughout the 1880s, but it was more specific. The accusations were more concrete, and when he accused those who sat in the state legislature of oppressing the farmer, he was, in effect, condemning the established leadership of the state.

Populist leaders like Omar Kem based many of their arguments for reform on the assumption that the farmer provided the backbone of American life

and that the future of the nation rested with the tough, vigorous West rather
than with the effete East.[21] This argument pervaded the whole Midwest and
was familiar to most village inhabitants. "The seat of the empire has come
west of the Alleghenies to remain forever" wrote the editor of the *Hayes
County Republican.*[22] Such pretensions and hopes of the Midwest, however,
were magnified in the often bombastic Populist rhetoric of those leaders carried away with their hostility toward the system. The boiler-plated, or nationally syndicated, section of Populist county papers were particularly violent. An item in the *Hamilton County Register* read:

> the beast of private property. . . the plutocrats have thought-
> lessly laid aside law and logic and impatiently appealed to
> an ignorant force known as "mob violence" which will turn
> on them and smash them out of existence. . . . Individualism
> must soon go, or Communism will soon come.[23]

Other Populist spokesmen went beyond the vague blanket condemnations
characteristic of the 1880s and attacked the institutions that were closely related to the life and prosperity of village Nebraska. During the campaign of
1890 at a meeting in Dannebrog, Howard County, the Populist candidate for
lieutenant-governor proclaimed "that the people had been fed by the politicians these many years upon sophistry [*sic*] history while the real problem
was the alarming and constantly increasing inequalities of the distinction
[*sic*] of wealth in the U.S."[24] The Populist *Hamilton County Register* compared the decline of equality in the United States with the decline of Rome:

> Already a few thousand men own more than half the wealth
> of the country. And nearly all this concentration has taken
> place in a quarter of a century. . . . The concentration of
> power keeps pace with the concentration of wealth. . . the
> policy of the nation is molded by the few who own this
> vast wealth.[25]

This process was visible to the editor of the *Register* in the long lists of trusts
organized between 1889 and 1891—seventy-one in all.[26] He believed that
these conditions must be relieved or another "French Revolution" would result in sweeping the "beast of private property and profitable religions from
the face of the earth."[27] Another item in the *Hamilton County Register*
sounded frankly revolutionary: "The bloody work of capitalism continues
unchecked. In Denver last Monday, a brick manufacturer and eight Negro
scabs. . . opened fire. . . . Two men were killed outright."[28] Populist rhetoric
as reflected in the boiler-plated sections of their county press (they comprised

about 70 percent of most weekly papers) was considerably more radical than that encountered in locally edited sections. Occasionally a local Populist editor would comment on the immoderate statements of national leaders, as when the editor of the *Hamilton County Register* admitted that "most agreed that she [Mrs. Lease] handled the truth with too much vigor."[29]

Although Populist editors reflected the economic miseries and antagonisms of their agrarian readers, a call for the radical renovation of the social order was used more as a threat than a specific program. They mentioned violence chiefly to denounce it; they suggested the downfall of capitalism only if it were not modified to meet their petty-bourgeois demands.

After initial approval of the aims of the farmers' movement, many regular party editors began attacking the wild "rantings and ravings" of the radical Populists. Although there was no united Democratic and Republican opposition to the Populists, most village leaders soon became concerned over the volume and extremism of some of the Populist demands. Since most Nebraskans were united at least theoretically against trusts and railroads, it was not so much the Populists' attack on the excesses of capitalism as an economic system that bothered village leaders as it was their belief that Populist descriptions of bad economic conditions discouraged the flow of investment capital into the state. Most village leaders believed that eastern capital had played a significant part in Nebraska's phenomenal growth during the 1880s Consequently, the reaction of village leaders to Populist "calamity howling" paralleled the view of the editor of the *Sutton Advertiser*:

> Emigration is turning away in disgust and capital is packing
> its grip and preparing to go home. The man who is willing
> to aggravate and lead the overwrought public clamor for the
> sake of office deserves more scathing ridicule than the feeble
> ability of the *Advertiser*.[30]

Many village leaders would have also agreed with the editor of the *Minden Gazette* when he explained that while "one class of our citizens try to build up the state and encourage home enterprises to keep as much of the wealth at home as possible, another class is clamoring for laws which would prevent such conditions."[31]

In addition to the businessman's fear that Populist furor would scare away eastern capital, he worried that Populist legislators might impose stringent usury laws to accomplish the same purpose. The *Omaha World Herald* presented the following point of view:

> There seems to be a feeling among eastern investors that the
> present legislatures of South Dakota, Kansas and Nebraska

> will make laws so radical and of such a stringent nature that
> in the future it will be impossible to obtain a dollar of east-
> ern money for investment. This impression has been strength-
> ened by resolutions passed by the Alliance Clubs and from
> interviews had with leading members of the Alliance Party.[32]

Village leaders had condoned agrarian complaints against railroads or the
money power of eastern capitalists as long as these complaints did not endanger the flow of capital from the East to the West. When they did endanger
capital procurement, the businessman's initial approval of many Populist programs turned to frankly expressed hostility.

Of even greater concern to the village leaders were those Alliance activities
that aimed at replacing the villages' primary function as the supplier of goods
and services to their immediate trading area. Much of the farmers' program
was directed toward this end, for the farmers did not direct all of their attacks against railroads, moneylenders, or eastern monopolists. The local merchant, elevator operator, banker, or lawyer received a good share of agrarian
hostility. When many Populist orators spoke against the monopolies, they
had in mind the conditions that existed in their locality; for example, it was
assumed that local elevator operators worked closely with the railroads to set
prices at the elevator and facilitate efficient handling of the grain.[33]

Farmers mistrusted middlemen in general, and they believed that they
reaped large profits from their merchandising and service activities. Undoubtedly, this feeling received added strength when the farmers observed the pre-
tentious Victorian houses that village leaders erected after they had achieved
a measure of success.[34] In order to fight what they considered to be excessive
profits of local businessmen, the Alliances began an ambitious program of cooperative activity, the most common of which was the Alliance store. Many
farmers considered this type of activity the most significant part of the Alliance's program. In Hayes County, a correspondent addressed the farming
population in this vein:

> we shall call a meeting. . . and see what the people think of
> organizing a Farmers' Alliance the object of which would be
> to put a store in Fairfield to be owned in shares by the or-
> ganization. We can talk for ourselves, let us do for ourselves.[35]

Even more to this point was a letter from a Populist farmer addressed to M. J.
Abbott, editor of the *Hayes County Republican.*

> We're going to have a paper here before long and then things
> will pop. We'll have an Alliance Store too, at Hayes Center,

and back these merchants off the track. You just wait till
we control things and we'll make you town fellers hump
yourselves.[36]

The Alliance store was a popular remedy for the farmers' grievances, and, in
nearly all of the counties studied, the farmers attempted to use this method
to lower their costs.[37] Usually the county Alliance hired a local businessman
or former clerk to manage the store or elevator.[38] In some counties where its
strength was not great, the Alliance operated through a purchasing agency instead of the store, while in others it endorsed a local merchant who priced his
goods to their liking.[39]

As the Alliance grew in strength it expanded its economic activity. In
Hamilton County, the farmers expanded their merchandising activities to all
four villages in the county and, in January 1891, organized the Farmers' Alliance Mutual Insurance Company. The Farmers' Alliance also showed interest in these mutual insurance associations, which were intended primarily to
provide protection to crops and farm property.[40] In other counties, the pattern was much the same. Cuming County farmers formed the Swedish Farmers' Mutual Fire Insurance Company of Cuming and Burt counties in the
spring of 1890, while Kearney County farmers formed a mutual insurance
company shortly after the first Alliance store opened.[41] Other Alliance projects included a grain elevator in Hamilton County and a cooperative loan
agency in Hayes County, which hoped to obtain eastern capital and loan it at
6 percent.[42]

County editors at this time were not openly hostile to the Alliance but
they increasingly pointed out the shortcomings and difficulties inherent in
the farmers' movement. In 1890, the editor of the *Cuming County Advertiser*
expressed doubt that the Alliance stores would really lower costs much "even
though such co-operative enterprises are working well in Germany."[43] In
Scotts Bluff County, A. B. Wood, editor of the *Gering Courier*, counseled the
farmers against letting demagogues turn the "country people" against the
"town people."[44] The villages' admiration of agrarian attempts to cut their
production and marketing costs soon turned to outright hostility. The villagers resented and feared the displacement of their retail establishments. The
editor of the *Aurora Sun* expressed this feeling in the following manner:

> At present the Alliance seems to be working to abolish the
> "middle man" and to transact their business through alliance
> stores, elevators and other cooperative enterprises. In some
> places the old dealers have been formally boycotted. Under
> such circumstances the alliance newspapers cannot expect

the support from the townspeople needed to insure their financial success. The newspaper. . . is. . . a part of a grand
system of specialized industry that has been built up by the
demands of modern life. A blow aimed at the old and well
established methods of buying and selling goods strikes the
county newspaperman even harder than it does the merchant or the grain and stock dealer. A few alliance papers
may gain a circulation large enough to justify their continued publication, but a fight between the farmers and the
townspeople means that the paper devoted to the alliance
must go along without much home advertising.[45]

The *Aurora Sun's* attitude was not an isolated example. The *Hamilton
County Republican* joined in the attack and foreshadowed the coming breach
between villager and farmer:

businessmen have acknowledged that it is not good policy. . .
to support a paper that is always using its influence to separate the farmers of the county and the businessmen of the
city. It is the wild harpings of the would-be McKeighan
stripe of newspapers that breeds most of the dissatisfaction
between the farmer and the businessman. This stripe of
newspaper are always preaching to the farmer that there is
a combination somewhere to rob the farmer. . . . This
"newspaper" then prints mail order ads and the farmer
sends for it and ends up with the goods our merchants
would not sell at any price.[46]

Villager opposition became such a political liability to Populist political
success that Populist leaders repeatedly attempted to mollify villagers. J. W.
Edgerton, secretary of the Douglas County Convention, assured the citizens
of Omaha that farm and urban interests remained the same even though, he
admitted, "some farmers seemed to distrust the city."[47] John Powers assured
an urban audience in 1892 that "we make no attempt to make merchants of
ourselves. The mercantile business should be left to them [*sic*] merchants. . . .
The interest of the merchants is the interest of the farmer."[48]

Village merchants did more than protest verbally against the farmers' entry
into competition with them. Managers of Alliance stores soon found themselves unable to secure many items from wholesalers who sympathized with
established village retailers. When the Victor Alliance at Lawrence, Nebraska,
ordered a barrel of oil from the Standard Oil Company at Hastings, they were

refused service on the grounds that they were not engaged in the "regular trade."[49] Paxton Gallagher, a wholesale merchant in Omaha, refused to deal with the Alliance store at Oak, Nebraska, on similar grounds:

> December 26, 1889
>
> Dear Sir:
> We have just been informed for the first time that you are operating a grange store. This being the case, we cannot fill any more orders from you as much as we would like to do business with you. If the information we have received is not right please let us hear from you.[50]

County Alliances replied with the only weapon at their disposal; they organized boycotts of merchants and wholesalers who engaged in such practices. When the state Alliance passed a resolution calling for the use of the boycott, village merchants became even more antagonistic.[51]

The struggle for the control of the county press became the most sensitive area of competition between village leaders and farmers during the Populist era, since most county editors wielded great influence in local political affairs. Metropolitan dailies did not reach into many rural areas, so the local editor was much more of an opinion molder than is the case in the twentieth century.[52] Most of the county papers operated on a meager profit margin and consequently pursued every new source of revenue. The economic prize in any county was the county and city printing contract, which was awarded solely on the basis of partisan political considerations. The number of newspapers started after 1890 illustrates the fact that many enterprising young editors realized that the success of the new party in county elections made the publishing of new Populist-oriented papers profitable. The *Hamilton County Register* originated under such conditions. The founder of the paper, George L. Burr, had been the editor of a Republican paper in Blue Hill, Nebraska. Shortly after the Populist victories in the 1890 elections, Burr underwent a transformation in political ideology, moved to Aurora, and established the Populist *Register*. His newspaper was not fully accepted by the rather suspicious farmers until the spring of 1891 when Fred Newberry and other Populist leaders indicated their approval by taking out subscriptions. Later in the year, the *Register* became the official paper of the Independent party, and the party central committee voted unanimously to pay for enough three-month subscriptions to give the *Register* the largest circulation in the county. These subscriptions were given to farmers who let their subscriptions to the *Sun* and the *Republican* lapse. The *Register* eventually became the dominant paper in the community and is the only one which has survived.[53]

In Cuming County, county patronage remained securely in the hands of the *Cuming County Advertiser,* a paper which never swerved from its appeals to the German majority of the county. The *Advertiser* became the official county paper after the prohibition issue became acute, and prohibition always was more important to its editors than economic reform.[54] Significantly, no Independent or Populist paper was established in West Point.

In strongly Populist Kearney County, J. I. Frederick and J. M. Hamilton bought the Republican paper, the *Kearney County Gazette,* in the spring of 1890 and gave to it a Populist stance. In their initial statement as publishers, they stated what they believed to be the position of the majority of Nebraska's newspapers:

> The county press of Nebraska is almost a unit in denouncing extortionate railroad rates, and in urging that the severe exactions of monopolies are the supreme causes for the present agricultural depression. When we take into consideration the real condition of these papers and the leverage that is used to throttle them it is surprising that such unanimity should exist.[55]

The editors of the *Gazette* were further strengthened in their allegiance to populism when, after a disagreement with Alliance leaders, the Alliance threatened to withdraw its membership's support of the *Gazette* and establish its own paper.[56] On other occasions, Alliances would sponsor formal boycotts of hostile papers.

In heavily Populist Howard County, the Republican *St. Paul Phonograph* changed publishers in 1890 and became Populist-oriented. Thus, the major papers in the Populist counties studied became Populist in sympathy. Western counties that remained Republican kept their Republican, but reform-inclined editors, while Cuming County, with its heavily Democratic German population, supported no Populist paper at all.

The Alliance papers found themselves in a desperate situation, and a perplexing dilemma, when their editorials and boiler-plated material alienated local merchants. If they espoused the antibusiness ideology of the agrarian radicals, they were in almost certain danger of losing their advertisers since most advertising was local in origin. In six issues of the Populist *Hamilton County Register* selected at random between 1891 and 1893, local advertising accounted for 76 percent of the column inches of advertising. On the other hand, if they made ideological concessions to the advertisers, they stood in real danger of losing Alliance support as did the *Minden Gazette* in Kearney County. For this reason, even the county press preferred to talk in terms of eastern monopolists rather than in terms of monopolies and price fixing in their own communities. Populist papers faced with this dilemma sought to allay the fears of village merchants:

> The attitude of the retail dealers toward the Independent
> movement is one of the mysteries of this generation. We
> can understand something of the feeling against the farmers'
> Alliance because the Alliance at its inception. . . before it
> was properly informed as to where the blow came from. . .
> under the effects of which they complain, took a hostile at-
> titude to the retail dealers but with the Independent Party
> this does not exist. The Independent Party is formed for the
> purpose of making money plentiful and relieving the general
> public. . . among which are towns and its businessmen. . .
> from the grasp of monopoly.[57]

When attempts to conciliate the merchants failed to attract more advertising, the Populist editors turned to economic measures. At a meeting of Populist editors at Aurora in December 1891, the editors concluded that "businessmen discriminated strongly against them on account of political prejudices." After serious discussion, they felt that the only remedy was direct action by the local Alliances. The farmer, they felt, paid indirectly for most advertising, so he should patronize only those merchants who supported his newspaper.[58] There is no way of knowing how effective such Populist boycott campaigns were, but, in the three Populist counties in this study, the significant fact stands out that the newspapers that have survived were the three which supported the Populists. The Republican papers that have survived were decidedly reform inclined;[59] the only paper that was hostile to the basic reforms advocated by the Populists and has survived is the Democratic *Cuming County Advertiser.*

In addition to direct agrarian competition with their businesses, the villagers complained about the farmers' lack of interest in projects considered vital to village growth. A case in point is the villagers' frequent attempts to acquire state institutions. During most of the period covered in this study, the citizens of Aurora, the county seat of Hamilton County, made repeated attempts to obtain a state normal school. Despite some sympathy for the farmers' cause, the Democratic and Republican leadership in Aurora was much more interested in the immediate, more tangible problem of obtaining the school than in fighting for the causes of the farmer. In 1886, A. W. Agee, a village leader, ran for the legislature on the normal school platform. He won, but the school never materialized.

The leaders of Aurora did not give up their desire for a state normal school, and, during the 1891 session of the legislature, they descended upon Lincoln in an effort to lobby the bill through for their city. Hamilton County, by this time, was represented by two rural Populists, and even though they supported the Aurora Normal Bill, they were attacked in the regular Democratic paper for their ineffectiveness in aiding the village:

> His [Fred Newberry's] opposition to the measures was vin-
> dictive. He used strong invective in place of argument. At-
> tacked Douglas and Lancaster County delegations alluded
> to them as "robbers of the state." Newberry is so violent
> that he lost all support even among Alliance-men, and the
> Aurora Normal Bill was defeated.[60]

The bill was of vital importance to Aurora's leading citizens, many of whom took the trouble to travel to Lincoln to lobby for the school. Both Democrats and Republicans were equally interested; only the Populists dragged their feet. The Democratic weekly fumed and sputtered at both of the Populist representatives from Hamilton County, and it concluded an attack upon them by suggesting that the next representatives from the county be selected on the basis of attitude toward the normal school. Representative Newberry, the editor thought, had spent too much time attacking the railroads.[61]

The Populists came into further conflict with many village promoters when they opposed the bounty on beet sugar production, which had been en-
acted by the 1889 legislature, because they felt that the direct subsidy to the manufacturer rather than to the beet producer was another example of the exploitation of the farmer.[62] County Populist papers complained that the Alliance was being labeled as the fomenter of opposition to beet production, but they held that the Grand Island refinery itself brought on the attacks. The Populist *Hamilton County Register* argued that the factory was efficient, for the beets in that area had an above-average yield, but the manufacturers, who received bounties of one cent per pound of sugar from the United States and two cents per pound from Nebraska's government, did not share this with either the producers or consumers. Populist Senator Switzler claimed that the Grand Island factory controlled the market price and that if the farmers of the area were to rebel against this arrangement, the company had options on enough land around Grand Island to raise beets itself.[63] The Populists argued that if the refineries would not lower prices, then the legislature could by lowering the bounty.[64] The Populist-dominated legislature in 1891 repealed the bounty, an action particularly unpalatable to city and village boards of trade. Henry Oxnard, president of the Grand Island Sugar Beet Company, had threatened his Populist opponents that he would build no more plants in

other Nebraska cities if the bounty were repealed.[65] He kept his word and the sugar beet boom in central Nebraska came to an end.

The extent of conflict between the villager and the farmer is illustrated by voting statistics from the six sample counties. In these counties, there were ninety-nine precincts; seventy-four were completely agricultural, eighteen were mixed between farmers and villagers, and eight represented the larger county-seat towns.

Before the election of 1890, when the farmer was not active in politics, there was a striking similarity between agrarian and village voting behavior. In the gubernatorial election of 1888, the Republican vote was highest in the county seat towns with 58 percent of the two-party vote. The mixed precincts voted 52 percent Republican, while the agrarian precincts returned 49 percent for the GOP.[66]

In the critical election year of 1890, the split between farmers and villagers reached its greatest proportions. In the villages and towns, the vote for the old parties held up well. The Populists, who appealed little to these people, won only 20 percent of the vote in the mixed precincts and 10 percent of the vote in the county seat. However, they carried rural precincts in all but the Catholic and far-western counties. In the six-county sample, they polled 39 percent in the rural precincts compared with 35 percent for the Democrats and 25 percent for the Republicans.

The election of 1896 illustrates the division between the village and the countryside more emphatically than that of 1890 because the prohibition question was no longer an issue. By 1896, fusion between Populists and Democrats was effected and the Popocrats carried the agrarian precincts with 63 percent and the mixed precincts with 53 percent, but lost in the county seats with 46 percent of the vote.[67]

The election statistics cited for the three elections confirm the commentary noted in the county press. Populism tended to polarize political allegiance between the village and the countryside. Between 1888 and 1896, Republican support declined 12 percent in rural precincts and 5 percent in the county seat precincts. After 1890, agrarian antagonism to the villages grew until a difference of nearly 20 percent existed between the votes that the Republicans were able to capture in the towns and the votes they could command in the rural areas.

It is evident that all the enemies of the farmer were not the tools of the railroads or of Wall Street. Many townspeople were sympathetic with some of the farmers' goals, but quarrels over local economic issues and political leadership caused them to oppose populism. A few years after opposing the farmers in 1890, many of the same village leaders became Progressives and championed many of the same reforms.

6

The Populists in County and State Politics

The election of 1890 was called a "revolution" by Nebraskans of the time. Not only did a new party gain control of the state legislature, but, for the first time in Nebraska's history, actual farmers held positions of power in the state. This dramatic change in political leadership applied to the state as a whole, but it is especially noticeable in the central portion of the state and in Hamilton and Kearney counties.

Nebraska farmers had engaged in politics previously. The Grangers of the late 1870s fought the railroads and then formed the core of the Greenback movement in the state, while the Alliance in the early 1880s closely aligned itself with the Anti-Monopoly party. Both the Alliance and the Anti-Monopolists won few political victories in the mid-1880s, a condition probably related to prosperity and the preoccupation of many Nebraskans with cultural conflicts, but attributed by some to be the result of the Alliance's overinvolvement in politics during the early years of the decade. Despite these reservations concerning the effectiveness of farmers' political activity, the mixing of agriculture and politics was common during the entire period. Many county Alliances, such as those in Kearney and Hamilton counties, never shunned political action during the middle and late 1880s.[1] The decision to move into state politics in 1890, then, was hardly a new or novel move for Nebraska's farmers to make. Both veteran leaders and rank-and-file members were readily available from previous political movements. Although there were those in the Alliance who opposed political action, they were easily overruled. In the perspective of post–Civil War Nebraska history, when any farmer's organization became strong enough to portend effectiveness in politics, the farmers usually took the risk and resorted to political action.

In many of the counties in Nebraska, the organization of the Alliance and the organization of a third party occurred simultaneously. This proved particularly true of the counties in the western part of the state where Alliance organizers were not active until the spring of 1890. Even in the central area, the bastion of the Alliance, the anticipated movement into politics greatly stimulated the growth of the Alliance.[2]

A few county Alliance organizations became involved in political action in 1889. Omar Kem had been instrumental in organizing the Custer County farmers into their first Alliances during the winter of 1887–1888, and Kem always counseled immediate political action. In 1888, he ran for regent of the state university on the Union Labor ticket, and in 1889 he prodded the farmers into running an Alliance ticket for county offices. The officials of the state Alliance protested the move into politics, but the Custer County farmers nevertheless entered the 1889 county election race. Several candidates, who were all farmers, won, carrying the county by a two-to-one majority. The Alliance victory in Custer County attracted statewide attention and strengthened the position of those who agitated for statewide political action.[3]

In many counties, the first signs of political revolt appeared in 1889, long before the drought of the summer of 1890. In the 1889 election, the Hamilton County Alliance fused with the Democrats to win the county treasurer's office from the entrenched Republicans.[4] The Kearney County Alliance was also politically active throughout the late 1880s, and in 1889 sponsored Union Labor candidates.[5] In Adams County, the local Alliance, too, joined with the Democrats in 1889.[6]

In the six-county sample, economic activity did not clearly precede political activity. In fact, the majority of farmers joined the Alliance for political reasons. Thus, when the Alliance leadership decided that its program would include political action, even third-party political action, a great surge in Alliance membership took place. Indeed, many counties did not have county Alliance organizations until after the decision to enter into political action was made.[7] But not all farmers or farm leaders preferred political action. State leaders Jay Burrows, editor of the *Alliance,* and John B. Powers, president of the state Alliance, witnessed the decline in power after the last statewide political campaign, and they hoped to direct the Alliance toward cooperative and pressure group activity. Burrows had been one of the leaders in the Alliance's catastrophic affiliation with the Anti-Monopoly party. He believed that political action would inevitably involve the Alliance with the Rosewater-Van Wyck or Anti-Monopoly wing of the Republican party and result in the destruction of the Alliance as an independent political force. Thus, neither Burrows nor Powers wanted to risk the organization again in open political disputes.[8] On the other hand, Edward Rosewater, leader of the Anti-Monopoly wing of the Republican party, counseled the Alliance men to work through the Republican party by controlling the county conventions.[9]

Acting against the advice of the state leaders, county Alliances increasingly engaged in political action. After the Alliance sweep in Custer County, Kem and other county leaders set out to win over the state leaders to direct political action. The Custer County Alliance, without authorization from the state organization, called the Third District Congressional Convention at Columbus, asking the various county Alliances in the district to send delegates; all but one complied. Kem described the grass-roots nature of the convention and its participants:

> There were two unique features about this convention, it was made up of delegates by invitation and there was not a delegate in it that had ever been heard of out of his county and many of them not outside their immediate neighborhood, and no member of any delegation had ever heard of any member of any other delegation.[10]

The convention took a militant position for political action and helped push the state leaders toward direct involvement in politics. After a conversation with Burrows, Kem reported that "Burrows still demurred about taking any action without sanction by the state officers." Kem then "terminated the gabberfest by telling him frankly that we proposed to make the fight and that we would take the Alliance of the west and north part of the state with us whether the State Alliance went with us officially or not." Soon afterward Burrows wrote to Kem that the state Alliance would enter politics.[11] Whether Kem's story about his influence on the Alliance leadership is true, it illustrates the turmoil within the Alliance concerning this vital decision. In some counties, the breech caused by the decision to move into politics was never healed.

The farmers of Hamilton County divided on the subject of independent political activity. During the spring of the year, they debated the subject at their local Alliance meetings. By June, their attitudes had crystallized, and, at the county Alliance meeting, they decided by a vote of 413 to 83 to form a third party.[12] In July, the county organization called for a primary election in each precinct to select delegates to the county convention, but the factional split over the Alliance's entrance into politics continued to plague the organization. The county Alliance leaders, F. M. Howard and M. H. Severy, apparently did not approve of independent political activity. Severy attempted to nominate a man who was the nominee of the Democrats and was rebuffed by the convention. Howard remained a Democrat until the time of fusion. Neither of these Alliance leaders played a prominent part in the campaign.[13]

Throughout the state, pressure from local Alliances helped mold the state Alliance into a political organization. On April 22, 1890, a convention of county Alliance organizers and presidents decided that if the strength of the Alliance increased impressively in the ensuing few weeks, statewide political action would be advisable.[14] Alliance membership continued to grow, and, after the annual state Alliance meeting in May, county Alliances circulated petitions calling for an Independent political convention. By June 21, 1890, ten thousand signatures were obtained. The convention was called, and the Alliance embarked in third-party politics.[15]

The Nebraska Populists had great difficulty securing adequate leadership for their political crusade. Of necessity, they had to draw upon leaders who had participated in the abortive political revolts of the 1880s. Most notable among these was former Senator Charles H. Van Wyck, who, along with Edward Rosewater, had led the Anti-Monopoly wing of Nebraska Republicanism, a thankless political task. As evidenced in the preferential ballot for United States Senator in 1886, Van Wyck had wide popular support among farmers, but his followers were unable to wrest the party organization away from the village leaders.[16] A lifelong reformer, Van Wyck had been a Liberal Republican, Greenbacker, Anti-Monopolist, and Populist; he finally became a Roosevelt Progressive after the turn of the century.

Van Wyck had been a Republican Senator, but he showed little hesitancy in embracing the new political movement, even though the Anti-Monopoly wing of Nebraska Republicanism still existed and retained its powerful voice in Rosewater's *Omaha Bee*. He soon added his voice to the local Alliance leaders who advocated statewide involvement in politics. As early as March 21, 1890, in a speech at Genoa, Van Wyck called for the organization of a third party. Van Wyck's call occurred about the time Kem threatened Jay Burrows with revolution within the Alliance and about six weeks before state leaders openly advocated forming a third party.[17] Van Wyck helped to force Burrows and Powers into endorsing third-party action by threatening to undercut their leadership in the Alliance. After his Genoa speech, the county press in the state began speculating about the possibility of Van Wyck's accepting the Alliance nomination for governor.[18]

Since Van Wyck had not been a leader in the state Alliance, Alliance officers at the state level and in many counties opposed his candidacy. Burrows and Powers regarded him as an opportunist who embraced the Alliance only when it could be used as a vehicle for his own political ambitions.[19] Later, after Van Wyck's unsuccessful bid for the gubernatorial nomination at the Populist state convention, Burrows openly attacked him in the *Farmers' Alliance* for not supporting some Populist candidates during the 1890 campaign.[20] The feud between Van Wyck and Burrows divided the Populist party and emphasized the split between the Alliance hierarchy, represented by Burrows, and the great bloc of farmers and reformers, who entered the Alliance only when it was committed to political action.

Burrows represented the leadership which had developed within the growing Alliance organization. He had been among those leaders who, in 1887, had revolted against the centralized direction of the Alliance's founder, Milton George. At that time, state leaders assumed the direction of the northern Alliance, gave George a life membership, and installed Burrows as president of the organization.[21] Burrows hesitated in the movement toward political involvement during the spring of 1890, and after his grudging endorsement of the Alliance's entry into politics, he vigorously attacked the Van Wyck group in the new coalition. He packed the Alliance State Nominating Convention with delegates favorable to the state leaders and insured that state Alliance president John B. Powers would gain the nomination for governor.[22] After the convention, he continued his attack on Van Wyck in the *Farmers' Alliance* and finally persuaded the state chairman to read him out of the party.[23] Burrows' plan for maintaining the Alliance organization's control of the Populist party backfired, however. The ferocity of his attacks on Van Wyck weakened his position in the party, especially among those members who had joined in 1890 because political action seemed imminent.[24] After Powers' defeat in the election of 1890, Burrows' influence in the party rapidly declined as newer, often non-Alliance, leaders began to wield greater influence in the movement.[25]

John H. Powers, president of the state Alliance, was a mild-mannered farmer from heavily Populist southwestern Nebraska. He symbolized the farmers' difficulties, for even while he engaged in state and national politics, he continued to live in a sod house on a newly acquired homestead. Although closely allied with Burrows, Powers adopted a more moderate tone toward the Van Wyck faction of the party. On several occasions, he withdrew his candidacy for office to avoid factional disputes and, by doing so, illustrated that he was more dedicated to Alliance objectives than to personal power. Powers remained the leading spirit of the Alliance faction in the Populist party, but his influence waned as more adept politicians won control of the party after 1892. His dedication and selflessness won him support and admiration, but he never possessed the ability or background to be an effective leader.[26]

Van Wyck, Powers, and Burrows were the only leaders of statewide reputation representing the Populists in 1890. By and large, the future Populist leaders in the state did not participate actively in the "revolution" of 1890. Silas A. Holcomb, who became the first Populist governor of the state, remained a Democrat until 1891, while William A. Poynter, the second Populist governor, had only a local reputation in 1890.[27] William V. Allen, the future Populist United States Senator from Nebraska, did not become a Populist until 1891 when he ran for district judge.[28]

The less important state leaders during the early years of populism were men who had long been active in reform politics. Joseph W. Edgerton, reputedly the only lawyer in the state who became a Populist in 1890, was closely connected with the Knights of Labor in Omaha. He had made feeble races for the state supreme court and congress on the Union Labor ticket before running for attorney general as a Populist in 1890.[29] A contemporary's description reveals Edgerton's appeal to the farmers:

> About the only Populist lawyer in the state when the Farmer's Alliance began was J. W. Edgerton ("Our Joe") of Osceola, father of Mrs. Maud E. Nyquist. . . . He was a plain country lawyer, without any town frills, who could talk to the cornfield farmers in their own dialect; who dressed in cornfield clothes and used his own grammar when deeply stirred.[30]

The two Populist Congressmen elected in 1890 were even more obscure although both had participated in reform efforts immediately prior to 1890. Omar M. Kem was a farmer in Custer County prior to Populist successes there in 1889. William A. McKeighan had been a minor Democratic leader from Red Cloud. He was a farmer when not engaged in politics and, as Powers, enjoyed the distinct political advantage of living in a sod house.[31]

Populist leaders at the county level were also often unknown before 1890. For example, the Populist county convention in Hamilton County nominated Henry England and Fred Newberry for the state legislature. England, a prominent farmer of Phillips precinct, resigned in a few weeks and was replaced by J. T. Vorhes. Neither man had ever been mentioned previously in the Aurora papers. Newberry owned one hundred and sixty acres seven miles northwest of Aurora and had lived in the county only eight months.[32] The nomination of Vorhes evidently resulted from the refusal of any other man to accept the nomination; he was unknown, and, judging from his record in the legislature, he was also undistinguished.

The other Allianceman in Hamilton County to win nomination to a state office, however, was a well-known and respected citizen of the county, Valentine Horn of Phillips. Horn, a prominent farmer, had served as president of the county Alliance and as vice president of the state Alliance, and had political ambitions. After being defeated for the congressional nomination for the Second District, he won the nomination for state senator.[33]

Howard County Populists also nominated two men with little political experience for state representative. Henry C. Parker and T. F. McCarty were both farmers from the county-seat precinct, but they had not played a prominent part in the Alliance or in the formation of the new party. The more important figures in Howard County populism did not seek public office in 1890.[34]

The Kearney County Alliance, on the other hand, was among the most politically active Alliances in the state; consequently there were a number of experienced farmer–politicians to supply leadership for the new political movement. Edward Krick, a prominent farmer and Allianceman of Liberty township, became the Independent candidate for state representative, while other Alliance leaders, such as Pat H. Driscoll, president of the county Alliance, and T. E. Hecox, county organizer of the Alliance, became leaders in the Populist party. J. T. Kellie, an Anti-Monopoly candidate for state office in 1886 and former president of the county Alliance, maintained his position of leadership in the state Alliance and the new party. Kearney farmers also worked closely with county Democratic leaders during the late 1880s, and after 1890 they found the Democrats eager for fusion.[35]

In Hayes County, too, the Populists recruited several important political leaders directly from the older parties. John H. Wiswall, for example, who led the dry faction in the Democratic party, served as president of the village-dominated County Agricultural Society, and acted as secretary of the county Alliance.[36] When the county Alliance decided to enter politics, Wiswall abandoned the Democrats and became a Populist. Jasper Koontz converted from Republicanism. He lived in Hayes Center precinct and served on the Republican Central Committee in 1889. In 1890, he turned Populist and became a popular and respected state senator.[37]

Wiswall and Koontz were exceptions to the rule; the other Populist leaders of Hayes County came from the Alliance. Henry Wiswall, president of the county Alliance in 1890, had been affiliated with an independent People's party in 1885. J. E. Buzzell served as secretary of the Alliance and won a position as county commissioner in the 1890 election. Other Alliance leaders served as delegates to the representative and senatorial district conventions.[38]

The Alliance in Scotts Bluff County shared the honor of forming the Independent party with the old Union Labor party, which had run a ticket in the county elections of 1889 and had supplied much of the impetus in the organization of the new party.[39] Indeed, the Independent convention held in the summer of 1890 to nominate county candidates was originally billed as a Union Labor convention. The major Union Labor politician, Judge J. M. King, proved to be an important figure at the convention, as well as in the future of the Independent party in the county. Alliance leaders had abstained from the Union Labor movement in 1889 but joined wholeheartedly in political action in 1890. C. F. Berry, the Alliance county organizer served as secretary of the county convention, while Lee A. Christian, a farmer from Highland precinct, became the county chairman of the new party. County candidates were split between the two founding groups.[40]

The Cuming County Alliance was the weakest in this study. Most of the German farmers in the area thought the Alliance simply meant prohibition, and their fears were confirmed when a leading prohibitionist, Henry Oakes, became president of the county organization.[41] After 1894, Cuming County became a bulwark of fusionist electoral power, but this was effected by the conversion of large segments of the Democratic party rather than through the Alliances.[42]

In the first years of their political revolt, farmers produced the bulk of both leadership and candidates for the Independent party. A few prominent politicians at the county level joined in the movement, but it was mainly the Alliance organization that filled the Populists' ranks and supplied the bulk of political leadership. Since populism was a movement that pitted the politically disenfranchised farmer against village groups who were long accustomed to political and economic leadership, Populists either had to develop effective leaders from among the farm population or recruit them from the villagers. As the movement became more institutionalized, the farmer and Alliance leaders, such as Fred Newberry, were often replaced by either sympathetic or opportunistic villagers, both at the state and local levels.

Examples of the influx of village leaders into the Populist movement were found in most of the counties in this study. Before the Populist landslide of November 1890, the farmers of Hamilton County gained no support from the ranks of the politicians and professional men of the area. With their triumph, however, a good many leaders and politicians began to look more deeply at the Independent cause. The charge of opportunism filled the air, and the farmers viewed every latecomer to the Populist ranks with some distrust and hostility.

George L. Burr was the most important late immigrant into Hamilton County. As noted previously, Burr had been the editor of a Republican paper in Blue Hill, Nebraska, but changed his residence and politics in 1890 when he established the *Hamilton County Register*. After a hesitant acceptance by the Populists, Burr became a leading figure in the Independent party.

In Howard County, two editors, Peter Ebbeson and J. L. Chaflin, became leading Populists after 1892. Populists in Kearney County also rallied around their own newspaper. The temptation for some editors to join the farmers' movement must have been irresistible; Nebraska had an abundance of county newspapers at the time, and the only chance of survival for many was to become the semiofficial publication of a political movement.[43]

Politicians also joined the movement. The most influential to come over to the Hamilton County Populists after 1890 was W. L. Stark, the incumbent county judge, a long-time Republican, and a popular and successful politician with the farmers of Hamilton County. According to one contemporary, his "strongest opposition came from the Republicans of the city of Aurora."[44] Stark's conversion to populism was a propitious move, for in 1892 he was elected to the United States Congress by the Independents. W. H. Fall, a former Democrat and Alliance leader, joined the Populists when Governor Boyd vetoed the Newberry Maximum Rate Bill, and other Democrats became prominent in the People's party after fusion.

Later Populist leaders in Hamilton County were, for the most part, business and professional men, occupational groups that were well represented in the leadership of the older parties. For example, J. H. Grosvenor and W. L. Stark were lawyers; David S. Woodard was a medical doctor. The Populists never elected another farmer to the house after Newberry stepped down in 1895.[45] The trend toward village leadership might have been a calculated move, for the Populists realized the lack of support in the villages and in the spring of 1891 organized a "Citizens Alliance" for village and city dwellers.[46]

The deluge of aspiring village editors, lawyers, politicians, and businessmen into the Populist ranks caused bitterness and dissension within the party. In many ways, this conflict resembled the earlier quarrel between the Van Wyck reformers and the Burrows Alliancemen, which had taken place at the state level in 1890. The Alliancemen tried to keep the organization in agrarian hands, while both the newcomers and the old reformers were willing to make concessions to other groups in order to gain political power. The struggle over fusion with the Democratic party, to a significant degree, represented a struggle for leadership between these two groups in the People's party. Joseph

Maycock, an early leader of the Scotts Bluff Alliance, quit the party in disgust in 1896 because he felt the "office seekers" and fusionists had betrayed the ideals of the party.[47] The theme was repeated often during the mid-1890s; another Populist leader withdrew from the party because "the middleman, the jackleg lawyers and the town loafers are more influential in controlling the People's Party than the farmer."[48] Even the delegates to the state Alliance meeting at Lincoln in 1892 were not spared a reference to the conflict which raged over Populist leadership and goals when the official greeter warned the delegates of the "camp followers and political foragers from the old parties" who sought to displace farmer leadership in the movement.[49]

Agrarian disillusionment with their leadership was an important factor in the sharp decline in the Populist vote toward the end of the decade. This decline is illustrated by the vote in Hamilton County. The increasing village domination of leadership, together with the infusion of Democratic leadership into the party, were important reasons for the decline of the Populists' role in the rural areas of Nebraska.

Many Nebraska historians have described the Populists' colorful campaign prior to the election of 1890, and it is unnecessary to expand their thorough description of events during that memorable autumn. The Republicans rejected the candidate of the skeletonized Rosewater–Anti-Monopoly faction of the party and nominated a regular Republican, Lucius D. Richards of Fremont, a moderate who ran on a platform advocating railroad regulation, the Australian ballot, and other planks nearly as liberal as those found in the Populist platform.[50] However, he was a past chairman of the Republican State Central Committee, a banker, a moneylender, and a real-estate promoter. All of his associations linked him with the village and corporate groups, against which the farmers rebelled. In addition, Richards had known prohibitory inclinations.[51]

The Democrats largely ignored the Populist revolt in 1890 as they concentrated their attacks on the prohibition amendments, which the Republican legislature had placed before the voters. As J. Sterling Morton still languished in retirement, the Democrats nominated James Boyd, a popular Omaha mayor, a wet, and a stalwart in the Miller faction of the party. The whole Democratic state campaign focused on the prohibition issue. The Omaha newspapers, and especially the county newspapers in the German counties, gave more space to the prohibitory amendment and the candidates' position on the amendment than they did to the problems of the farmers.[52]

The results of the election of 1890 show that Populist strength rested in those central and southwestern counties that had previously been the bulwark of Nebraska Republicanism (Figures 1 and 6). The Republican vote in

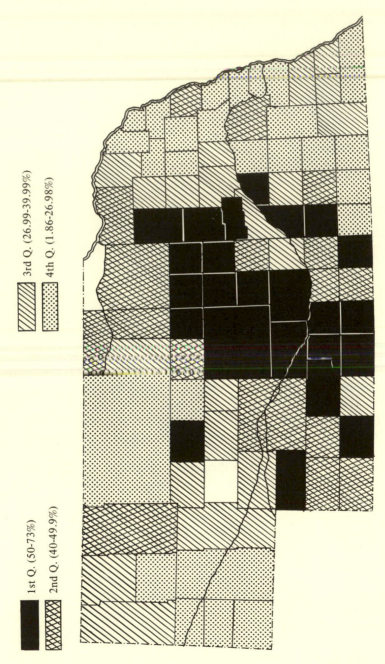

1st Q. (50-73%)

2nd Q. (40-49.9%)

3rd Q. (26.99-39.99%)

4th Q. (1.86-26.98%)

State Average Independent Vote: 32.78 %

Figure 6: Independent Vote, 1890, by Quartile

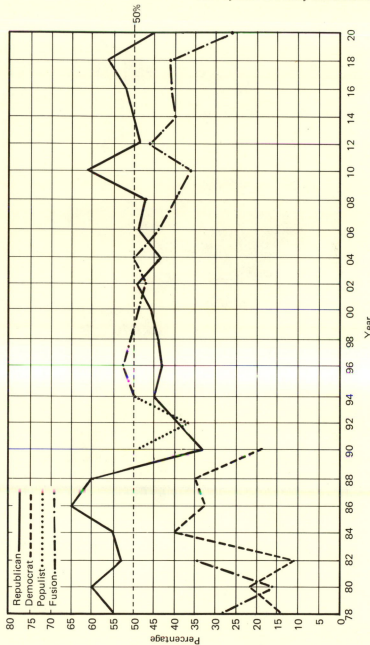

Figure 7: Hamilton County: Percentage of Vote for Governor (A Sample Populist County)

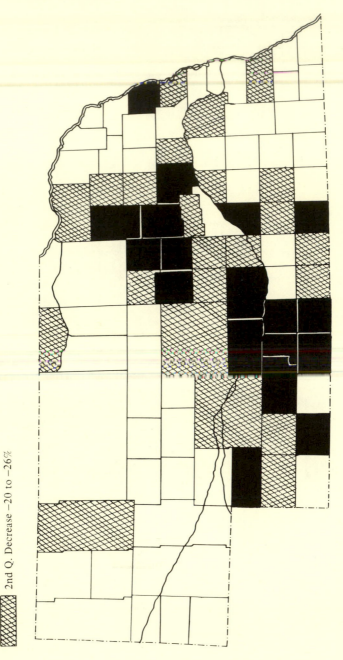

1st Q. Decrease −27 to −47%

2nd Q. Decrease −20 to −26%

NOTE: The decrease calculated is simply the raw decline in Republican vote, e.g., from a 60-percent vote to a 30-percent vote would be a 30-percent decline.

Figure 8: Decrease in Republican Voting Strength, 1888–1890

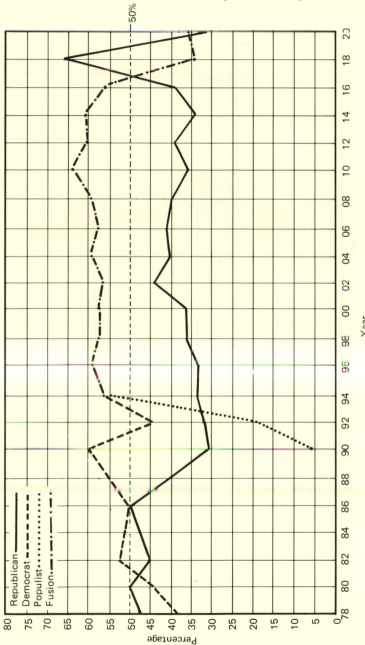

Figure 9: Cuming County: Percentage of Vote for Governor (A Sample Democratic County)

the state as a whole declined 19 percent, but in many of the counties in central and southwestern Nebraska it declined from 25 to 50 percent (Figure 8).[53] The loyalties engendered by the Civil War, cultural loyalties, and the aggressive settlement policies of the Republicans after the Civil War failed to meet the economic needs of Nebraska farmers who were faced with high transportation costs, drought, low commodity prices, and high fixed costs. In the eastern part of the state, economic conditions were not as critical as the central area, and this, together with the prohibition issue, helped maintain Democratic strength in the German counties (Figure 9). In the far western section of the state, which still lacked transportation and other capital improvements, farmers also tended to maintain their old voting patterns (Figure 14). The following chapter more precisely analyzes the basis of Populist support in the election of 1890.

The Populist movement in Nebraska reached its zenith in 1890. At that time, more than any other in its history, populism reflected agrarian aspirations and responded to exclusively agrarian leadership. After 1890, populism continued to be a force in the state, but Populists increasingly depended upon leadership and votes supplied by the Democratic party. Figures 7 and 9 illustrate the increasing influence of the Democrats, together with the decline of the fusionist vote in a typical Populist county.

The last attempt the Populists made to win the governorship in Nebraska without Democratic help took place in 1892, only two years after their initial political successes. In the gubernatorial contest of that year, the Republican party showed some of the vitality which, prior to the Populist era, had made it more responsive to western economic needs than the more culturally oriented Democratic party. The spirit of revolt that pervaded the state enabled the Rosewater faction to gain control of the state convention and name the reform-inclined former congressman, Lorenzo Crounse, as the Republican nominee for governor. Rosewater shrewdly selected Crounse because of his appeal to reform groups and because he was also the father-in-law of Gilbert Hitchcock, editor of the powerful reform Democratic paper, the *Omaha World Herald*. Hitchcock predictably did not oppose Crounse.[54]

Even in 1892 the future of Nebraska populism rested to a large extent upon the political fortunes of a Democrat, William Jennings Bryan, who had emigrated from Illinois to Nebraska in 1887 and, with the help and advice of J. Sterling Morton, swiftly became a prominent figure in the Nebraska Democracy.[55] In 1890, he won the congressional race in the First District (Omaha and Lincoln) with the support of the Bourbon Democratic leaders. However, Bryan soon departed from Bourbon orthodoxy, and, by 1892, he openly advocated the free coinage of silver.[56] Bryan had great appeal to many rank-

and-file Democrats within the party, but in 1892 he had no organized following in the state. County leaders such as Judge J. C. Crawford in Cuming
County and the Glover brothers in Hamilton County remained solidly at-
tached to the old state leadership for several reasons. They felt that Bryan's
program too closely resembled that of the Populists and consequently would
choke off economic development in the state. The Bourbon leadership also
had no desire to make any accommodation with the reformers that might en-
tail the danger of the Democracy being swallowed up by the Populist movement.[57]

The Bourbon Democrats dominated the Democratic state convention of
1892, but Bryan emerged as the first and greatest champion of reform in the
Democracy. His eloquence and personal magnetism nearly succeeded in per-
suading the Democrats to place a free-silver plank in the state platform.[58] But
Morton won the Democratic nomination for governor, with Bryan again being
the candidate for Congress. The breach in the Democracy had become permanent. Morton conceived of his campaign primarily in terms of defeating the
Populists, while Bryan ran with Populist support.[59]

In the November election of 1892 Lorenzo Crounse easily defeated Van
Wyck and Morton for the governorship, but the Bryanites had laid the ground-
work for fusion between Populists and Democrats.[60] Fusion became a fact in
1894. Populist leaders realized that they needed Democratic electoral support,
and the Bryan forces captured the Democratic party in the cause of reform
and fusion. Bryan was an astute politician whose ambitions were not satisfied
by a marginal seat in the House of Representatives. Early in 1894, he realized
that the depression would seriously endanger any Democratic congressional
candidate and that a possible defeat would harm his chances in the senatorial
election in the 1895 session of the legislature.[61] Consequently, he did not
seek the Democratic nomination for Congress. Instead, he accepted the offer
of Gilbert M. Hitchcock to become editor of the *Omaha World Herald*, a position which gave his advocacy of fusion a wide hearing in the state.[62] By the
late summer of 1894, the Bryan forces in the party were strong enough to
control the state convention, and the Bourbon Democrats withdrew to a
rump convention, where they named a Gold Democratic ticket.[63]

Republican factionalism also aided the fusionists' cause. Edward Rosewater never became a Populist, but he still led the reform wing of the Republican party. When the Republican state convention in 1894 nominated his old
antagonist, the "regular" Thomas J. Majors, for governor, Rosewater
bolted the party. Shortly afterward, all of the reform elements in the state,
the followers of Powers, Van Wyck, Bryan, and Rosewater, united behind the

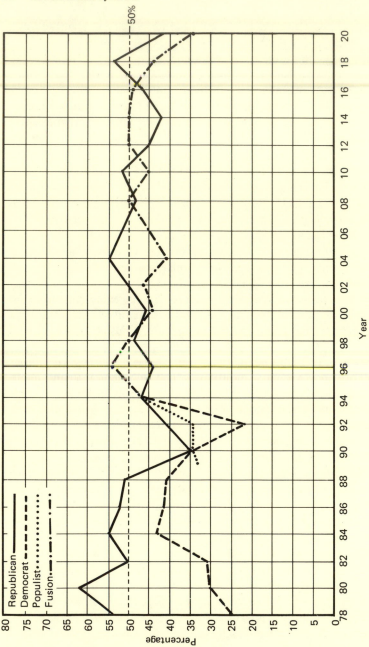

Figure 10: Nebraska: Percentage of Vote Received by Major Political Parties in Gubernatorial Elections

Populist nominee for governor, Silas A. Holcomb of Broken Bow. Fusion, with the aid of Edward Rosewater, became a victorious reality.[64]

After fusion and with the return of prosperity following 1896, Nebraska politics retained characteristics of both the more culturally oriented politics of the late 1880s and the more economically oriented politics of the Populist years. Nebraska did not return to the overwhelming Republicanism of the 1870s and 1880s but as Figure 10 shows, remained a closely contested state well into the twentieth century.[65]

The Populist revolt, by its effective emphasis on economic concerns, had shaken many Nebraskans away from their traditional allegiance to the Republican party. The new coalition, as it emerged, can be seen visually in Figure 11 as a fusion of the Democratic German and ritualistic counties of the late 1880s with the strong Populist counties of 1890. This visual correlation is confirmed by election graphs from several of the sample counties. Howard County (Figure 12) represents those counties which had been closely contested during the 1880s because of their ethnic mix, but with the upheaval of 1890 moved away from the GOP and into Populist ranks and then strongly into Populist-Democratic fusion. Hamilton County (Figure 6) illustrates the behavior of those Populist counties that had been the native American, Protestant bastions of Republican strength during the 1870s and 1880s. There the equilibrium reached after 1894 became one of virtual stalemate. Douglas County (Omaha), the most populous and ethnically diverse county in the state, after being evenly matched during the Populist era, moved into a period of slowly increasing Democratic strength (Figure 13). The Republican sample counties in this study (Figure 14) remained staunchly Republican well into the new century, while the German counties (Figure 9) retained a sizable proportion of the large Democratic majorities of the late 1880s and early 1890s.

The most significant change in the voting behavior for Nebraskans during the era had resulted from the economic conditions and political frustrations that had propelled the farmers into the Populist revolt. The combination of the two issues worked to modify the influence that village business and professional men exerted on public policy and gave the farmer his first opportunity in the state's history to participate effectively in politics. Table 12 illustrates the greater political role of the farmer after 1890. With fusion, the farmers in central and southwestern Nebraska lost some of their ardor for reform politics, but they were never again as voiceless in Nebraska politics as they had been before 1890. After 1890 the voting behavior of the Nebraska farmer reflected more clearly his political and economic desires. Fusion, third-party action, or the Democratic ballot were always possibilities after 1890. Wartime loyalties and cultural politics had been significantly modified by the economic crises of the nineties.[66]

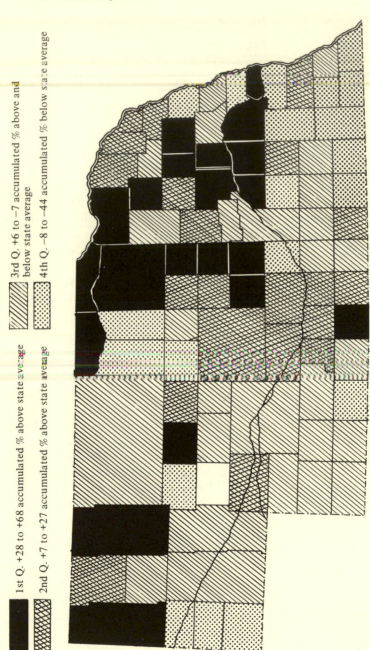

1st Q. +28 to +68 accumulated % above state average

2nd Q. +7 to +27 accumulated % above state average

3rd Q. +6 to −7 accumulated % above and below state average

4th Q. −8 to −44 accumulated % below state average

Figure 11: Fusion Tendencies, 1894–1900

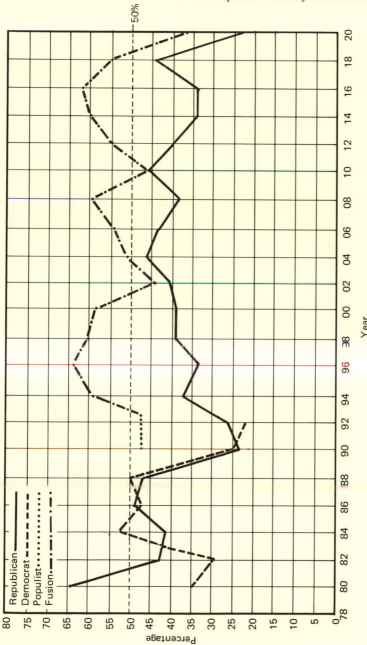

Figure 12: Howard County: Percentage of Vote for Governor (A Sample Populist County)

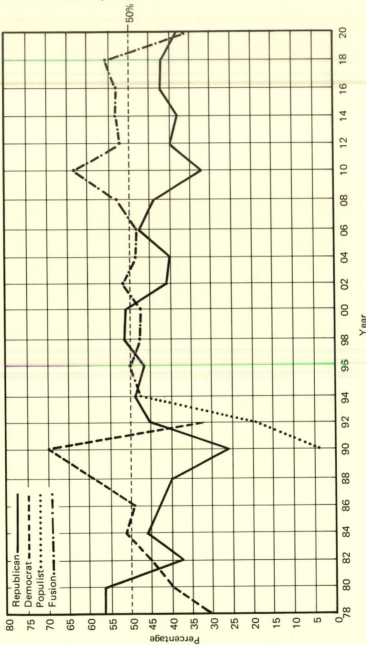

Figure 13: Douglas County (Omaha): Percentage of Vote for Governor

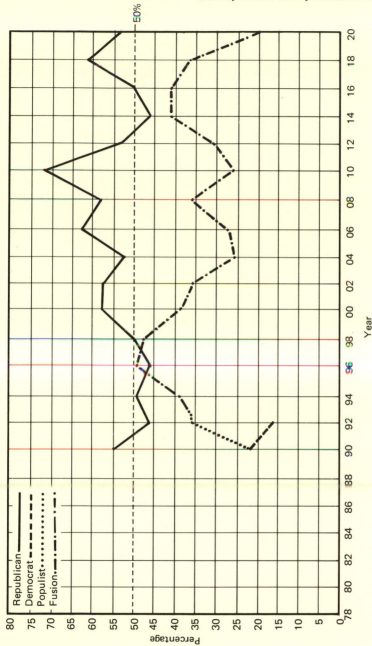

Figure 14: Scotts Bluff County: Percentage of Vote for Governor (A Sample Republican County)

Table 12: MEMBERSHIP IN NEBRASKA HOUSE OF REPRESENTATIVES, BY OCCUPATIONAL GROUP AND POLITICAL PARTY

Legislatures		Republicans	Democrats	Third Party
1885	Farmer	39%	7%	1% (Independent)
	Town: professional and business	42	11	0
1889	Farmer	39	7	0
	Town: professional and business	41	11	1 (Union Labor)
1891	Farmer	13	9	51 (Populists)
	Town: professional and business	8	16	1
1893	Farmer	23	5	37
	Town: professional and business	24	7	4
1897	Farmer	12	6	36
	Town: professional and business	18	11	11
	Unidentified (6)			

Source: Journal of the House of Representatives of the State of Nebraska (Lincoln), 1885, 1889, 1891, 1893, 1897.

PART III
CROSS PRESSURES

7

Cultural Conflict During the Populist Era

Populism involved elements other than the economic complaints of the farm population. The struggle for political and economic power played a significant part in the Populist movement, and it helps explain the feelings of alienation of many farmers. Populists vigorously attacked the village leaders for their part in denying the agrarians a role in the political process and for the villagers' domination of the economic life of Nebraska. However, some of the Populists' explanations of their difficulties went beyond attacks on village leaders. Historians have adequately documented Populist attitudes toward railroads, trusts, and moneylenders, but the nativistic and anti-Semitic aspects of the movement have only recently received attention. Illustrative of these Populist inclinations is an item that appeared in the Populist *Hamilton County Register* in June 1891:

> Dear Uncle Sam;
>
> Your dream, I fear, is to be verified very shortly. The English Jew bankers own the earth. They have mortgaged mankind. . . . You may not know it, but those same English Jew bankers supplied certain persons in this country whom we know as monopolists with the money with which to buy the stocks and bonds of the corporations of this country for them.[1]

Other contemporary sources link populism to nativism. The Populist candidate for governor in 1890, John Powers, led in the prohibition movement in the state, and many Nebraskans believed that their candidate for the state supreme court in 1891 was a member of the notoriously anti-Catholic American Protective Association.[2] Moreover, Populists were overwhelmingly rural and of Anglo-Saxon descent, factors that would, at least theoretically, make them prey to nativistic leanings during times of economic distress.[3]

Most of the evidence of Populist orientation toward nativism comes from agrarian participation in several nativist-tinged movements that coincided with populism. The prohibition movement, the movement for restriction of immigration, and the American Protective Association all had nativistic undertones. The question becomes, to what extent did Populists participate in these concurrent movements? Do the occasional items about English Jewish bankers indicate Populist support for nativistic causes, or do they simply reflect the views of a small number of men working unsuccessfully to align populism with the nativists?

The ethnic origins of Nebraska's population had as much effect on Nebraska politics as did the economic difficulties associated with populism. During the Populist era, the largest and most significant immigrant group in Nebraska were the Germans. German immigration to Nebraska began in the mid-1870s and continued until the collapse of the real-estate boom in the late 1880s. The German settlers were fortunate, for they settled in the fertile and easily accessible northeastern section of the state. Northeastern Nebraska was also less affected by drought than the central counties because it had a higher annual rainfall and a higher humus content of the soil. These factors were of political significance in later years when the German farmers did not face the economic hardships of the farmers in central Nebraska.[4]

The major German counties and the percentage of the German foreign-born population residing in them follows:[5]

Cuming	22.8%
Stanton	17.4
Pierce	16.6
Dodge	15.4
Platte	14.5
Cedar	13.1
Hall	12.8
Sarpy	12.6
Madison	12.2
Wayne	12.0

The German influence in these counties was actually much higher than the percentage figures indicate. In Cuming County, for example, the foreign-born figure of 23 percent represents adults who were usually the middle-aged heads of families. Since each family had from three to six children, German foreign-born or first-generation stock approached 75 percent of the county's population, or three times that indicated by the census statistics. Examination of the census manuscripts corroborates this.[6] A more accurate indication of the voting strength of any major ethnic group can be obtained by multiplying the census figure by three.[7]

The German population in the state was evenly divided between Catholics and Lutherans, but more Catholics congregated in the dominant German areas. The two German counties used in this study, Cuming and Colfax, had among the highest percentage of Germans in the state; the Catholic population in each comprised about three-quarters of the German population.[8]

Bohemians and Irish comprised the other significant Catholic immigrant groups in Nebraska in the 1880s and 1890s. Large numbers of Bohemians settled in Butler, Colfax, Saline, and Saunders counties in the late 1870s.[9] The Bohemian population was also significant in Omaha (Douglas County).[10] The Irish made up a considerable part of the population in only two counties, Greeley and Holt, but their ability in politics and their position of leadership in the Democratic party helped make them influential in many counties. This was especially true in Omaha.[11]

Other important Protestant immigrant groups were largely Scandinavian in origin. Swedish immigration to Nebraska reached its peak after the Populist era, yet by 1890 Swedish stock in Phelps and Kearney counties accounted for over 25 percent of the population. Danish immigrants comprised about 25 percent of the population in Howard and Kearney counties.

Immigrants to Nebraska faced most of the frustrations and hostilities common to immigrants in other sections of the country. Because of language and cultural barriers, they often existed apart from the native Anglo-Saxon community. At the first opportunity, they established their ethnic churches, newspapers, and parochial schools in which the mother-tongue was the language of instruction, and, next to prohibition, the most potent cultural issue.[12] They clung to their cultural traditions and maintained a deep affection for their native country. Some of the more successful immigrants returned home occasionally to visit friends and relatives.[13]

As soon as immigrants constituted a significant proportion of the population in any county, they usually made vigorous attempts to enter into political activity. In some cases, they were rebuffed by the older settlers. John Dethlefs, a German candidate for county office in Lancaster County, expressed political frustration in a letter to the *Omaha World Herald*: "I think the Republican Party in Lancaster County made a studied effort to ignore us in politics. My candidacy in the late Republican convention was urged as a recognition of the German people."[14] Despite some barriers, most of the new immigrant groups managed to win significant political power. West Point and Norfolk had German mayors; the Irish in Omaha dominated several city administrations; and the Bohemians consistently placed their countrymen on local tickets in Butler and Douglas counties.[15]

A majority of Nebraskans approved of the progress and Americanization of the different immigrant groups in the state. Many new citizens themselves agitated for speedy assimilation into American culture by emphasizing the similarities of religious traditions, by stressing the use of the English language, and by praising the vitality of a pluralistic America.[16] Catholic editors often attempted to mollify Protestant fears of Romanism with patriotic statements from noted Catholic clergymen. M. O. Gentzke, editor of the *Cuming County Advertiser* and *Nebraska Volksblatt*, frequently quoted Cardinal Gibbons' statements to illustrate Catholic patriotism. Gentzke proudly reproduced Gibbons' statement that "indeed to proclaim loyalty to a government like ours ought to be a spontaneous act of love, as well as a duty to all who preach the gospel."[17]

Although most Nebraskans gave verbal encouragement to the ideal of America as the haven of the oppressed and downtrodden, they had serious reservations about some of the cultural traditions of the new Americans. These reservations revolved around two dominant characteristics of the immigrant: his Catholicism and his attitude toward liquor.

The most violent manifestation of cultural conflict in Nebraska during the late nineteenth century involved anti-Catholic nativism and culminated in the formation of the American Protective Association. The APA was not indigenous to Nebraska. Founded in Clinton, Iowa, it soon extended in a belt across the Midwest from eastern Michigan to central Nebraska. In Nebraska, it became a significant force in the early 1890s, after a prohibitory amendment to the state constitution had been defeated. The APA received added impetus in 1891 when John C. Thompson and W. C. Kelly established the *Omaha American* as a semiofficial organ of the movement in the state.[18]

Nativistic sentiments grew from several sources. Many Nebraskans who did not join the nativists felt the cultural and political antagonisms responsible for its growth, but channeled their feelings into other movements, such as prohibition. However, some Nebraskans expressed their hostilities openly and attacked immigrant groups which they felt were undermining American cultural values and were responsible for the corruption in political life. Resentment toward immigrants and minorities existed among most native-born groups in Nebraska in the late nineteenth century, and the minority groups even attacked each other.

The reform-inclined and Democratic *Omaha World Herald* represented much of the press when it referred to the increasing number of "undesirables" among immigrants and felt them to be "an infusion which seems to threaten deterioration."[19] The editor of the Populist *Hamilton County Register* editorialized that "whatever may be said of them [*sic*] immigrants as a class, we have too much reason to believe that many of them are people of a kind that are very undesirable."[20] The *Register* heartily approved of the lynching of eleven Mafia members in New Orleans. Other editors, like Asa B. Wood of the Republican *Gering Courier*, often referred to Jews as "Shylocks" or made mildly derogatory remarks about immigrant groups. Wood once mentioned a new store in Broken Bow as having "electric lights on the outside, and Israelites on the inside," a statement which recognized the existence of the Jew, but certainly was not violently anti-Semitic.[21] Most Nebraskans in the late nineteenth century had not benefited from the "brotherhood" programs which have since discouraged expressions of cultural antagonisms. Although few Nebraskans were entirely free of cultural hostilities, only the avowed nativists were obsessed with them.

Cultural conflict existed as one important element in the social and political life of the 1890s, but it constituted only one element for most Nebraskans. The nativists, however, made it the central element in both their analysis of the troubles of society and in their proposed solution. To members of the APA, the domination of Omaha politics by Irish Catholics was symptomatic of the troubles facing the nation as a whole. Omaha housed a significant Irish-Catholic community, and, to a great extent, the Irish existed apart from the older Anglo-Saxon group that had long dominated the city's economic and political life. The Irish were denied social recognition and were looked upon with hostility because of their opposition to prohibition, their Catholicism, and their political power.[22] In other areas of Nebraska, the APA crystallized opposition to the Irish in particular and Catholics in general, making explicit the feelings of many Nebraskans and appealing to those citizens who were desperate enough or fatuous enough to accept a very simple explanation for social distress.

The major complaint verbalized by APA members against Catholics centered upon the Irish responsibility for the degeneration of American urban politics. The APA paper in Omaha, *The American*, expressed this dogma:

> Year after year you complain of poor government: the high
> taxes and the hard times! What causes this? Romanists! Who

> are your officials? Romanists in the main! Why are your taxes
> high? Because there are thousands of dollars worth of prop-
> erty being held by the Roman church for speculative purposes,
> which does not bear one cent of taxation. . . . Will you con-
> tinue to growl and grumble at the way things are run? Many
> of you will. . . . Many of you are Americans and will purify
> the politics of the city.[23]

After exposing the causes for urban problems, the editor of *The American* explained that all of these problems resulted from a Catholic plot:

> The critics of the APA ought to go to the root of the mat-
> ter. The average citizen looks with disgust and alarm at the
> condition of things in all our good cities. He sees these
> cities in the hands of Roman Catholics. Almost every office
> is controlled by them. Everyone knows that it is the result
> of Jesuitical scheming.[24]

Omaha proved to be fertile ground for such complaints. By the early 1890s,
Catholic politicians in the Democratic party exercised considerable power in
city affairs. Although the city had had no spectacular scandals, there were continued rumors of bribery and graft, as well as Protestant complaints about
prostitution and drunkenness. In addition, several major strikes added to the
social disorder of the period.[25]

Some contemporaries accused the Populists of participating in the nativistic
movement. These accusations had a certain amount of logic and some fact behind them, for the Populists had many similarities with the groups that embraced nativism. Both Populists and nativists were deeply concerned with what
they considered to be the decline of American democracy and the inability of
the common man to realize the American dream promised by liberal democracy and capitalism. In their public pronouncements, both groups tended to
see sinister interests as a factor in this decline. Furthermore, both groups
were largely Anglo-Saxon and Protestant in ethnic and religious orientation.
To some extent, individual Populists participated in movements that received
support from the nativists. John Powers, the Populist candidate for governor
in 1890, had been a leading prohibitionist, and many Populist county newspapers supported prohibition at the county level, just as they did immigration
restriction.[26]

Nativists recognized the similarities between the two movements and repeatedly attempted to cultivate Populist support. The *Omaha American* continually emphasized these similarities:

> The Populists are in the main, Americans, native born, who
> have nothing in common with ecclesiastical politicians and
> if they will stand for principle. . . . The people will soon ap-
> preciate the fact that they are reformers and not office
> seekers.[27]

The Populists, while they sympathized with some nativist projects, such as
the compulsory use of the English language in the public schools,[28] did not al-
low themselves to become embroiled in cultural conflicts. In 1891, Populist
Joseph M. Edgerton engaged in a three-party race for justice of the state supreme court. During the campaign, his opponents circulated rumors that he was
a member of the APA, and he consequently lost most of the Catholic vote.[29]
Edgerton's defeat reinforced earlier Populist desires to emphasize only economic issues. Antagonism also grew between nativists and Populists because
several Populist politicians had had long associations with Catholics. Charles H.
Van Wyck, through his close association with the Knights of Labor, had both
Catholic and Protestant followers in Omaha, while a few Populist politicians
and nominees were themselves Catholic.[30]

By 1895, sentiment against nativists was so strong in the Populist party that
a resolution condemning nativism passed in the state convention.[31] Fusion with
the Democratic party in 1894 also showed Populist concern over economic
rather than cultural issues, for in fusion, Anglo-Saxon and Teutonic Protestants
united with German and Irish Catholics. Protestant Populist opponents to fusion never opposed fusion with the Democrats on ethnic grounds, although some
Catholics seem to have had some reservations concerning the Populists. By 1893
The American was lamenting about the number of "Romans" in the Populist
party.[32]

Most Populist newspapers participated in the conspiracy of silence that en-
veloped the APA in Nebraska. Nativism was generally considered disreputable,
and most editors tried to ignore it, but occasionally nativist outbursts brought
some comment from Populist papers. The editor of the *Granger* expressed the
feeling of most Populists when he wrote:

> We have no apology to offer for what we have said relative to
> APAism. We are not of the faith of the Roman Catholic Church
> nor is it true that our father, nor mother or grandmother were
> any of them Roman Catholics, yet we are not to be governed
> or swayed by the prejudice engendered between Catholics
> and Protestants in the unrighteous and unholy conduct in
> years gone by, nor today so long as the constitution and laws
> of this country guarantee free and untrammeled thought and
> worship in any religion, free thought and speech.[33]

It was the Republican party, not the Populists, that received the greatest amount of support from the nativists. Like the Populists, most Republicans were native-born Protestants, but Republicans were not faced with the economic hardships that confronted the Populists. Cultural conflict was also largely confined to the cities of the state where the native-born Republican businessman or clerk came into contact with the Irish-Catholic Democrat. Anglo-Saxon businessmen formed the core of the APA; a list of advertisers compiled from the 1891–1896 files of *The American* shows that a large number of urban business and professional men regularly advertised in the paper.[34] A. B. Morearty states that the APA recruited most of its membership from naturalized former British subjects.[35] His analysis was colored by his Irish partisanship, but he was correct in detecting a pro-English bias in *The American.*

The APA never entered politics itself; instead, it endorsed those men whom it considered worthy candidates of any party. In fact, it almost universally endorsed Republicans. In Omaha, an APA-endorsed candidate was often asked to sign a pledge that he would employ only Protestants formally approved by the APA.[36]

The election of 1890 in Omaha centered on the prohibition issue and therefore had some nativistic overtones; however, nativism did not become a significant force in the city until the 1891 mayoralty election. At that time, the Republicans, who had been excluded from city office since the mid 1880s, united with the APA to win the election. The Republicans stressed the corruption in the city council, while their APA allies linked the corruption to the Irish.[37] Democrats, on the other hand, made a fatal blunder and concentrated their campaign on attacking the nativistic overtones in their opponents' campaign. Their rather abstract defense of a "religious sect and a particular nationality" could not withstand the concrete attack of the Republicans and the APA.[38] John Williams, a noted Protestant preacher, analyzed the Democratic defeat in the following manner:

> The Democratic city council, with its rings and ringsters . . .
> its infamous confessions of licentious immorality, its charges
> and counter charges of bribery and corruption . . . nomin-
> ated men whose delights would be in the burnt district.
> . . . It nominated for mayor a representative . . . of the
> saloon element. . . . The APA used most outrageous slanders
> to arouse Protestants' alarm, but all they said was not false,
> one thing they said was too true. . . . The city and county
> offices were crowded full with Irishmen and Roman

Catholics . . . "home rule" is as good a thing to cherish for
America as for Ireland.[39]

The election of 1891 showed that nativism was a popular issue in Omaha.
Prior to 1891, and especially in the election of 1890, Omaha had been a source
of great Democratic strength in Nebraska. Then nativism and populism realigned
Omaha politics, and, throughout the populist and fusion era, Omaha voted Republican (see Figure 13). Anti-Irish sentiment, goether with an antiagrarian
feeling, had caused significant numbers of urban dwellers to forsake the Democracy for the Republicans.[40] It was the Republicans, not the Populists, who
were the beneficiaries of nativism in Douglas County.

After the election of 1891 the *Grand Island Independent* commented that
the Republican–APA alliance seemed to have aided Republicans across the
state.[41] Governor Boyd (Democrat) was quoted in the *Omaha World Herald* as
saying the APA was the decisive factor in the election because it had successfully linked corruption and Catholicism. Ironically, Boyd had risen to power
in Omaha during the mid-1880s as the mayoral candidate of a reform group,
the Democratic Citizens Coalition.[42]

APA activity on the state level, too, usually benefited the Republicans. In
1892, however, *The American* endorsed both J. Sterling Morton (Democrat)
and Lorenzo Crounse (Republican) for the major party nominations for governor, but it refused to endorse the Populist candidate, Charles H. Van Wyck,
because of his Catholic associations. Since Morton also had numerous Catholic
associates, some of *The American*'s antagonism to Van Wyck might have been
due to Populist economic doctrines, as well as to their Catholic following.[43]

The nativists generally approved of candidates from the more conservative
railroad wing of the Republican party. On various occasions, *American* editorials endorsed John M. Thurston for public office.[44] On other occasions, it
flailed the Rosewater-*Bee* reform wing of the party.[45] Some Democrats accused Rosewater of using the APA to get rid of the Irish and then discarding
the organization in his political feud with Omaha Democrats, but he certainly
never joined the APA.

Although the APA was strongest in Omaha, it had significant influence
throughout the state. In 1894, it made its greatest bid for statewide power
when it enthusiastically endorsed and supported Thomas Majors, the Republican candidate for governor.[46] Majors did not disavow APA support, and his
rumored membership in the organization became the most important campaign issue in Catholic counties.[47] Many Republicans hoped that Majors would
make deep inroads into the Protestant wings of both the Democratic and
Populist parties. Election returns fulfilled their hopes. Although Majors lost,

the Republicans did increase their percentage of the vote in the old Populist counties. In only a few counties did the Fusionists' vote in 1894 equal the combined Populist and Democratic vote in 1892. On the other hand, fusion succeeded in Nebraska when the Catholic–Democratic counties wholeheartedly joined the Populists because of the APA issue. Catholic Democrats in 1894 had no place to go besides their coalition with the Populists. Far from being a haven for nativistic sentiment, Populists increasingly found themselves cast as the defenders of immigrant religion and traditions, and the APA played a significant role in cementing fusion. Those newer immigrants who did not become fusionists voted Republican because of their belief in the gold standard rather than fear of Populist nativism.[48]

All of the evidence discovered in this study points to the conclusion that Populists did not display the nativistic and anti-Semitic characteristics that often have been attributed to them. Aside from the vague distrust of foreigners, which was felt by most Nebraskans, Populists avoided overt manifestations of ethnic hostility. Finally, their single-minded concern with economic issues led them to an alliance with the great bulk of the Catholic and immigrant population in the state.

The prohibition movement was more closely related to populism than was nativism, but just as they had done with nativism, the Populists had to reject prohibition in order to become a viable force in Nebraska politics. Prohibition became an issue in Nebraska in the late 1870s, and, in 1881, the Slocumb High License Bill allowed any incorporated municipality in the state to exercise local option on two specified alternatives. The municipality could license saloons for any fee from a minimum of five hundred dollars to a maximum of three thousand dollars, or it could entirely prohibit the sale of alcoholic beverages within its limits.[49]

The sponsors of the Slocumb Act intended it to put the prohibition controversy to rest in the state, but, contrary to their expectations, the local-option provision caused the opposite to occur. The next three decades saw increased conflict over prohibition, especially on the local level. Every village and city in the state had to decide its policy in the matter and then withstand renewed attacks from the opposition.

Agitation for prohibition came from a dedicated and articulate segment of Nebraska's citizens. Protestant ministers, teachers and professors, country churches, sabbath schools, Demorset medal societies, Chautauquan societies, and a few professional politicians led the movement.[50] The election of 1884 marked the first appearance of a strictly prohibition vote. Then, in numbers of votes cast, the prohibitionists rapidly increased their strength through the elections of 1886 and 1888. The vote in 1888 was so large that prohibitionists brought great pressure upon the Republican legislature of 1889 and coerced the somewhat reluctant politicians into voting for the submission of a prohibitory amendment to the state constitution.[51]

The militancy and ardor of the prohibitionists rivaled similar feelings held by the Populists and nativists. Theirs was a simple faith and a simple program, which they felt would uplift a wretched mankind and solve the problems that buffeted society.[52] The reasons behind this fervor are difficult to assess. Various contemporary observers noted the large numbers of women who participated in the movement. These women, such as Helen Gougar, a spokeswoman for prohibition forces, frequently exhibited feelings of alienation toward the rapid changes occurring in late nineteenth-century society. Speaking to a prohibition rally largely composed of women in 1890, Mrs. Gougar gave some of the reasons for her fervor: "I don't wonder that we have Bob Ingersolls, and that the growing generations are showing a growing disrespect for Christianity, and that our boys are playing baseball on Sunday rather than being in church."[53]

Mrs. Gougar and her fellow prohibitionists felt that sinister forces were at work producing the alleged degeneration. First among these was the atmosphere of the city of Omaha. Vice President Woodward of the WCTU from Seward voiced this aversion to Omaha during the fight over the prohibition amendment to the state constitution when she said: "We know of the wicked city of Omaha. We know if it were not for the few faithful ones here it would have gone the way of Sodom and Gomorrah."[54] However, most prohibitionists felt that Omaha held some good Christian people. It was the foreign element that often worried Mrs. Gougar. It was they who were "leading our sons to destruction"; it was they who championed demon rum and lawlessness. "American saloon keepers tell me that if the amendment is carried they will go out of business and obey the law, but the foreign born tell me they will disobey the law and continue to sell liquor." For Mrs. Gougar, the "foreigners" problem went beyond the liquor question; they were a threat to America itself: "These foreigners are all anarchists and by the eternal and the American flag let the Americans rise up and compel them to obey the American law."[55]

In addition to teaching the foreigners respect for American law, the prohibitionists saw another solution to the temperance problem: give women the vote. Women's suffrage and the temperance effort were inextricably bound together, and, for leaders such as Mrs. Gougar, one logically followed the other: "If you give women the vote," she said, "you will have prohibition."[56]

Dedicated prohibitionists made determined foes for all those Nebraskans who did not participate in their crusade. The Omaha newspapers, which defended the wet beliefs of most of their urban readers, were accused of being agents of the powerful "liquor lobby"—a lobby which rivaled the Populists' "railroad lobby" in the magnitude of nineteenth-century conspiracy. Editor Edward Rosewater of the *Bee* became a favorite target of the ladies, while other Omaha leaders, such as Dr. George Miller and Herman Kountz, reigned as leaders of the sinister "liquor league."[57]

Statewide legislation was the only method the prohibitionists had to attack their powerful Omaha antagonists, but the fervor of the movement produced violent conflicts in the villages of Nebraska. In Crete the militant prohibitionists showed hostility

> to every businessman and every business interest that does not array itself on the side of fanatical prohibition. Their leading organ, the *Globe,* has repeatedly vilified and abused honorable citizens of this city for the sole reason that they were not prohibitionists. Not content with that, it advised its prohibitionist readers, happily few in number, to boycott all the businessmen of Crete who do not believe in Prohibition, at least nine-tenths of the businessmen in Crete. The businessmen have withdrawn patronage from the paper, which has retaliated by getting Lincoln merchants to advertise and telling Cretans to go to Lincoln to shop. This doctrine is openly preached by leading members of the third party here.[58]

Politicians who opposed the prohibitionists were often branded as alcoholics.[59]

Prohibitionists usually preferred to operate within their own party, but, in the southern and western sections of the state, they comprised a vociferous and powerful segment in the Republican party. The *Kearney County Gazette* reported that about three-fourths of the Republican county papers of the state supported a prohibition amendment.[60] In the six counties of this study, the Republican papers in the county-seat towns of Aurora, Hayes Center, St. Paul, Gering, and Minden supported prohibition. Only the Republican paper in heavily Democratic—and German—Cuming County did not support the movement.

Pressure from the prohibitionists continued to increase throughout the 1880s until the Republicans had to face the issue in their 1888 state convention. Many Republicans felt the extreme danger of their position, looking to the example of Iowa, where the issue of prohibition resulted in the election of a Democratic governor.[61] After a hard fight on the convention floor, the Republicans passed a resolution calling upon the legislature to submit a prohibitory amendment to the voters in the next election. But many realized that their moderate proposal would receive little help from the hard core of militant prohibitionists, a prediction which proved true.[62]

Prohibition split the Republican party in the state and, to a large extent, contributed to their defeat by the Democrats and Populists in the elections of 1890. If the Republican candidate for governor, Lucius D. Richards, had received the 9,000 votes given to the prohibition state ticket, he would have been elected.[63]

Prohibition divided Republicans and confused Populists, but it helped save Nebraska's outnumbered Democrats. With a significant number of Irishmen already in the party, the Democrats became the instrument new immigrant groups used to defend their cultural traditions. The reaction to the prohibition question was far different in northeastern Nebraska than in the central and western counties. In Cuming, Howard, and Colfax counties, the new German, Bohemian, and Irish immigrants soon learned that it was the Democrats who opposed the prohibitionists. When prohibition first became an issue, the Democratic *Cuming County Progress* read dark forebodings for the German population: "The prohibition craze has swept Iowa. The indicators point to a similar result in Nebraska. Threatening mutterings of fanaticism portend an outbreak in the state of all the elements of puritanism and proscriptive bigotry."[64]

During the debate over the Slocumb Bill, Democratic leaders, including James E. Boyd, John A. McShane, and John A. Creighton, called a protest meeting in Omaha on September 11, 1882.[65] It was the Democrats who led the opposition to it in the legislature and voted against its final passage. The Democrats also organized groups, such as the Personal Rights League in West Point, to fight prohibition.[66]

The Democratic position on prohibition lost some votes in southern and western Nebraska, and it helped earn the party the "Bourbon" tag from the prohibition groups both in and out of the Republican party. They pictured the Democrats as the party of drunkenness and lawlessness, hardly a proper political affiliation for a prosperous, God-fearing citizen of rural Nebraska. The *Gering Courier* spoke with scorn:

> The democracy has a fighting chance in the eastern part of the state. . . . This is due in great measure to the enviable position of the democratic saloon party upon the temperance and morality plank of the Republican party. The loafer element, the street bum and the drunken class in a large city are always the adherents of the rum shop and vote the same way. . . . A vote for St. Rayner is a vote against temperance.[67]

On another occasion, Editor Wood of the *Courier* could not refrain from mentioning: "Last Saturday a saloon was opened in Gering and a Democratic caucus was held. Quite a coincidence."[68]

The Democrats received the brunt of the prohibitionist attack, but they fought back with a zeal born of the hope that the issue would win the votes of the new immigrants in the state. Republican politicians were wary of the issue and realized the effect it was having on immigrant voters.[69] However, they could do little to counter the obvious connection of their party with the prohibitionist sentiment. The Republican editor of the *Schuyler Sun* realized the role the issue had in Democratic Colfax County:

> Several causes have here-to-fore not figured in, helped greatly
> to decrease the Republican vote. The German and Bohemian
> newspapers brought considerable prestige to bear on their
> readers by the cry of the Republicans being Prohibitionists
> and allied with that party. Germans in Wilson who had al-
> ways voted Republican tickets before cast straight demo-
> cratic ones this time.[70]

Prohibitionists realized the attitude of the newer immigrant groups and in retaliation sought to ban them from the ballot. In one instance, prohibitionist officials tried to secure an injunction restraining over six hundred Omaha citizens from voting in the election of 1890.[71] This move only increased the tendency of the German, Bohemian, and Irish population to move into the Democratic party.

The Democrats gained some followers in other sections of Nebraska because of their championing of "personal rights." They appealed to many businessmen, such as Asa B. Wood of Gering, who were temperate themselves, but who were afraid of the economic dislocations that might accompany prohibition. The single most effective argument used against the prohibitionists was that prohibition would hurt business, and it was reproduced in nearly all of the county Democratic papers examined in this study and in metropolitan papers, such as the *Bee.*[72]

A second argument advanced by the antiprohibitionists stressed individual rights. The Reverend B. Sproll expressed this viewpoint in a letter to the editor of the *Hamilton County Register*:

> We have no use for prohibition in Nebraska. No liquor man
> ever forced a cold water man to drink beer . . . but you want
> to force others to abstain from it. What an injustice . . . .
> May the Lord grant . . . the Prohibitionists will soon be

bowed to the ground and unable to injure the innocent, and to deprive them of their rights.[73]

A prohibition amendment to the state constitution was the ultimate goal of the prohibitionists, but in the interim they made a concerted attempt in many communities to enact the local-option provision of the Slocumb Law. Throughout the 1880s, the most significant elections for village officials centered around the local-option aspect of the prohibition issue. In 1883, the Minden village board set the liquor license fee at five hundred dollars for six months, while Axtell, a neighboring village, permitted no saloons.[74] Every village had to make and remake its policy concerning prohibition. Far from solving the liquor problem, local option became a constant source of conflict and dominated other issues in most of Nebraska's municipal elections.[75]

In most villages, the city elections were not under the regular party labels, but were under a temporary party alignment which reflected attitudes toward the prohibition issue. Party lines were not exactly reproduced since a significant number of Republicans usually joined with nearly all of the Democrats to form the antiprohibition forces. The issue for a struggling community involved more than the moral and cultural factors usually associated with prohibition. A very practical consideration, which the antiprohibitionists always stressed, concerned the effect that the high license fee had upon village finances. Most leaders realized that several licenses at a thousand dollars a year went a long way toward meeting a village's financial obligations. In Aurora, the City Improvement party campaigned on the platform that high license fees brought three thousand dollars annually into the city treasury. The new mayor, a Democrat, used the slogan "License the saloon for public improvement."[76] These arguments carried a great deal of appeal and logic; in this instance, the City Improvement party carried the 1891 election by a two-to-one majority.[77] In the counties examined for this study, prohibition forces were not generally successful locally and turned to agitation for statewide amendments.

In the western section of the state, prohibition became an issue soon after settlement, but it met with little success since village leaders hesitated about losing any buisness, even a saloon, from the sparsely settled business districts. In Gering, there was little agitation among the prohibitionists for any local policy other than their insistence that the license fee be collected.[78] However, when a constitutional amendment became a possibility, a number of the leading citizens, including Asa B. Wood, editor of the *Courier*, and Lot L. Feltham, one of the two local attorneys, founded the Prohibition League to support the amendment. In Minden, town father Joel Hull and long-time state representative Otto Abrahamson organized a similar league.[79] The citizens of the other western county, Hayes, showed somewhat less interest in prohibition than those who lived in central Nebraska, but, even in Hayes County, prohibition was an important issue and the Democratic paper carried a WCTU column edited by the wife of a local minister. Temperance workers met frequently in Hayes Center, especially during the critical election year of 1890.[80] The other two counties in this study, Cuming and Howard, contained large numbers of militantly antiprohibitionist German or Polish immigrants; consequently no local agitation existed either for the submission of an amendment to the state constitution or for local option.

The election of 1890 proved to be critical for the prohibition forces throughout the state, just as it was for the Populists. The Aurora municipal election of that year hinged solely on the prohibition question. When the City Improvement party held its nominating convention, town leader Edward J. Hainer offered a resolution asking that prohibition not be the only issue discussed during the election. The convention voted down Hainer's motion and went on to select a wet Democrat as its candidate.[81]

The news of municipal prohibition elections elicited great interest in the state during the fall of 1890. The *Omaha World Herald* kept a score, showing the choice each municipality had made. High license towns included Aurora, Norfolk, Plainview, Talmadge, Sutton, Minden, Albion, Ord, Springfield, Ainsworth, Avoca, Tecumseh, Auburn, North Platte, Orleans, Gibbon, Wayne, and West Point. Only Beatrice and Osceola voted to be dry.[82]

The Republican party hesitantly supported statewide prohibition. The Republican convention, which approved of the submission of a prohibitory amendment to the state constitution, split on the issue, and the vote for submission was close. Then the Republican platform of 1890 straddled the issue as did their candidate for governor, Lucius D. Richards, a known prohibitionist, who became the object of Democratic amusement as he vainly tried to please both wets and drys during the campaign:

> There is one question, a non-partisan one which many of our
> people consider of paramount importance. I refer to the pro-
> hibitory amendment. Our democratic friends seem to think
> it would help their cause to have me publicly define myself
> on that question. . . . If the platform was good enough to ac-
> cept nomination on it was good enough to go before the
> people on.[83]

Republican attempts to disassociate themselves from prohibition had little effect on the foreign born. The Democrats had an issue that served them well in the German, Bohemian, and Irish counties. The discouraged editor of the *West Point Republican*, who lived in a virtual sea of Germans, forlornly defended the remnants of Republicanism in Cuming County: "Democrats out in county townships are still using the prohibition racket against Republican candidates . . . last year the Republican party did more to defeat prohibition than the combined efforts of all other parties.[84] Republican politicians in central Nebraska possibly benefited from the prohibition issue, but agitation for prohibition certainly did not aid their Republican brethren in the Northeast. The prohibition issue all but obliterated the Republican party in the heavily German and Bohemian counties.

Nebraska's farmers were not drawn into the battle that raged around the liquor question as were the city and village dwellers. Under the Slocumb Law, decisions affecting this problem were shunted to urban residents, for the decision rested with each municipality as to whether it would license or prohibit the sale of alcohol. However, the prohibition question proved to be most significant in those areas in which the Populists showed greatest strength. Prohibitionists had considerable success among the rural population by arguing that, while all the county residents supported the jails into which the drunks were thrown, only the cities received the benefit of the high license fees. The *Kearney County Gazette* stated it this way: "The sentiment is growing among the farmers that license is robbery for the benefit of the municipality and the detriment of the farming community."[85] Another prohibitionist writer turned the same argument against Omaha: "If Omaha likes high license to support her schools, you people of the state are not going to help support the penitentiary which her citizens fill."[86] Prohibitionists attempted to capitalize on this sentiment. The *Central City Courier*, a prohibitionist newspaper, advocated a coalition of the prohibitionists and the farmers. Assuming that the farmer would not want to "ally himself with the saloon," the *Courier* observed that the prohibitionists were "drifting" toward national control of the railroads, "the only true solution to the railroad problem."[87]

A. B. Wood, editor of the *Gering Courier*, supported the prohibition amendment, and he, too, hoped for Alliance support:

> It is now confidently claimed that the farmer's Alliance will roll up a tremendously solid vote for prohibition. The prominent leaders . . . of the farmer's movement denounce the saloon as being responsible for an enormous percent of the agricultural depression on [*sic*] existing throughout the county. They point to the injustices of the Slocumb laws' provisions that turn all license money into the city and village school funds, yet taxes the criminal costs of the liquor traffic up to the whole county, thus saddling the main

burden on the farmer . . . about three-fourths of all alliance
men feel this way.[88]

Many farmers sympathized with the prohibitionists, and they lent them
their speaking platforms at local Alliance meetings In Kearney County, the
county Alliance passed resolutions favoring the prohibition amendment; however, these resolutions never reached the state level.[89] The leaders of the state
Alliance realized that bringing this issue into the campaign would weaken their
chances in the eastern part of the state. Consequently, the Nebraska State Alliance never took a position on the prohibition amendment. This proved to be
a wise tactical move, since election statistics indicate that prohibition meant
more to German farmers than economic factors.[90] Nevertheless, the Populists'
attempt to disassociate themselves from prohibition did not prove altogether
successful in 1890, for their gubernatorial candidate, John B. Powers, was a
known prohibitionist.[91] As a result, the Populists received very few votes in
the heavily German counties and in Omaha.[92]

The importance of the prohibition issue during the era, especially to the
German population, is illustrated by voting statistics from heavily German precincts in the northeastern part of the state. In these precincts, the German
farmer did not react to economic depression as did the farmers of other local-
ities, but because of the prohibition crisis, German precincts actually increased
their Democratic pluralities. Nine rural precincts that averaged 85 percent
German voters illustrate this tendency.[93] In 1883, these precincts averaged
73 percent Democratic. In 1890, even with economic conditions vying with
prohibition as an issue, the Democrats raised their share of the vote to 79 percent; the Populists polled a mere 12 percent, while the Republicans won only
9 percent. After 1890, when prohibition became less important, the German
counties increased their Populist vote, but, by and large, the German voters
remained suspicious of the Populist interest in prohibition. The Bohemians in
the northeastern part of Nebraska also refused to join the Populist cause because of the prohibition issue. Four heavily Bohemian rural precincts in Colfax County gave the Populists only 0.1 percent of the vote in 1890. The
Danes, on the other hand, switched from the Democratic party to the Populist
in 1890. In two heavily Danish precincts in Howard County, the Democrats
won 64 percent of the vote in 1888, but the Populists carried them with 69
percent of the vote in 1890 and 76 percent in 1896.

Of the major immigrant groups in Nebraska, the Swedes showed the most
pronounced Republican and prohibitionist proclivities. In six rural precincts,
the Republicans received 65 percent of the vote in 1888. In 1890 the Populists
carried these precincts with 45 percent of the three-party vote, but, by 1896,

the Swedes had returned to their previous pattern by giving Republicans 65 percent of the votes.

The Swedish population, which generally supported prohibition, was the only major immigrant group in Nebraska not affected by the prohibition issue. Unlike the Germans and Bohemians, they were more concerned with economic, rather than cultural, problems.

Census statistics have to some extent presented a misleading impression of the significance of the various immigrant groups during the Populist era. By reporting the numerous children of immigrants as native-born, the domination of several counties by immigrants has been obscured. Consequently, the role of ethnic and cultural conflict in the state has usually been minimized. Actually, many areas in Nebraska and the Midwest witnessed the solidification of immigrant political loyalties, which were as significant as those described by Samuel Lubell in metropolitan areas during the 1920s.[94] This process occurred at about the same time as the Populist movement, but was basically cultural, not economic. In Nebraska, it resulted in the solidification of German political loyalties in the Democratic party.

Some historians have mistakenly tended to combine populism and the various forms of cultural conflict. Inevitably, there was some interaction between the two movements, but most Populists attempted to concentrate almost solely on economic reforms. Populism existed at the same time as conflicts that grew from cultural differences, but instead of participating in these movements, the Populist movement in the state was hampered by outside cultural conflicts. Rather than being a part of the major thrust of populism, nativism and cultural conflict temporarily diverted many Nebraskans from the economic reforms which assumed such great importance after 1890.

8

The Nebraska Populists: A Statistical Description

Previous chapters of this study have described various factors that affected the course and values of Nebraska populism. Farmer–village conflict, cultural tensions, and economic conditions have been treated by using evidence derived from traditional historical sources and using narrative techniques of presentation. Another approach to the problem of historical interpretation is provided by various statistical techniques. These techniques do not attempt to reduce all history to a simple formula, but can be used in conjunction with more traditional methods to provide a higher degree of probability concerning historical relationships. In this chapter, two statistical approaches will be used: the Pierson product–moment correlation statistic, which measures the strength of the relationship between two electoral or demographic variables, and various methods of legislative roll-call analysis, which can be used to measure the attitudinal positions and groupings of legislators.

The Pierson product–moment correlation coefficient used in the first part of this chapter is expressed numerically—from an absolute "one-to-one" relationship (+1.0) to a similar inverse relationship (–1.0). Of course, such absolute relationships seldom occur in political behavior; consequently, most coefficients are expressed decimally on a scale between two poles. For the purpose of this study, coefficients above plus or minus 0.20 are considered to be theoretically significant.

For the Piersonian correlation analysis, the dependent variable, or the factor being investigated, was the percentage of the vote the Populists received in each county of Nebraska in the gubernatorial election of 1890. Variables that might be related to the Populist vote are political, cultural, and economic factors obtained from the United States census.[1] The object of the problem is to indicate which social, economic, and political factors are most closely related to a high percentage of Populist votes in Nebraska's eighty-nine counties.

The election of 1890 was chosen as the best index of Populist strength in Nebraska. The movement at this time was still in its initial stages of development and was not yet influenced by other political groups. The 1890 vote also marks the greatest strength the Populists ever showed in the state. Never again were they able to poll such impressive majorities in most counties. Later, when they finally captured the governorship, they did it only with the aid and direction of the Democratic party. After populism's first successes, a new group of leaders took control, and the movement lost much of its initial fire and vigor. Farmers were often deprived of leadership as village groups, which were more familiar with political action, gained influence in party councils. The "farmers' movement," then, was in its purest state in 1890.

The election of 1890 in Nebraska was one of the most colorful in American history. Because of a drought and the resultant crop failure, the farmers were free to swarm into town and hold emotion-packed political rallies.[2] All of the parties in the campaign damned the railroads and the East, but the Populists seemed the most sincere in these views. A prohibition amendment to the state constitution added cultural conflicts to the boiling economic issues. Neither the Republicans nor the Populists took a firm stand on prohibition, but the Democrats staunchly opposed it and carried Douglas County (Omaha) by such an enormous margin that they were able to capture the governorship for the first time in Nebraska's history. The Populists, however, won control of the state legislature. Most observers regarded the election as the Populists' greatest triumph, but because of the Bourbon Democratic governor's effective use of the veto, the victory did not bring the Populists the reforms they wanted.

Some of the factors associated with the Populist revolt cannot be set to a statistical model. For example, historians who have been greatly influenced by Frederick Jackson Turner emphasize the closing of the frontier safety-valve and the subsequent channeling into politics of much unrest, which before 1890 might have been expended in expansion. John D. Hicks states this point of view in his preface to *The Populist Revolt.* There is no way to test Hicks' hypothesis concerning populism statistically. There are, however, many variables that can be quantified. Those which can be tested statistically have been divided into three major groups: economic factors, social–cultural factors, and political relationships. These factors, together with the rationale for selection, follow.

I. Economic Factors

A. Wealth

1. *Average value of farm products per farm.* Obviously the Populist farmers were not affluent in comparison to some other farm groups in the United States. However, there is little information showing how they compare with other farmers in the same state. Assuming the Populist farmers were the poorest in the state, then the Populist vote would vary inversely with the average value of farm products per farm in each county.

2. *Percentage increase in tenant farmers, 1880–1890.* Tenant farming has been associated with declining agricultural prosperity. Hypothetically, counties showing the greatest increase in tenant farmers should have a tendency to return a larger Populist vote.

B. Type of Farming

3. *Wheat.* Nearly all historians who have chronicled the Populist movement have noted that the wheat farmer was particularly vulnerable to economic disaster at this time. Hicks, who often gives credence to the Populist analysis of the economic situation, mentions:

> Such crops as wheat and cotton, of which the United States
> had had an excess for export, must now often come into
> competition with these tremendous outpourings from other
> parts of the world, and the prices must be fixed accordingly.
> It was the price brought by this exportable surplus that set
> the price for the entire domestic output.[3]

James Malin has also stressed the influence of changing market conditions on the plains farmer.[4] If such a relationship existed between wheat farmers and the agrarian movement, then the Populist vote should vary directly with the percentage of arable land in each county devoted to the cultivation of wheat.

4. *Corn.* Corn was the major crop in Nebraska during the 1890s as it is today. Only in the extreme western part of the state was corn production a less important crop in terms of acres planted than was wheat. But corn production also characterized Iowa and Illinois, states with insignificant numbers of Populist voters. Corn production has been called a more mature type of agriculture than wheat production because it requires that a considerably larger amount of capital be spent in the purchase of livestock, fencing, and the like. Once an area adopts a corn–livestock economy, it is generally considered somewhat more stable than a wheat-growing area. The reason for this is that livestock

constitutes a relatively concentrated commodity and requires proportionately less in freight expenditure. The corn–livestock economy is also less liable to be an easy victim of wide market fluctuations.[5] This condition proved particularly true in the late 1880s when the international wheat market was glutted and prices were low. Since populism is often related to less prosperous farmers, it was hypothesized that the Populist vote would vary inversely with the percentage of arable land in each county devoted to the cultivation of corn.

5. *Cattle.* Closely associated with corn production is the average number of cattle per farm. As stated above, a larger number of cattle per farm indicates a more prosperous agricultural community. Consequently, the Populist vote should vary inversely with this variable.

C. Interest

6. *Interest rates.* The Populist press placed great emphasis upon high interest rates as a factor behind the farmers' movement. This variable represents the average interest rate per county as recorded by the census.

7-8. *Interest charges as a percentage of value of farm property* and (another variable) *interest charges as a percentage of farm income.* Because interest charges did not vary a great deal in Nebraska at this time, these two variables were constructed to represent the percentages of net income or farm value required to pay interest charges. If high interest charges, together with low income, or farm value, are important variables, then the Populist vote should be directly related to these two factors.

D. Stages of Growth

9-10. *Population increase, 1885-1890, and 1880-1890.* Several studies of populism in other states have established a relationship between counties experiencing a rapid population growth and the Populist vote.[6] A rapid rate of growth was a frontier phenomenon and might be related to populism.

E. Transportation Costs

11. *Zonal distance from Chicago.* Populist spokesmen complained about high transportation costs, and the narrative portion of this study shows that it naturally became more expensive to ship commodities east the farther west the farmer moved. Simple distance from markets could be a factor in producing the farmer's crisis. For this variable, Nebraska was divided from east to west into seven zones, each averaging two counties wide. Theoretically, the farther from market, the higher the freight charges, the higher the Populist vote.

II. Social Variables

F. Cultural

12–13. *Pietistic and ritualistic cultural background.* Several recent studies, as well as the narrative portions of this study, have shown the importance of cultural elements in the politics of the era. Some historians have suggested that populism had important cultural roots, or that it was strongly associated with nativism and even anti-Semitism. If cultural animosities are related to populism, there should be a statistical relationship between the movement and a pietistic Protestant cultural background. Conversely, there should be an inverse relationship between populism and a ritualistic cultural background. Since these factors are difficult to define in the religious census, those Nebraskans with a German, Irish, or Bohemian ancestry were classified as ritualists; all others become pietists.

14. *Native birth.* If populism can be associated with native birth, then the Populist vote should vary directly with percentage of native-born residents of a county.

15. *Relationship to the vote for the prohibition amendment.* A more sensitive gauge to the pietistic elements in populism might be the relationship between the Populist vote and the vote for the prohibition amendment to the state constitution in 1890. If populism were related to pietistic values, then there should be a positive relationship between the two voting patterns.

G. Residential

16. *Rural and urban voting behavior.* William Diamond, in his influential article on rural–urban tensions in 1896, concentrates on large urban centers and uses a population of 40,000 to separate urban from rural.[7] He does not deal with smaller urban areas in the plains area. Although it is a valuable model, Diamond's rural–urban tension dichotomy has a strong large-city bias, as it classifies many large towns as "rural." Historians agree that the Populists were farmers. But to what extent? What was their appeal to urban and village inhabitants? Can Diamond's model of city–outstate tension be expanded to include all townspeople against all farmers? If Populists were solely farmers, then counties with the highest percentage of farmers would have the highest percentage of Populist vote.[8] The percentage of the three-party vote won by the Populist gubernatorial candidate will then vary directly with the percentage of the farm population of each county.

III. Relationship with Other Voting Patterns

17-20. *Voting comparisons.* The correlation statistic can also be used to help analyze similarities and differences between voting behavior between several elections. If, for example, the Populist gubernatorial vote in 1890 correlates highly with the Populist gubernatorial vote in 1892, it is an indication that county voting patterns are substantially the same for the two elections. Comparisons were made between the Populist gubernatorial vote for 1890 and: (17) *Populist gubernatorial vote, 1892* (3 parties on ballot); (18) *Fusionist gubernatorial vote, 1896* (2 parties on ballot). (19) *Republican gubernatorial vote, 1888.* (20) *Democratic gubernatorial vote, 1888.*

Table 13 suggests some of the characteristics of Nebraska populism, derived from the correlation analysis.[9] Taken together, the coefficients relating to economic conditions are consistent enough to indicate that populism received its greatest support in the counties that were experiencing the most severe economic crisis. Nebraskans did not raise much wheat during the era; consequently, the 0.34 correlation with wheat acreage probably indicates the undercapitalized position of many farmers in the Populist counties. This analysis is substantiated by other coefficients. The -0.24 with cattle per farm further suggests a marginal type of operation, in which farmers had to plant staple crops because of lack of capital to purchase livestock. The low, but probably theoretically significant -0.17 for average value of farm products per farm and the 0.17 for increase in tenant farmers give some minor evidence for this contention. The average interest rate paid per county indicates that there is no direct relationship between interest rates and populism, but the other interest variables—0.24 for percentage of income paid as interest and 0.28 for interest payments as a percentage of farm value—suggest that when even average interest rates were operant with low income the debtor perceived interest rates to be as high as Populist orators claimed. This undercapitalized frontier farmer picture of Populist counties is further corroborated by the growth variables. The 0.25 coefficient with population increase, 1880-1890, indicates that the newly settled counties had a marked inclination to become Populist. The counties undergoing settlements, with a large population growth after 1885, did not correlate highly with the Populist vote. One other variable— distance from Chicago—with a coefficient of 0.24, illustrates that there was a tendency for counties in the western part of the state to vote Populist. Perhaps this was a result of the higher freight charges to be expected from areas a great distance from a major market. Such a theory is more plausible when it is remembered that populism thrived on the western fringe of the Midwest—that area which was the farthest from major markets.

Table 13: PIERSON PRODUCT-MOMENT CORRELATION COEFFICIENTS
BETWEEN POPULIST VOTE FOR GOVERNOR, 1890, AND
SELECTED ECONOMIC, CULTURAL, AND ELECTORAL
VARIABLES (by county units)

	Description of Variable in Each County	*Correlation Coefficient with Populist Gubernatorial Vote, 1890*
(I)	Economic variables	
	(A) *Wealth*	
	(1) Average value of farm products per farm	−0.17
	(2) Percentage increase in tenant farmers	0.17
	(B) *Type of farming*	
	(3) Percentage of land in county devoted to raising wheat	0.34
	(4) Percentage of land in county devoted to raising corn	0.16
	(5) Average number of cattle per farm	−0.24
	(C) *Interest*	
	(6) Average interest rate per county	0.06
	(7) Interest payments as a percentage of farm value	0.28
	(8) Interest payments as a percentage of farm income	0.24
	(D) *Stage of growth*	
	(9) Population increase, 1885–1890	0.10
	(10) Population increase, 1880–1890	0.25
	(E) *Transportation*	
	(11) Zonal distance from Chicago	0.24
(II)	Social variables	
	(F) *Cultural*	
	(12) Percentage pietistic cultural background	0.08
	(13) Percentage ritualistic cultural background	0.05
	(14) Percentage native-born	−0.13
	(15) Vote for prohibition amendment, 1890	0.36
	(G) *Residential*	
	(16) Percentage in county residing on farms	0.06
(III)	Relationship to other voting patterns	
	(17) Populist gubernatorial vote, 1892	0.64
	(18) Fusionist gubernatorial vote, 1896	−0.02
	(19) Republican gubernatorial vote, 1888	0.48
	(20) Democratic gubernatorial vote, 1888	−0.47

Social variables as a whole did not correlate as highly with the Populist vote
as did economic factors. In all of these cases—pietistic cultural background,
ritualistic cultural background, native birth, and rural or urban residence—so
many other cross-pressures appear to have been operant that it was impossible

to secure meaningful coefficients. Although in 1890, for example, most Populists were probably Protestants, still most Republicans and many Democrats also kept that faith. A similar condition probably existed for the native-birth variable, although foreign birth did correlate highly with the Democratic vote. Finally, for the state as a whole the percentage of the population living on farms proved of little value in analyzing Populist voting behavior. This fact is not startling, for voting returns from the eastern and the northwestern parts of the state indicate that many farmers were not interested in populism. The Populist was a farmer, but a farmer living in a particular environment. County voting maps have revealed a tendency of counties in the central third of Nebraska to vote Populist. To test the statistical significance of rural–village cleavage in the Populist counties the Pierson statistic was used for only the counties occupying the central third of the state. In these counties the Pierson coefficient between percentage living on the farm and the Populist vote was +0.60. Taken together, the coefficients indicate that not all farmers were Populists. Populism had the greatest appeal to those farmers in central Nebraska with a certain set of social and economic characteristics. This is substantiated in the narrative portions of this study. Counties in the far western part of the state were the most rural and voted heavily Republican because they needed capital, while German farmers in the populous eastern counties voted heavily Democratic because of prohibition.

The voting pattern established by the Populists in the 1890 gubernatorial campaign lasted until fusion with the Democrats. The 1890 vote correlates with that of 1892 at 0.64, but when the Democratic counties joined in coalition in 1896, the pattern collapsed and the coefficient became 0.02.

The two correlations with both the Democratic and Republican gubernatorial vote in 1888 illustrates that Populist strength came from the former heavily Republican counties in central Nebraska.

The table in the appendix presents a matrix of coefficients between later elections and many of the variables presented here. It shows that when the cultural issues of 1890 were removed from consideration, the importance of the economic variables increased.

Election analysis at the county level can be helpful and suggestive in analyzing nineteenth-century politics, but counties, even then, were heterogeneous, a fact that makes generalization difficult. Data secured at the precinct level, however, are more precise and homogeneous and can both act as a check on the county data and add refinements to interpretation. Table 14 was compiled using precinct voting returns and manuscript census reports which listed the nativity and residence of voters.

Table 14 illustrates the significant difference between the rural and city acceptance of populism. This is most pronounced in the native American precincts

Table 14: RESIDENTIAL AND ETHNIC VOTING PATTERNS USING SAMPLE PRECINCT DATA: FORTY-SIX PRECINCTS, NEBRASKA, 1888–1900

Ethnic Background and Residence	Number of Precincts	1885 Gub.	1890 Gub.	1892 Gub.	1892 Pres.	1894 Gub.	1896 Gub.	1896 Pres.	1900 Gub.
					Elections				
URBAN									
Bohemian (Omaha)	3	No Data	81.4 D	50.0 D	47.8 P	ND	57.8 F	54.4 F	ND
American (Omaha–middle class)	4	ND	62.7 D	57.5 R	58.0 R	ND	63.4 R	65.0 R	ND
American (Omaha–laboring)	5	ND	64.6 D	40.9 R	43.7 R	ND	57.4 R	58.1 R	ND
RURAL									
American (Platte, Howard, and Hamilton counties)	14	59.2 R	63.5 P	49.5 P	56.1 P	58.1 F	62.2 F	60.2 F	59.2 F
German									
Protestant	4	66.2 D	78.3 D	40.0 D	33.9 D	45.2 F	61.6 F	53.4 F	52.9 F
Catholic	4	66.5 D	80.9 D	65.8 D	68.0 P	67.1 F	68.5 F	68.3 F	61.7 F
Volga-German	1	70.2 R	52.3 P	50.4 R	51.3 R	56.4 R	50.8 F	49.6 R	51.2 R
Swedish	5	71.8 R	44.1 P	44.2 P	54.9 P	ND	52.4 R	56.1 F	ND
Danish	1	70.7 D	69.4 P	65.8 P	66.9 P	75.7 F	75.2 F	72.9 F	ND
Bohemian	5	69.1 D	87.4 D	74.3 D	76.3 D	70.1 F	67.5 F	77.3 F	85.6 F

Note: The first letter after each figure in the table indicates the party receiving the plurality of votes: Republican (R), Democrat (D), Populist (P), Fusionist (F).

Source: County election returns secured from county clerk's offices in the respective counties or from local newspapers. Demographic data for the precincts used were secured from the *Schedules of the Nebraska State Census of 1885.* To qualify as a sample precinct, over 60 percent of males over twenty-one years of age had to belong to the same cultural group. Precinct uniformity ranged from 65 to 90 percent. Most of the rural population were farmers.

of Omaha, particularly when the middle-class designation is added, but it also holds true for the only ethnic community (the Bohemians) that could be clearly distinguished in the urban area.

In the rural areas, the most significant voting switch of the era came from native Americans in central Nebraska, who in 1888 averaged 59.2 percent Republican, but by 1900 voted the same percentage fusionist. The only other cultural group to swing from Republican to Populist to fusionist was the Swedish, almost all of whom lived in the Populist areas of the state. On the other hand, the one precinct with a large number of Volga Germans maintained a Republican inclination. The rural and ethnic portion of the table shows that most rural Germans and Bohemians came to populism through fusion after the cultural furor of the early 1890s had abated. They were clearly concerned with the cultural issues of the era and maintained their heavily Democratic voting commitment through the election of 1892. Only the German Catholics broke ranks and voted for Weaver that year. Of the staunchly Democratic precincts of 1888, the Danish were the only ones who switched to populism in 1890 and maintained the position throughout the 1890s.

Finally, Table 15 illustrates the variation observed in one county because of economic variables. When Roscoe Martin conducted a similar study in Cooke County, Texas, for his book, *The Peoples Party in Texas*, he found a startling difference in the Populist vote between the richer and poorer precincts. This was less so in Hamilton County, Nebraska, where there was a statistical relationship between the Populist vote per precinct and income per precinct of -0.32.

Although statistical analysis has not accounted for all of the variables related to the Populist vote, it has suggested some generalizations about the demographic background of the Populists. From the statistical evidence it can be inferred that the Nebraska Populist was likely to be a pietistic Protestant who lived on a farm in the central part of the state. This environment proved particularly conducive to populism. In the first place, it was not the newest settled area in the state. Settlement had begun one or two decades earlier and growth had been rapid between 1880 and 1890. The inhabitants of areas in the far-western part of the state, settled after 1885, were often less radical than the more established operator because the far-western farmer still needed the capital, railroads, and aid of the more affluent East. Central Nebraska, however, was an area inhabited by farmers who had recently undergone the transition to a more commercial agriculture. Being but fledgling entrepreneurs, they were particularly susceptible to economic disaster. They were not the poorest nor did they pay the highest interest rates in the state, but the fact that they grew more wheat than other farmers emphasizes their meager

Table 15: VOTING AND INCOME DATA BY PRECINCT: HAMILTON COUNTY, NEBRASKA (PRESIDENTIAL ELECTION OF 1892)

	Percent of Populist Vote: 1892	Adjusted Income[a]
Orville Precinct	53.0	$1,459.75
Beaver Precinct	38.0	$1,440.96
Farmer's Valley Precinct	47.9	$1,403.38
Valley Precinct	36.6	$1,371.30
Grant Precinct	44.0	$1,243.29
Aurora Precinct	50.7	$1,137.23
Union Precinct	52.2	$1,120.63
Phillips Precinct	45.5	$1,095.35
Bluff Precinct	34.2	$1,048.13
Monroe Precinct	45.8	$1,026.91
Otis Precinct	43.0	$ 994.46
Hamilton Precinct	70.3	$ 979.29
Scoville Precinct	70.7	$ 946.23
Deep Well Precinct	63.1	$ 842.69
Cedar Valley Precinct	45.8	$ 841.61
South Platte Precinct	43.0	$ 761.81

[a]Value of farm products sold plus value of cattle held at time of census.
Source: Schedule of the Nebraska State Census of 1885.

resources of capital with which to engage in more profitable feeding operations. The amount of wheat they did grow, however, was so small that it symbolizes the difficulties they were experiencing in acclimating to their geographical environment and entrepreneurial position more than the fact that they were competing on the international wheat market. Thus, the "statistical" Populist tended to be a pietistic Protestant, low-capitalized, commercial farmer attempting to farm in a hostile environment while paying freight and interest rates that were not exorbitant, but still taxed his meager resources. Unlike his ritualistic neighbors, he could attack the economic difficulties in his environment rather than being compelled to defend his cultural tradition. The undertaking of commercial farming in a marginal area during a recession is a situation which understandably might bring on a political crisis.

Another readily available source for a statistical description of the nature of populism can be found in the legislative voting behavior of Populist legislators elected in large numbers after 1890. By analyzing roll-call votes for given interest areas, it is possible, within broad lines, to generalize about Populist attitudes in at least as accurate a manner as generalizations can be made from the Populist press or from the writings of important leaders. We can also define more precisely the attitudes of important Populists toward several different concepts of reform, and evaluate the relationship between the Populist legislative behavior and the farmers' general legislative concerns during the preceding decade.

The legislative sources of this section of inquiry comprise the lower house of the Nebraska legislatures of 1883, 1885, and 1891. The choice of these legislatures evolved from two considerations: availability of biographical data for all the members of the legislature, a relatively rare occurrence in the nineteenth century, and the nature of the legislatures themselves. The 1891 legislature marks the apex of Populist power in Nebraska. On the other hand, the legislature of 1885 reflects the power of those who had traditionally controlled the state—village and city businessmen. Finally, the legislature of 1883 represents a power position between the two other sessions; although farmers did dominate the lower house by a small margin, village and city business and professional men were still a powerful minority.

The first step in analyzing each of the legislatures involved selecting categories of legislation or issue areas. Although each of the legislatures had some of its own particular issues, there were issues in common to all three. The choice of issues relates closely to concepts of reform, for example, railroad regulatory legislation might be deemed worthwhile reform by some, while aid to state colleges might be more meaningful to others. How different groups reacted to different issue areas, then, to a large extent defines that group's definition of reform, just as a historian's conception of populism might be colored by the issues of his time. In the three legislatures studied, the unique and common issue areas and the number of bills considered in each legislature is seen in Table 16.[10] The total number of roll calls considered numbered 183 and represented 18,000 individual responses. Since every method of roll-call analysis has its own strengths and weaknesses, three different methods were used: analysis of categoric groupings, agreement scores, and Guttman scaling.[11]

The categorical groupings that might help to explain the polarities of political conflict during the period include six subjectively selected dichotomous categories: the voting patterns of third-party members against Democrats and Republicans, Omaha–Lincoln legislators against all outstate legislators, eastern Nebraskans against western Nebraskans, Democrats against Republicans, farmers against nonfarmers, and active members of the legislature against passive members of the legislature.[12] In order to measure conflict between the various categorical groups in the legislatures, three different scales were used: a comparison of simple percentages, the Rice Index of Cohesion, and the Index of Disagreement.[13]

The Nebraska legislature of 1891 marked the zenith of Populist influence in the state. Perhaps the legislature's most notable characteristics was a dramatic change in its personnel. For a quarter-century, farmers had been numerically outnumbered; but in 1891, they won control of the lower house

Table 16: SELECTED ISSUE AREAS AND THE NUMBER OF ROLL CALLS CONSIDERED IN EACH AREA (add)

Issues common to each legislature	1883	1885	1891
Railroad regulations	18	13	9
Culture	10	8	13
Finance	13	14	8
Education	6	13	12
Issues covered in one or more legislatures			
Government operations	–	7	3
Institutions	–	9	3
Resources	–	7	–
Interest	–	–	3
Militia	–	–	3
Relief	–	–	3
Sugar	–	–	4
Medical	–	–	4
Roll calls in each house	47	71	65
Total roll calls			183

Source: *House Journal of the Legislature of the State of Nebraska,* 1883, 1885, 1891.

and threatened to enact legislation that might radically alter the status quo. The increase in farmer power is illustrated in Table 17.

Table 17: OCCUPATIONAL GROUPS IN THE NEBRASKA LEGISLATURE

	1883	1885	1891
House			
Farmer	52	48	76
Nonfarmer	48	51	24
Lawyer	(14)	(17)	(5)
Business	(19)	(27)	(12)
Other	(15)	(7)	(7)
Senate			
Farmer	18	13	24
Nonfarmer	26	31	8
Total Farmer	70	61	100
Total Nonfarmer	74	82	32

Source: Nebraska Senate and House Journals for the appropriate years.

The actions of the agrarian majority in the 1891 house were consistent with their rhetoric and traditions. Railroads, a strictly economic concern, obsessed agrarian orators, and they were equally important to farmer legislators. The highest average indexes of disagreement between the groups in all three legislatures occurred over issues related to regulation of railroads, seen in Table 18.[14]

Table 18: MEAN DISAGREEMENT SCORES FOR ALL CATEGORIC GROUPS: MAJOR ISSUE AREAS

Issue Areas	1883	1885	1891	Average for Issues
Railroad	26.5	11.2	28.2	21.9
Cultural	15.7	15.2	31.0	20.6
Financial	21.2	12.6	28.0	20.6
Educational	12.4	16.1	24.5	17.6
Average score for legislature	18.9	13.7	27.9	20.1

Analysis by categorical groups of twelve railroad roll calls in 1891, presented in Table 19, reveals that the greatest disagreement or polarization came between the old party legislators from Omaha and Lincoln and outstate Populists.

Table 19: DISAGREEMENT SCORES BY CATEGORICAL GROUPS: RAILROAD ISSUES, 1891 HOUSE

Position Prorailroad	Antirailroad	Disagreement Score
Omaha–Railroad	Outstate	44.4
Democratic–Republican	Populists	43.5
Nonfarmer	Farmer	36.4
East	West	25.4
Democratic	Republican	10.8
Active	Passive	0.9

This general description of the position taken by different groups can be corroborated by other methods used in legislature roll-call analysis. These methods, agreement scores and Guttman scaling, were devised to identify groups of legislators who behaved in a similar manner. By using agreement scores, which are simply the percentage of times given legislators agreed on a series of roll calls, a matrix was constructed, which reveals those legislators who agreed with one another. Agreement scores of railway issues in the 1891 house revealed four groups of legislators who agreed on *all* railroad legislation at least 70 percent of the time. The largest prorailway group included eleven men. Of these, six were from Omaha or Lincoln, all were from eastern Nebraska, and nine were business or professional men. The antirailroad bloc—a powerful group in 1891—comprised forty legislators who agreed over 70 percent of the time. Thirty-eight of these men were farmers, thirty-six were Populists, and all but one lived outside the major urban centers. A moderately antirailroad group of ten included nine farmers, six Democrats, and four Republicans. Table 20 substantiates both of the other approaches and illuminates

Table 20: RAILROAD ISSUES: DISTRIBUTION OF CATEGORICAL GROUPINGS BY SCALE POSITION

Scale Position	F	NF	P	D-R	W	E	O	L-O	Total
				Categorical Groups					
Antirailroad 0	59	5	51	13	33	31	64	0	64
1	7	2	3	6	2	7	9	0	9
2	3	4	0	7	1	6	4	3	7
3	4	4	0	8	0	8	6	2	8
4	0	1	0	1	0	1	0	1	1
Prorailroad 5	2	8	0	10	0	10	4	6	10

Note: The abbreviations of the dichotomous categorical groups used on all the summaries of the Guttman scales are as follows:

column 1   farmer (F) against nonfarmer (NF) legislators
column 2   Populist (P) against Democratic and Republican legislators (D-R)
column 3   western (W) against eastern (E) legislators
column 4   outstate (O) against Lincoln and Omaha (L-O) legislators

several other characteristics of those who fought over railroad rate regulation. Although most antirailroaders were farmers and Populists, seven nonfarmers were shown to be in the two most antirailroad scale positions. The common tie between these men seemed to be that five of the seven were very active legislators, perhaps aspiring urbanites, who wanted to hitch their future to the militant new party. From the data presented, a rough description of a prorailroader would be an urban, eastern, nonfarmer who was a Republican or a Democrat. If he were from one of the two cities in the state, he was almost certain to be very sympathetic to the railroad position. The antirailroader was most likely to be from the western part of the state, a farmer, and a Populist.[15]

Obviously, the 1891 Nebraska legislature polarized on railroad legislation, but it is well known that Populists and/or farmers hated established railroads. Populist reactions to other types of legislation relating to social and cultural issues, such as divorce and women's suffrage, are less well known. Although such issues at first seemed only vaguely related, Table 21 revealed that voting patterns were essentially the same on six of the thirteen roll calls.[16] These six bills included four roll calls relating to women's suffrage and two relating to attempts to prohibit pool rooms and bookmaking in urban areas. Populists tended to fall into the native American pietistic position, that is, favoring women's suffrage and opposing loafing and gambling. They were joined,

Table 21: CULTURAL ISSUES: DISTRIBUTION OF CATEGORICAL GROUPINGS BY SCALE POSITION

Scale Position	*Categorical Groupings*								*Total*
	F	*NF*	*P*	*D-R*	*W*	*E*	*O*	*L-O*	
Native, pietistic values 0	20	2	18	4	10	12	22	0	22
1	10	0	9	1	7	3	10	0	10
2	19	3	11	11	5	17	21	1	22
3	14	3	10	7	7	10	15	2	17
4	3	2	2	3	1	4	4	1	5
5	0	3	0	3	0	3	2	1	3
Immigrant ritualistic values 6	7	9	3	13	4	12	10	6	16

however, by many nonfarm villagers in outstate Nebraska. Agreement scores of the 1891 house reveal that seventeen legislators consistently voted together for the cultural legislation favored by the shifting majority of the Populists. All of these men were Populists, all were farmers, and ten were from the western half of the state. The core of opposition to women's suffrage and for the support of pool rooms came from the Omaha and Lincoln delegations and from newly arrived ethnic groups which did not accept pietistic moral values.

Several individual bills in the cultural area did not form a scale, but do illustrate Populist cultural positions. One, a bill to provide matrons for female prisoners, received strong Populist support. Two roll calls on divorce issues produced no statistical significance between Populist legislators and any stand on divorce.

Although a limited number of roll calls concerning cultural issues were contested in the 1891 house, Populist legislators generally assumed a pietistic cultural position. They supported moves for women's suffrage and women's rights, they opposed a liberal stand on legislation involving blue laws or personal liberties, while on several other progressive issues their position was no different from that of other groups in the state.

A third major category of important legislation involved twelve roll calls on various educational measures. The average disagreement index was 24.5, and these roll calls ranked fourth in the degree of partisanship among major roll calls considered during the session. A general analysis of the conflict between categoric groups in Table 22 indicates that, although not exhibiting the conflict seen in railroad regulatory issues, the major division occurs on Populist-farmer versus old-party–businessman lines. Of the roll calls considered, House Resolution 10, a Populist-sponsored bill to provide textbooks at cost to school districts, produced the highest disagreement scores. The entire series of roll calls on this proved most partisan, with the Populists on one side and the old parties on the other. The Democrats in particular provided the core of the opposition to the move toward cheaper textbooks.

Table 22: 1891 NEBRASKA HOUSE DISAGREEMENT SCORES:
TWELVE EDUCATION ISSUES

	Position of Group	*Disagreement Score*
Third party	Democratic–Republican	33.0
Farmer	Nonfarmer	31.4
Omaha	Outstate	27.4
Democratic	Republican	24.6
East	West	16.1
Active	Passive	15.0

Another series of educational roll calls involved the creation of state normal schools. In four roll calls, the most important category for producing disagreement proved to be the Populist versus old parties category. Although voting was not nearly as polarized as on railroad issues, all of the normal school issues failed—with a majority of the Populists voting against all of them. Agreement scores indicate that the pro-school book–anti-normal school bloc numbered fifteen legislators, of whom fourteen were Populist farmers and one a lone Democrat.

Several other major issue areas characterized the legislature of 1891. In issue areas such as legislation restricting interest rates, Populist–farmer categories, as expected, were in sharp disagreement with nonfarmer–urban categories. Table 23 illustrates how western, Populist farmers sharply opposed nonfarmer, old party, eastern, and city legislators in this type of legislation. Populists and farmers also opposed state support to the fledgling sugar beet industry, an industry they believed aided only a few farmers and many urban promoters. Table 24 illustrates the voting patterns on these four roll calls.

Table 25 illustrates attitudinal positions on two roll calls concerning the establishment of a boys' reformatory. Here again, as in the roll calls on educational institutions, support for the institutions came from groups opposed to populism. The Omaha and Lincoln delegations in particular seemed concerned over this problem, while Populist–farmers perhaps looked upon such institutions as related to urban problems only.

Table 23: INTEREST ROLL CALLS: DISTRIBUTION OF CATEGORICAL GROUPINGS BY SCALE POSITION

Scale Position		F	N	P	D-R	W	E	O	L-O	Total
Low interest	0	23	0	23	0	15	8	23	0	23
	1	25	3	24	4	10	18	27	1	28
	2	21	13	6	28	9	25	28	6	34
High interest	3	3	3	1	5	1	5	4	2	6

Table 24: 1891 SUGAR ROLL CALLS: DISTRIBUTION OF CATEGORICAL GROUPINGS BY SCALE POSITION

Scale Position		F	N	P	D-R	W	E	O	L-O	Total
Antisugar	0	36	4	27	13	18	22	38	2	40
	1	20	4	17	7	11	13	21	3	24
Prosugar	2	18	16	10	24	7	27	27	7	34

Table 25: 1891 STATE INSTITUTIONS: DISTRIBUTION OF CATEGORICAL GROUPINGS BY SCALE POSITION

Scale Position		F	N	P	D-R	W	E	O	L-O	Total
Pro-state institutions	0	15	19	7	27	8	26	27	7	34
	1	25	4	13	16	10	19	24	5	29
Anti-state institutions	2	35	1	34	2	19	17	34	2	36

The 1891 house concerned itself with four bills related to medical care for Nebraskans. Of these, two scaled; both were bills proposing building construction at the Nebraska Institution for the Feeble Minded. Although the dichotomous groups did not polarize to the same degree they did on railroad legislation, Table 26 shows that neither farmers nor Populists exhibited the same degree of concern for this problem as nonfarmers or city inhabitants. The urban delegation, for example, voted unanimously for this addition to the state's health facilities.

**Table 26: 1891 MEDICAL CARE ROLL CALLS: DISTRIBUTION OF
CATEGORICAL GROUPINGS BY SCALE POSITION**

Scale Position	*F*	*N*	*P*	*D-R*	*W*	*E*	*O*	*L-O*	*Total*
			Categorical Groupings						
Pro 0	44		32		22		55		
		23		35		45		12	67
1	17		14		8		18		
		1		4		10		0	18
Anti 2	9		5		6		9		
		0		4		3		0	9

Other issues dealt with by the 1891 house cast some light on Populist attitudes. Populists, probably because of their support of the Knights of Labor's position against the use of the militia to break strikes, did not support the state militia in two roll calls to the same extent as the older parties or the non-farmer occupational group (see Table 27), nor did they support more autonomy for cities under 5,000 population in the government operations roll calls. As could be expected, they supported relief expenditures for drought victims in western Nebraska.

**Table 27: 1891 MILITIA ROLL CALLS: DISTRIBUTION OF
CATEGORICAL GROUPINGS BY SCALE POSITION**

Scale Position	*F*	*N*	*P*	*D-R*	*W*	*E*	*O*	*L-O*	*Total*
			Categorical Groupings						
Pro 0	33		17		14		42		
		19		35		38		10	52
1	10		8		4		10		
		0		2		6		0	10
Anti 2	29		24		18		30		
		2		7		13		1	31

The Populist house of 1891—although much of its work was emasculated by the senate or the conservative governor—revealed itself much as both liberal and revisionist historians have said. If "liberalism" today means opposition to corporate power, the Populists stand in sharp contrast to the Republican and Democratic small-town and city legislators who defended the railroads and bankers against many Populist proposals. On issues other than regulation of railroads, interest rates, or elevators, however, the Populist program did not anticipate twentieth-century concerns. Although they did support women's suffrage and a girls' reformatory, they showed little enthusiasm for better facilities for education or medical care. They opposed a chance for the state to attract the sugar industry. On several issues they showed a marked pietistic point of view—an inclination which must have confirmed German fears for their "personal liberty."

Analysis of the 1891 legislature suggests that Populist and farmer concepts of reform were practically synonymous. That is, populism seemed to be closely related to the way a country businessman perceived the world around him. If populism was a projection of purely farm discontent, there should be a similarity between Populist legislative interests and legislative interests of farmers in general during the preceding decade. The houses of 1883 and 1885 provide an opportunity to view any similarity between agrarian interests in those years and 1891.

Table 28 reveals that there was not the easy identification between antirailroad attitudes and farming in 1883 that there was in 1891. Farmers themselves were less polarized than the Populist legislators—so there were prorailroad farmers in 1883. Similarly, the antirailroad faction included more non-farmers than it did in the 1891 legislature. From these data and a similar scalogram for 1885, it appears that the Populist legislature of 1891 polarized around farm–nonfarm conflict more than earlier legislatures. In both of the earlier legislatures, farmers usually formed a major part of the coalition that voted against higher education, state hospitals, state boards of charity, and the like.

Table 28: 1883 RAILROAD ISSUES: DISTRIBUTION OF CATEGORICAL GROUPINGS BY SCALE POSITION

Scale Position	Categorical Groupings								Total
	F	N	3D	D-R	W	E	O	L-O	
Prorailroad 0	9	15	0	24	5	19	4	20	24
1	3	10	0	13	3	10	9	4	13
2	7	8	0	15	6	9	15	0	15
3	5	7	1	11	8	4	12	0	12
4	2	0	0	2	1	1	2	0	2
5	5	2	1	6	3	4	6	1	7
Antirailroad 6	18	3	14	7	5	16	21	0	21

Farmers did favor legislation aimed at restricting what they considered to be the "bad habits" of others—very often urban immigrants. They provided the hard core of support in several roll calls for retaining Nebraska's high license prohibition bill in 1883. They backed bills to teach the evils of narcotics and stimulants to public-school children and joined the small-town businessman in outlawing the sale of tobacco to minors.

In none of these cases was voting completely polarized, and, on some occasions, such as protection of female employees and maternal rights, farmers seemed as interested as their village neighbors. On the whole, however, farmer attitudes in both of the legislatures of the 1880s were similar to those held by the Populist legislators of 1891. Populists had approximately the same hostile attitude toward railroads, interest rates, and exploitation by eastern capitalists as did many of the farmers who sat in the legislatures of the early and mid-1880s. Time, the end of the boom cycle, the collapse of some of their markets, and the drought of 1890 intensified and somewhat polarized their attitudes, but their basic behavior remained unchanged.

Just as their concept of the economic nature of reform did not change, neither did their limited vision of a complex reality. The isolated farmer-legislator from Broken Bow, Nebraska, behaved as if he were somewhat indifferent to many of the urban and industrial problems that were beginning to make an impression on his village and city colleagues. He could appreciate the need for cheaper textbooks for his children, but the state university or normal school apparently seemed remote. He was probably somewhat less aware of the problems of the sick, poor, and misguided than his village and city fellow legislators, and he certainly was less able to pay for them. Culturally, farmer and/or Populist legislators provided a source of strength for the movement to give women the vote, a movement which had another facet, a strict moral code centering on prohibition. The harassed country businessmen were the great champions of many important economic reforms, but they appear to have been much less interested in many other needs of even a preindustrial Nebraska.[17]

PART IV
CONCLUSIONS

9

The Agrarian Myth
and Political Realities

The context of agrarian radicalism rests to a large degree in a political paradox: the vast difference between agrarian power and agrarian numbers during the final decades of the nineteenth century. The farmer was dominant numerically on the plains, but he was outmaneuvered, outfought and outwitted by more sophisticated village and urban groups who were more in tune with the growing industrial and commercial economy.

At the same time that the yeoman settled on his homestead, village and urban occupational groups occupied the sites that became the villages and cities of the American West. These merchants, professional men, and entrepreneurs performed a vital role in nineteenth-century America. They planned, promoted, and schemed to advance the interests of their town and the area in which they had settled. Numerically, they were of less consequence than the farmer, but their plans for railroads, factories, and real-estate developments showed a purpose and organization almost totally lacking among the farmers. Town fathers and other village leaders planned and promoted schemes ranging from the acquisition of the national capital to the seemingly endless variety of small manufacturing plants that dotted the rural areas of late nineteenth-century America. In Nebraska, this feverish speculative activity resulted in the real-estate boom of the mid-1880s, a boom that promised to reward richly many entrepreneurs and small town inhabitants.

The farmers on the plains eagerly pursued the chimera of development and speculation. Unfortunately, though, his position vis-à-vis the emerging industrial system was not as favorable as most of the other groups in the West. His continued prosperity was contingent upon a host of factors over which he had little control. Railroad rates, though hardly dictated by greedy plutocrats, took a large share of his gross product because of the distance to market in Chicago or Europe. Interest charges, taxes, and appreciation ate still further into the meager income of many farmers. Add to these the effect of the droughts of the late 1880s, the difficulties inherent in farming a new area, and the wide fluctuations in commodity prices during the period, and it is not difficult to appreciate the economic nature of agrarian revolt. The farmer, along with the great financiers, felt the difficulties of the competitive marketing system, but because he found it so difficult to organize to control prices, he was left isolated and ineffective in that system.

If the farmer had performed politically as Thomas Jefferson expected, or if he had been as important in the emergence of democratic government as depicted in the writings of the Turnerians, he might have been able to cope more effectively with the difficulties in an emerging industrial society. But farmers as a group proved as unable to perform effectively in the political arena as in the economic. The handicaps imposed by the necessities of constant husbandry, the difficulties of communication, and the distances to the seats of political power effectively limited their participation in western politics. Instead, the vaunted yeoman was usually content to follow the policies and leadership of the village and urban business and professional classes. It was these men, not the farmers, who wielded the power in late nineteenth-century politics. Village and city groups usually dominated the politics of the era. In Nebraska, the village businessmen and professional politicians dominated the political machinery throughout the first decades of the state's history. They, not the yeoman, served as the county chairmen, legislators and other political leaders of the time. Although they were not militantly antagonistic to the farmers' programs, they always evaluated them in the light of village and city needs. And to the typical promoter of the era, the most important need was increased economic growth, which would be gained through the encouragement of business and the acquisition of capital. In Nebraska during the latter part of the nineteenth century, these nonagrarian groups constituted the dominant political forces.

When economic conditions became unbearable, western farmers inevitably rose up and asserted some of the power attributed to them in the ritual expressions of the agrarian myth. To do this, they had to work outside of the established parties, for both the Democrats and Republicans were so blinded by the prevailing business consensus and cultural issues that they continually proved hostile to the farmer's unique interests. The usual example given by those who emphasize the irrational nature of the Populist movement is the farmers' use of conspiracy theory, which grew from the feeling that the yeoman was shamelessly manipulated by business-oriented urban interests. Such a belief is hardly irrational. Farmers did not exercise the power to which their numbers theoretically would have entitled them. Undoubtedly, as Richard Hofstadter suggests, some Populists went much further than this and claimed that all history is conspiracy. These men, of course, cannot be defended, but the fact remains that the control of government was not in the hands of the farmer, and the government of the new state basically responded to urban and village interests and needs. The last decades of the nineteenth century did not belong to the farmer; indeed, despite his great numerical strength, it is doubtful if any era did.

Populists, and farmers in general, accepted most of the hard facts of the new industrialism. Most of their own fathers had probably engaged in commercial agriculture. In few places in their literature does one ever find a plea for a return to subsistence agriculture. An overwhelming amount of evidence points to the fact that even though the western farmer had only a hazy idea of the real nature of the industrial society, he accepted it in its general outlines. His revolt simply grew from the desire to compete more successfully. Admittedly, when times were hard, he spoke harshly of many of his adversaries, but most farmers developed no real ideological commitment to any utopia other than the one they were hoping to create by modifying the existing system. A well-developed ideology can have a powerful hold on men, but the farmers' ideology was so weak that one good crop year sent them scurrying back to the major parties. This is hardly an example of an indigenous American radicalism. It is, instead, the temporary desperation of a frustrated, pragmatic capitalist. Unfortunately, in their spirited attack on the dominant groups of the era, the Populists often permitted their analyses of their difficulties to become overly simplified and interlaced with exaggeration and falsehood. This left them open to ridicule and criticism by both their contemporaries and later critics.

Many of the reforms that the farmers championed proved to be relevant to the emerging corporate and social order. Some of these programs, however, were not unique with Populists; other groups advocated them at the same time. If the antagonists of the Populists are viewed in the light by which the Populists saw them, and sometimes reproduced in the pages of John D. Hicks' *The Populist Revolt,* then their movement was a relevant attack on a plutocratic conspiracy that might have engulfed the whole nation. This study, however, indicates that many village "plutocrats" who were wholeheartedly dedicated to defeating populism were, in other ways, even more progressive than the radicals themselves. The village promoters of real-estate expansion, manufacturing, or sugar beet culture also shared many of the concerns of the Populists, and they enacted them later into the Progressive legislation of the first decade of the twentieth century. While the Populists often exaggerated in criticizing the existing economic system, the village leader tempered his criticism with a reality born of his promotional experience and his concern with attracting the capital and transportation facilities needed for economic growth. A quarrel over specific legislation, the rhetoric of reform, and leadership split the farmers and urban leaders into hostile camps. By the end of the nineteenth century, Nebraska's farmers had neither the ability nor the organization for political leadership. When, for a few short years, they did capture political power, their programs for reform did not alter the difficulty of their own situation. The solutions for most of the problems of the age awaited programs and techniques to be developed in the next century by a village- and urban-based leadership.

Other issues influenced Nebraska voters during the Populist era, but none directly affected populism. Nativism, recently associated with populism by some historians, had little influence on the economically oriented Populists. In fact, the Republicans were much closer to both nativist and prohibition groups than were the Populists. The farmers might have been disenchanted with the political and economic system, but they did not join those who attacked it in ethnic or religious terms. Many people of foreign birth joined the movement. Even the Catholic, German, and Bohemian groups, after some uneasiness about the Populist inclinations toward prohibition, found fusion with the Protestant Populists possible.

The militant organization, the fiery rhetoric, and the vivid symbolism of the farmers' movements were partially designed to hide the most grievous flaw in the agrarian political crusade: the extreme difficulty of organizing the farmers into an effective political or economic force during the nineteenth century. The farmer's poverty, his isolation, and his lack of experience in politics help explain why farm movements have been so extreme, so colorful, and so short-lived. The vaunted yeoman of Jefferson's dream often proved an unsuccessful performer in the late nineteenth-century struggle for political power.

Notes

INTRODUCTION

1. John D. Hicks, *The Populist Revolt* (Lincoln, 1961), 404-424. In the final chapter, "The Populist Contribution," Hicks sees the Populists as precursors of the reform movements of the early part of the twentieth century. Eric Goldman, *Rendezvous With Destiny* (New York, 1956), 327-347, expands on Hicks' thesis and articulates what New Dealers had felt all along—populism, progressivism, and the New Deal were all reform movements with a great many similar objectives and attitudes.

2. Richard Hofstadter, *The Age of Reform* (New York, 1955). The classic "fascist" interpretation is Victor C. Ferkiss, "Populist Influences on American Fascism," *The Western Political Quarterly* 1 (June 1957): 350-373. For more moderate, but still anti-Semitic, interpretation, see John Higham, "Anti-Semitism in the Gilded Age: A Reinterpretation," *Mississippi Valley Historical Review* 43 (1957): 559-578, and Oscar Handlin, "American Views of the Jews at the Opening of the Twentieth Century," *Publications of the American Jewish Historical Society* 40 (June 1951): 423-444.

3. Walter T. K. Nugent, *The Tolerant Populists* (Chicago, 1963); Sheldon Hackney, *Populism to Progressivism in Alabama* (Princeton, 1969). See also O. Gene Clanton, *Kansas Populism* (Lawrence, 1969) and Cedric C. Cowing, *Populists, Plungers and Progressives* (Princeton, 1965).

4. Robert A. Dahl, *Who Governs?* (New Haven, 1961); Nelson W. Polsby, *Community Power and Political Theory* (New Haven, 1963).

5. Robert R. Dykstra, *The Cattle Towns* (New York, 1968); Merle Curti, *The Making of an American Community* (Stanford, 1959). For the comprehensive picture of small-town life, see Lewis Atherton, *Main Street on the Middle Border* (Bloomington, 1954).

6. Hicks, *The Populist Revolt*, 54-95. In chap. 2, Hicks lists the complaints of the farmer. While he does not give credence to all of the allegations of the Populists, he does not emphasize the arguments of those groups in society which disagreed with them. Of the earlier works on populism in the Plains states, see John D. Barnhart, "The History of the Farmers' Alliance and of the People's Party in Nebraska" (Ph.D. diss., Harvard University, 1929), as the most pertinent for this study. Other studies, which emphasize the economic basis of western populism, are: Raymond C. Miller, "The Background of Populism in Kansas," *Mississippi Valley Historical Review* 11 (March 1925); Herman C. Nixon, "The Populist Movement in Iowa," *Iowa Journal of History and Politics* 24 (January 1926): 3-107; Hallie Farmer, "The Economic Background of Frontier Populism," *Mississippi Valley Historical Review* 10 (March 1924): 406-427; Robert Higgs, "Railroad Rates and the Populist Uprising," *Agricultural History* 44 (July 1970): 291-297.

7. Until recently the only work dealing with Populist leadership was Roscoe C. Martin, "The People's Party in Texas, A Study of Third Party Politics," *University of Texas Bulletin*, No. 3308 (February 22, 1933). Since 1965, several historians have studied Populist leadership at the state and county level. David Stephens Trask, "Formation and Failure: The Populist Party in Seward County, 1890-1892," *Nebraska History* (Fall 1970): 281-301, deals with both leaders and membership at the county level. Walter T. K. Nugent, "Some Parameters of Populism," *Agricultural History* 40 (October 1966): 255-270, studied county officers and state legislators. Both Clanton, *Kansas Populism*, and Hackney, *Populism to Progressivism in Alabama*, deal extensively with biographical data of state legislators.

8. The model for behavioral study at the county levels is Curti, *The Making of an American Community*. A noteworthy attempt at voting analysis on the county level is George Lundberg, "The Demographic and Economic Basis of Political Radicalism and Conservatism," *American Journal of Sociology* 32 (March 1927): 719-732 and Frederick C. Luebke, *Immigrants and Politics* (Lincoln, 1969). The pioneer, and only, study of local conditions in Nebraska during the Populist era is Arthur R. Bentley, *The Conditions of the Western Farmer as Illustrated by the Economic History of a Nebraska Township*, Johns Hopkins University Studies in Historical and Political Science (July-August 1893). Other works are suggestive of ways to approach power relationships in small communities: Arthur J. Vidich and Joseph Bensman, *Small Town in Mass Society: Class, Power and Religion in a Rural Community* (Princeton, 1958); Murray B. Levin, *The Alienated Voter* (New York, 1961); Peter H. Rossi, "The Study of Community," *Administrative Science Quarterly* 1 (March 1957); Rudolph Herberle, "On Political Ecology," *Social Forces* 29 (October 1952): 1-9.

CHAPTER 1: The Politics of Economic Development

1. Edward C. Kirkland, *Industry Comes of Age, Business, Labor and Public Policy, 1860-1879* (New York, 1961), 400.

2. Perceptive treatment of the cultural elements that were important in the politics of the states to the east of Nebraska can be found in Paul Kleppner, *The Cross of Culture: A Social Analysis of Midwestern Politics, 1850-1900* (New York, 1970), and Richard Jensen, *The Winning of the Midwest: Social and Political Conflict 1888-1896* (Chicago, 1971). Both works treat the cultural conflicts arising from a Protestant-pietistic world-view as opposed to the Catholic and Lutheran orientation toward a ritualistic religious outlook. Of the two, Kleppner places greater emphasis on cultural politics. David S. Trask, "The Nebraska Populist Party: A Social and Political Analysis" (Ph.D. diss., University of Nebraska, 1971), strongly emphasizes the cultural antecedents of Nebraska populism. Kleppner and Trask tend to see the politics of the 1880s in cultural terms and the 1890s in economic terms. I do not feel that the politics of either period was so polarized; there are many examples of economic conflicts in the 1880s, and cultural antagonisms remained important to many Nebraskans well into the twentieth century. The two forces operated concurrently, although economic concerns did assume greater importance after 1890.

3. *Nebraska Blue Book and Historical Register, 1918* (Lincoln, 1918). This work contains election statistics for counties, 1860-1918.

4. S. D. Mercer to R. M. Easley, Esq., March 28, 1892, in John Higham, "Party Problems in 1892," *Nebraska History* (1952): 56-57. Mercer's analysis of Republicanism parallels that which I deduced from Nebraska newspapers. See also *Omaha World Herald*, August 23, 1876, for a similar analysis.

5. See Eva May Fosbury, "Biography of John Miller Thurston" (Master's thesis, University of Nebraska, 1920), 98.

6. Thurston notebooks, State Historical Society of Nebraska Library, Lincoln.

7. *Omaha Bee*, August 20, 1888.

8. *Omaha World Herald*, April 11, 1890.

9. Ibid., April 11, 1890.

10. Fosbury, "John M. Thurston," 17-18.

11. *Omaha World Herald*, July 5, 29, 1891.

12. Ibid., February 26, 1892.

13. Ibid., April 29, 1891, June 29, 1892; *Omaha Bee*, January 3, 1889.

14. Van Wyck Collection, State Historical Society of Nebraska Library. This is a series of loosely organized notebooks.

15. Mercer, "Letter," 56-57: *Nebraska Blue Book and Historical Register, 1918*, 400-455.

16. See Helen Claudine Knollenberg, "The Political Career of Church Howe in Nebraska" (Master's thesis, University of Nebraska, 1933)

17. Ibid., 5*ff.*; *Omaha World Herald*, September 7, 1890.

18. Knollenberg, "Church Howe," 5*ff.*

19. *Omaha Bee*, February 28, 1881.

20. Ibid., February 13, 1886.

21. Ibid., January 30, February 3, 1885, February 13, 1886; Knollenberg, "Church Howe," 55-60.

22. *Omaha Bee*, January 24, 1889; Knollenberg, "Church Howe," 65-66, 68.

23. Knollenberg, "Church Howe," 63.

24. Ibid., 72.

25. Ibid.

26. *Omaha World Herald*, May 18, 26, 1890.

27. *Nebraska State Journal*, January 12, 1893; *Omaha World Herald*, April 13, 1891; Knollenberg, "Church Howe," 84. The *World Herald* was generally critical of Howe; consequently, their endorsement of him as a reformer indicated that he must have had a considerable change in his point of view.

28. *Omaha World Herald*, April 17, 1890.

29. Robert F. Patterson, "Gilbert Monell Hitchcock: A Study of Two Careers," *University of Colorado Studies* (November 1940): III, 4.

30. See Dale J. Hart, "Edward Rosewater and the Omaha Bee in Nebraska Politics" (Master's thesis, University of Nebraska, 1938), 45; *Omaha World Herald*, December 7, 1891.

31. *Omaha Bee*, March 18, 1889.

32. Edward F. Morearty, Sr., *Omaha Memories* (Omaha, 1917), 47.

33. *Nemeha County Granger*, October 16, 1891; Victor Rosewater "The Life and Times of Edward Rosewater," manuscript, 181-182, State Historical Society of Nebraska Library.

34. *Omaha World Herald*, July 9, 1890; Patterson, "Gilbert M. Hitchcock," III, 49.

35. When populism swept the state, Rosewater had to share the reformer's mantle with other reform leaders. Alliance leaders often ignored him and regarded him as a representative of Omaha's interests. See *Omaha World Herald*, July 14, 1890, for an account of Rosewater's attitude toward the Alliance.

36. Nebraska's Bourbon leaders have been treated in Horace Merrill, *Bourbon Democrats of the Middle West, 1865-1896* (Baton Rouge, 1953). The great similarity between northern and southern Bourbons can be seen in C. Vann Woodward, *Tom Watson, Agrarian Rebel* (New York, 1938), chap. 4.

37. James C. Olson, *J. Sterling Morton* (Lincoln, 1942), 209.

38. James C. Olson, *History of Nebraska* (Lincoln, 1955), 322. Olson does not emphasize the pro-village bias in the State Agricultural Society. The relationship, however, is clearly seen in any of the county papers used in this study.

39. Olson, *Morton*, 374; *The Atlantic* 77 (March 1896): 393-394.

40. *Omaha Bee*, June 24, 1885.

41. *Omaha World Herald*, May 31, 1891.

42. For a discussion of railroad influence on Nebraska politics, see George W. Berge, *The Free Pass Bribery System* (Lincoln, 1905).

43. Olson, *History*, 250.

44. Frederick C. Luebke, *Immigrants and Politics: The Germans of Nebraska, 1880-1900* (Lincoln, 1969), deals extensively with the cultural aspects of Nebraska politics during this period.

45. Morton to Boyd, July 16, 1882, Morton Letters, State Historical Society of Nebraska Library. Luebke, *Immigrants and Politics*, observes that the Bourbon-German-Irish-Bohemian alliance was very comfortable since all four groups were economically conservative. Although Luebke's work deals primarily with immigrant adjustment, his ideas concerning native American-immigrant conflicts parallel those presented here.

46. Boyd to Morton, September 4, 1882, Morton Letters.

47. Olson, *Morton*, 272.

48. Morton to A. L. Perry, October 12, 1882, Morton Letters; Olson, *Morton*, 272.

49. Morton to George W. Doane, September 18, 1882, Morton Letters.

50. Although parties contained a very strong cultural factor and divided far less on economic issues than those in the mid-twentieth century, I do not mean to imply that politics was devoid of economic content. Certainly large groups of Nebraskans were concerned with economic issues as *economic issues*, not only as cultural symbols as suggested by Kleppner, *The Cross of Culture*.

CHAPTER 2: The Farmers' Complaint

1. See Freida C. Keuster, "The Farmer's Alliance in Nebraska" (Master's thesis, University of Nebraska, 1927), 36. See also Rudolph A. Knudsen, "Regulation of Railroad Rates in Nebraska" (Master's thesis, University of Nebraska, 1937), 120.

2. *Omaha World Herald*, September 16, 1891.

3. *Omaha Bee*, March 29, 1889.

4. See *Omaha World Herald*, April 10, 1890, for the report of a "railroad convention" in which several villages in southwestern Nebraska agitated for a

railroad between Phillipsburg, Kansas, and Omaha. The *Omaha Bee*, September 2, 1885, carried an attack against the *Blair Republican* for not supporting a bond issue for building a railroad northwest from Omaha. The *Bee*, as a promoter of Omaha, showed great interest in using railroads to expand the trade area of the city.

5. The problem of equitable railroad rates is much too complex to be dealt with in any detail in this study. The farmer's contention that the railroads charged too much is very difficult to prove. My belief that there was much exaggeration in western claims of exorbitant freight rates is shared and documented by several recent economic historians. See Douglas C. North, *Growth and Welfare in the American Past* (Englewood Cliffs, 1966), and Fred A. Shannon, *The Farmer's Last Frontier: Agriculture, 1860–1897* (New York, 1945). Recent econometric studies, such as Robert William Fogel, *Railroads and American Economic Growth* (Baltimore, 1964), do not deal specifically with the justice of western rate structure, but Fogel's study is based on the assumption that rates were low enough to have opened the prairies and plains to profitable farming. Much of the rhetoric and conflict revolves around achieving a politically acceptable solution that balanced inter- and intrastate rates.

6. North, *Growth and Welfare,* 137–148, presents evidence that, during the entire postwar era, farm prices declined less than other commodity prices. He dismisses the role of poverty in producing Populism because he generalizes about the American farmer. These, of course, do not apply to particular areas such as the drought-stricken plains or the poor upland areas in the South.

7. *Omaha World Herald*, April 29, 1890. The editor noted similar sentiments in the *Saunders County Leader* and *Leigh Herald.*

8. *Omaha Bee*, July 8, 1885, April 4, 1889; *Omaha World Herald*, March 4, 1892.

9. Knudson, "The Regulation of Railroad Rates," 10.

10. Ibid., 9.

11. See William F. Zimmerman, "The Legislative History of Nebraska Populism, 1890–1895" (Master's thesis, University of Nebraska, 1926), 18–20.

12. Albert Watkins, *History of Nebraska* (Lincoln, 1913), 606; James C. Olson, *J. Sterling Morton* (Lincoln, 1942), 188.

13. *Omaha Bee*, February 7, 1886.

14. Watkins, *History of Nebraska*, 604.

15. *Journal of the House of Representatives, 1883* (Lincoln, 1884), 640.

16. See Lawrence Logan Durisch, "Judicial Review of Administrative Discretion in Nebraska" (Master's thesis, University of Nebraska, 1928), 149; Watkins, *History of Nebraska*, 608.

17. Knudsen, "The Regulation of Railroad Rates," 69-70; see also Solon J. Buck, *The Agrarian Crusade* (New Haven, 1920), 171.

18. *Fifth Annual Report of the Board of Transportation, 1891* (Lincoln, 1892), 86.

19. *Laws of Nebraska, Twentieth Session, 1887* (Lincoln, 1888), 561.

20. *Farmers' Alliance*, August 12, 1889; *Omaha Bee*, February 14, 1887.

21. Arthur F. Bentley, *The Condition of the Western Farmer as Illustrated by the Economic History of a Nebraska Township*, Johns Hopkins University Studies in Historical and Political Science (Baltimore, 1893), 51.

22. U.S., Department of Interior, Bureau of the Census, *Eleventh Decennial Census of the United States, 1890* (Washington, 1895), V, 402-403. For a discussion of farm-making costs, see Clarence H. Danhof, "Farm-Making Costs and the Safety-Valve: 1850-1860," *Journal of Political Economy* 49 (June 1941): 317-359.

23. See Allan G. Bogue, *From Prairie to Cornbelt* (Chicago, 1963), 176. Bogue gives a detailed account of the capital needs of early settlers in the tier of states to the east of Nebraska.

24. *Hamilton County Register*, September, 1891.

25. See Omar M. Kem, "Memoirs," I, 91-93, owned by Claud J. Kem, Cottage Grove, Oregon; *Omaha Bee*, July 13, 1890.

26. See Bureau of the Census, *Eleventh Decennial Census*, V, 449-450; *Hamilton County Register*, January 10, 1891; *Kearney County Gazette*, March 19, 1891; *Cuming County Advertiser*, September 13, 1892. Rates of under 8 percent are found in the majority of county papers I examined. The more moderate view of interest rates is confirmed in Allan G. Bogue, *Money at Interest* (Ithaca, 1955). A much more detailed table showing midwestern interest rates can be found in Bogue, *From Prairie to Corn Belt*, 178. Rates in three sample Iowa counties ranged from 6.4 to 7.8 percent in 1890.

27. When confronted with data showing that interest rates were not as high as they claimed, Populists or their defenders often admitted that the rates themselves were not so high, but that the commissions paid to loan agents raised the real rates to usurous levels. This argument is reproduced in Raymond Curtis Miller, "The Background of Populism in Kansas," *Mississippi Valley Historical Review* 11 (March 1925), 482. Miller claims rates of 8 percent and commission fees of 13 percent for a total of 21 percent. Miller distrusted census material and placed his trust in two interviews. I could find no concrete evidence of commission rates this large. Bogue, *Money at Interest*, 70, puts commission rates at about 2 percent in 1889.

28. *Hamilton County Register*, January 10, 1891.

29. *Hayes County Register*, February 21, 1891.

30. John D. Barnhart, "The History of the Farmers' Alliance and People's Party in Nebraska" (Ph.D. diss., Harvard University, 1927), 24, holds that the chattel was not a "serious difficulty"; Bentley, "The Conditions of the Western Farmer," 337-338.

31. *Omaha World Herald*, July 22, 1890.

32. Bentley, "The Condition of the Western Farmer," 45.

33. *Omaha World Herald*, July 22, 1890.

34. U.S. Department of Agriculture, *Yearbook of the United States Department of Agriculture, 1901* (Washington, 1901), 699, 709, 754.

35. North, *Growth and Welfare*, 138, shows that farm purchasing power for all United States farmers rose substantially during the postwar years. This fact, of course, does not necessarily apply to farmers in central Nebraska.

36. Floyd M. Farmer, "The Land Boom in Southwest Nebraska" (Master's thesis, University of Nebraska, 1936), 74.

37. *The Conservative*, January 19, 1899.

38. James C. Olson, *History of Nebraska* (Lincoln, 1955), 206.

39. Richard Hofstadter, *The Age of Reform* (New York, 1955) has been the most consistent advocate of the cultural origins of populism; however, Hofstadter's concern is primarily with the anti-Semitic nature of some of the Populist ideology, not with conflict between socioeconomic groups at the local level.

CHAPTER 3: The Village

1. U.S., Department of Interior, Bureau of the Census, *Eleventh Decennial Census of the United States*, 29, 260-273. I did not use the rural-urban classification which the Bureau of the Census used in the late nineteenth century. My rural precinct is one with no village of any size in it. If the precinct contained farmers and villagers, I classified it as "mixed." The town precincts represent the voters in the larger county seat towns. The same classification of rural and town dwellers is used in the statistical portion of this study. The census classification has caused much confusion among social scientists. William Diamond in his well-known article, "Urban and Rural Voting in 1896," *American Historical Review* 46 (January 1941) is careful never to use "rural" and "farmer" interchangeably. He does, however, set very high limits on "rural," any village up to 45,000 in population, and implies that his "rural" areas are basically interested in agricultural pursuits.

Leon E. Truesdell, chief demographer of the Bureau of the Census, dealt with the problem of rural-urban classification in *Current Population Reports*,

"The Development of the Rural-Urban Classification in the United States: 1874-1949," Series P-23, No. I. Truesdell noted the confusion in the bureau and attributed some of the difficulty to the European-type village in which agricultural workers comprised the major population group. Although this type of village never achieved importance in this country, this imported concept of the village as primarily agricultural remained to confuse commentators on American life.

Using the 2,500 figure used by the Census Bureau as the dividing line, Truesdell gives the following statistics for the rural percentage of the population in Nebraska and two other midwestern states:

	Nebraska	*Kansas*	*Missouri*
1880	86.4	89.5	74.8
1910	73.9	70.9	57.7
1940	60.9	68.1	48.2

After 1920, the bureau began using the rural nonfarm category. Although this was too late to help for the nineteenth century, the breakdown of the rural classification into three parts gives some idea of how late nineteenth-century America divided between the three residential groupings.

	Urban	*Rural-nonfarm*	*Rural-farm*
1920	51.2	19.1	29.7
1930	56.2	19.3	24.6
1940	56.5	20.5	22.9

The groups which are the major interest of this study, farm and village America, were still obscured by the census takers. The village over 2,500 was still included with the city. The farm categories, however, give some idea of the relative numbers of villagers and farmers during the latter part of the nineteenth century.

A view close to my own is seen in Charles Tilly, *The Vendée* (Cambridge, 1964). In this study of the social organization of western France, Tilly defines urban as any "outside interested" village. Tilly holds that the village middle class were the most active leaders in the Revolution in western France. I believe that many American villages because of their commercial and promotional nature would be "outside interested" and hence could be classified as urban on many specific issues.

2. *Cuming County Advertiser*, May 27, 1890, October 13, 1896. Those men who were constantly active in local affairs, generally participated in politics, and associated with others in the same category were held to be com-

munity leaders. The town fathers very often received universal acclaim; lesser leaders were more difficult to locate.

3. Ibid., October 13, 1896. See also R. J. Krause, "The History of West Point, Nebraska" (Master's thesis, University of Nebraska, 1935), 35.

4. *Gering Courier,* December 27, 1889, June 6, 1890.

5. George L. Burr and D. O. Buck, *History of Hamilton and Clay Counties* (Chicago, 1921), 287.

6. *Hayes County Republican*, October 24, 1889; *Hayes County Herald*, June 14, 1888.

7. *St. Paul Republican*, October 24, 1894, August 19, 1896. This is indicated by the fact that the Pauls' name did not often appear in political news.

8. Roy T. Bang, *Heroes Without Medals: A Pioneer History of Kearney County, Nebraska* (Minden, 1952), 112.

9. I did not mean to imply that factions did not exist within parties, but that, in terms of community development, there was a great area of consensus. Undeniably some conflicts grew out of struggles which revolved around personality differences. See Krause, "History of West Point," 59, for conflict over the postmastership.

10. Krause, "History of West Point," 55.

11. *Cuming County Advertiser*, May 27, 1890, March 18, 1899; Krause, "History of West Point," 1-15.

12. *Aurora Sun*, July 9, 1890.

13. The activities of this group are mentioned periodically in the county's Democratic paper, *The Aurora Sun*. See for example, *Aurora Sun*, September 16, 1890.

14. See the files of the *Minden Gazette* or the *Kearney County Democrat.*

15. Counties with inclinations toward one party seemed to produce the most numerous state leaders. Cuming County, which was strongly Democratic, produced many Democratic leaders at the state level. State leaders also seemed to come from areas that emphasized manufacturing or food processing, rather than farming.

16. See especially the files of the *Cuming County Advertiser*. Cuming County, in particular, produced leaders of national reputation.

17. See H. L. Glynn, "The Real Estate Boom in Southwestern Nebraska" (Master's thesis, University of Nebraska, 1927), 21-24. Richard Lowitt, *George W. Norris, The Making of A Progressive, 1861-1912* (Syracuse, 1963), 14, quotes Norris as saying about Nebraska in the late 1880s, "The first money I made in Nebraska was in the land business, and often I made more money in the land business than in the law business."

18. *Omaha Bee,* May 3, 1886.

19. The history of urban promotions by aggressive entrepreneurs is a major concern of urban historians. The "winning" cities are those which have naturally received the most attention. See Richard C. Wade, *The Urban Frontier: The Rise of Western Cities* (Cambridge, Mass., 1959). For a history of a less successful urban promotion, see Lawrence H. Larsen and Charles N. Glaab, *Neenah–Menasha, Wisconsin. A Study in Urbanization and Industrialization* (Madison, 1968).

20. *Cuming County Advertiser*, May 20, 1890; *Gering Courier*, April 11, 1890.

21. Village leaders frequently owned substantial amounts of farm land in their counties. Many even referred to themselves as farmers, although they seemed to gain their livelihood from village-based activity.

22. *Cuming County Advertiser*, August 2, 1892.

23. *Hamilton County Register*, August 8, 1891.

24. Ibid., February 28, 1891.

25. *Hayes County Republican*, August 29, 1889.

26. Thomas L. Green, *Scottsbluff and the North Platte Valley* (Scottsbluff, Nebraska, 1950), 76.

27. *Kearney County Gazette*, December 2, 1886.

28. Ibid., June 12, 1891. Antipathy toward government ownership was not as great as in the middle of the twentieth century, for those at the meetings thought that the state should build and operate this road.

29. *Hayes County Republican*, April 27, 1890.

30. Krause, "History of West Point," 83.

31. Ibid., 35.

32. *Hamilton County Register*, May 7, 1890.

33. Green, *Scottsbluff,* 79.

34. *Gering Courier*, April 4, 1889; Green, *Scottsbluff,* 79-80.

35. Green, *Scottsbluff,* 76.

36. Ibid., 80, 86-87.

37. *Omaha World Herald*, January 29, February 8, 1891.

38. Green, *Scottsbluff,* 80.

39. Nebraska, *Laws of 1889* (Lincoln, 1889), chap. 70; *Omaha World Herald*, February 23, 1891; *Hamilton County Register*, January 17, 1890.

40. *Minden Gazette*, December 18, 1888; *Hayes County Republican*, November 27, 1890.

41. *Omaha World Herald*, September 11, 1890, February 23, 1891, January 26, 1892. Villages often offered free land and exemption from taxes.

42. *Omaha World Herald*, May 31, April 2, 1891.

43. Ibid., January 26, 1892.

44. *Gering Courier*, April 11, 1889.

45. Green, *Scottsbluff*, 80ff.

46. *Gering Courier*, October 7, 1892; *Hayes County Republican*, July 31, 1890; *Cuming County Advertiser*, March 11, 1890; *Minden Gazette*, February 4, 1892.

47. *Hayes County Republican*, July 3, 1890.

48. *Cuming County Advertiser*, February 18, 1890.

49. *Kearney County Gazette*, April 13, 1886.

50. *Hayes County Republican,* May 8, 1890.

51. *Hayes County Herald*, September 12, 1888; *Hamilton County News*, January 28, 1886.

CHAPTER 4: The Political Leadership of the Village

1. *The National Cyclopedia of American Biography* (New York, 1904); J. Sterling Morton and Albert Watkins, *History of Nebraska* (Lincoln, 1918). Both works contain data on all state officials during the era. O. Gene Clanton, *Kansas Populism, Ideas and Men* (Lawrence, 1969), 21, 137, reaches similar conclusions about Kansas.

2. Several recent studies deal with nineteenth-century rural leadership. The most methodical of these is Merle Curti, *The Making of an American Community: A Case Study of Democracy in a Frontier County* (Stanford, 1959). Curti's findings do not parallel mine in that leadership in Trempealeau County rested more with the farm population than is the case in this study. The Trempealeau study, however, covered an earlier time period and involved a county which was more agricultural than most of the Nebraska counties covered in this study. See pp. 420, 422–423.

The criteria used for determining leadership were similar to those used by Curti in his pioneering work. The criteria were (1) officeholding, (2) prominence in social and economic life, (3) frequent mention in newspapers. I dropped Curti's monetary worth criteria because of my larger sample, but added (4) participation in party machinery.

3. *Aurora Sun*, July 9, 1890.

4. *Aurora Republican*, September 23, 1886.

5. The files of the *Hamilton County Republican*, 1880–1895, were used in compiling this list.

6. A. J. Spanogle and Joshua Cox are examples of this group. Cox might have been a farmer, but the extensive amount of his land holdings, together

with the fact that these holdings were scattered through the county, suggest that he can be identified with the "monied" class. Perhaps he was engaged in speculation.

7. *Hamilton County Republican*, 1880-1892. The office of state representative was chosen for the sample for several reasons. First, county offices required residence in the county seat town, a fact which tended to exaggerate the importance of Aurora. Second, the duties of state representative demanded a comparatively short period of absence from the county and consequently might be held by any citizen. The office of state senator usually went to Clay County, the other county in the senatorial district.

8. *Hamilton County Republican,* September 23, 1886.

9. *Hamilton County Register*, November 21, 1891.

10. See W. F. Porter, "Populism and What It Stood For," manuscript, 91-93, State Historical Society of Nebraska Library, Lincoln, for Populist expression of this condition.

11. See the files of the *Kearney County Gazette*, 1885-1890.

12. *Minden Gazette*, October 11, 1894; *Kearney County Gazette*, September 25, 1890.

13. *Minden Gazette*, August 21, 1891; *Workman*, September 25, 1890, September 2, 1891.

14. *Minden Register*, March 21, 1890.

15. See the files of the *Kearney County Gazette*, 1881-1890.

16. *Inventory of County Archives of Nebraska, No. 47, Howard County* (The Nebraska Historical Records Survey, WPA, 1941), 13-15.

17. For a history of St. Paul and its early leaders, see Robert Harvey, "Howard County," manuscript, State Historical Society of Nebraska Library.

18. *St. Paul Phonograph*, November 1, 1889, September 19, 1890.

19. Ibid., November 1, 1889.

20. Ibid., September 19, 1890, September 25, 1891; *St. Paul Republican*, September 9, 1896.

21. The list of county officeholders comes from the files of the *Gering Courier*, 1888-1895. The farm population was more active in Scotts Bluff County than in any other county in the study. Perhaps agrarian concern with irrigation projects and the sugar beet bounty promoted a greater political involvement.

22. *Gering Courier*, 1888-1895.

23. *Hayes County Republican*, October 24, 1889. The discussion of Hayes County is based on the files of this newspaper, 1885-1895.

24. Ibid., November 5, 1891.

25. The relationship between populism and progressivism in Nebraska is

the subject of Robert Wallace Cherny, "Populist and Progressive in Nebraska, 1885-1912" (Ph.D. diss., Columbia University, 1972).

26. *Aurora Sun*, August 16, 1890; Dale P. Stough, ed., *History of Hamilton and Clay Counties, Nebraska* (Chicago, 1921), I, 420.

27. Bourbon Democratic newspapers continually emphasized the tariff issue but later pro-Bryan editors with their agrarian-based following largely ignored it.

28. Stough, *History of Hamilton and Clay Counties*, I, 422; *Aurora Sun*, September 28, October 12, November 9, 1889.

29. *Aurora Sun*, October 12, 1889.

30. Sherman, Casino, Grant, and Liberty townships were all poor and Danish.

31. *Kearney County Democrat*, November 16, 1886; *Kearney County Gazette*, October 11, 1886.

32. *St. Paul Phonograph*, November 1, 1889.

33. Ibid., August 15, 1890.

34. *Hayes County Republican*, October 24, 1889.

35. *Cuming County Advertiser*, 1885-1896.

36. Ibid., 1885-1896.

37. *Aurora Sun*, October 12, 1889.

38. W. F. Porter, "Populism and What It Stood For," manuscript, State Historical Society of Nebraska Library. Porter was a contemporary.

39. *Omaha World Herald*, October 21, 1890.

40. The evidence presented in this chapter is similar to that used by Roger Louis Hart, "Bourbonism and Populism in Tennessee, 1875-1896" (Ph.D. diss., Princeton University, 1970). Hart emphasizes the alienation related to status conflicts more than I have done in this chapter.

CHAPTER 5: The Populists and the Village

1. It is a serious error to confuse the misfortunes of Nebraska farmers with the prosperity of many farmers in the eastern parts of the Midwest or the East. Allan Bogue, *From Prairie To Cornbelt* (Chicago, 1963), shows that despite Populist rhetoric about the poverty of the American farmer, farmers east of the Missouri River were entering a "Golden Age" after the mid-1880s.

2. The general nature of the real-estate boom is discussed in chap. 3.

3. See Freida C. Keuster, "The Farmers' Alliance in Nebraska" (Master's thesis, University of Nebraska, 1927), 25-28.

4. *Biographical and Historical Memoirs of Adams, Hall and Hamilton Counties, Nebraska* (Chicago, 1890), 714.

5. See the files of the *Hamilton County Register*, the Republican paper, and the *Aurora Sun*, the Democratic paper, 1886-1890.

6. *Biographical and Historical Memoirs*, 714*ff.*

7. Ibid., 714-715.

8. *Aurora Sun*, July 19, 1890.

9. For information on the Alliance in Kearney County, see various issues of the *Kearney County Democrat*, especially issues for July 13, October 5, and November 16, 1886, and the *Minden Gazette*, June 12, 1890, August 20, 27, 1891.

10. *Minden Gazette*, August 20, 1891.

11. *Hayes Herald*, February 7, March 21, 1889.

12. *Hayes County Republican*, November 14, 1889, March 24, 1890, October 15, 1891.

13. *Gering Courier*, March 28, May 16, 1890.

14. *Cuming County Advertiser*, December 9, 1889, June 17, 1890.

15. *St. Paul Phonograph*, August 22, 1890.

16. *Hayes County Republican*, March 24, 1890.

17. Ibid.

18. *St. Paul Phonograph*, August 22, 1890.

19. *Hayes County Republican*, July 10, September 4, 1890.

20. Omar M. Kem, "Memoirs," I, 74-88, owned by Claud J. Kem, Cottage Grove, Oregon.

21. Paul Glad, *The Trumpet Soundeth* (Nebraska, 1960), 33.

22. *Hayes County Republican*, March 6, July 16, 1890.

23. *Hamilton County Register*, June 13, 1891.

24. *Omaha World Herald*, September 22, 1890.

25. *Hamilton County Register*, September 26, 1891. For similar sentiments in Iowa, see E. S. Micklin to L. H. Weller, April 5, 1888, Weller Papers, Box 9, State Historical Society of Wisconsin Library, Madison.

26. *Hamilton County Register*, August 22, 1891.

27. Ibid., June 13, 1891.

28. Ibid., July 4, 1891. See also *Hayes County Republican*, September 30, 1890.

29. *Hamilton County Register*, April 25, 1891.

30. *Omaha World Herald*, June 18, 1890, reprinted from the *Sutton Advertiser*. See also *Hayes County Republican*, April 24, 1890, and *Omaha World Herald*, January 14, 1891. J. Sterling Morton described the Populists as "libelling the financial conditions of the citizens of Nebraska and lowering

the individual and collective credit of the commonwealth." Morton to David Brown, September 3, 1894, Morton Collection, State Historical Society of Nebraska Library.

31. *Minden Gazette*, March 3, 1892. Village leaders were also skeptical about much Populist legislation. Most of them wanted railroad rate regulation, but they felt that the Populist bill provided for much too drastic reductions. *Omaha World Herald*, March 5, 1891.

32. *Omaha World Herald*, January 14, 15, 1891.

33. *Hamilton County Register*, May 9, 1891.

34. *Cuming County Advertiser*, June 16, 1891.

35. *Hayes Herald*, March 7, 1889.

36. *Hayes County Republican*, August 13, 1891.

37. *Aurora Sun*, September 27, 1890; *Hayes County Republican*, March 6, 1890; *Aurora Republican*, December 20, 1889. See also Robert Krause, "The History of West Point, Nebraska" (Master's thesis, University of Nebraska, 1935), 18-19.

38. *Hayes County Republican*, March 6, 1890; *Aurora Sun*, September 27, 1890; *Aurora Republican*, December 14, 1889.

39. *Hamilton County Register*, May 28, 1891; *Hayes County Republican*, April 27, 1890.

40. *Aurora Sun*, January 17, 1891.

41. *Cuming County Advertiser*, March 25, 1890.

42. *Aurora Republican*, December 14, 1889; *Hayes County Republican*, February 24, 1891.

43. *Cuming County Advertiser*, February 18, 1890.

44. *Gering Courier*, November 6, 1890.

45. *Aurora Sun*, February 21, 1891.

46. *Hamilton County Republican*, April 2, 1891.

47. *Omaha World Herald*, July 27, 1890.

48. Ibid., January 28, 1892.

49. *Alliance*, January 18, February 8, March 8, 1890.

50. Ibid., Feburary 15, 1890. See also *Omaha World Herald*, July 27, 1890.

51. *Hayes County Republican*, July 3, 1890; *Omaha World Herald*, May 31, 1891. Though few denied the antagonism between the two groups, some businessmen tried to ease the tension. In Butler County, the Businessmen's Association sponsored a picnic to "modify class prejudice and antipathy." *Omaha World Herald*, August 31, 1891.

52. *Omaha World Herald*, May 31, 1890. The paper contains a statement by Governor John M. Thayer saying that the county newspaper is the power in the land.

53. *Hamilton County Register*, February 7, 1891, August 1, 1891, August 22, 1891.

54. *Cuming County Advertiser*, June 11, 1889.

55. *Kearney County Gazette*, March 19, 1890.

56. Ibid., July 17, 1890. See also *Omaha World Herald*, September 30, 1890.

57. *Hamilton County Register*, September 5, 1891. See also *Omaha World Herald*, January 28, 1892.

58. *Hamilton County Register*, September 29, 1891.

59. *Aurora Sun*, November 2, 1889.

60. Ibid., April 4, 1891.

61. Ibid., March 14, 1891.

62. *Hamilton County Register*, January 17, 1891.

63. *Omaha World Herald*, February 23, 1891.

64. *Hamilton County Register*, January 17, 1891.

65. *Omaha World Herald*, February 3, 27, 1891.

66. Frederick C. Luebke, "Main Street and the Countryside: Patterns of Voting in Nebraska During the Populist Era," *Nebraska History* (Fall 1969): 157-275, confirms this analysis and extends its duration to 1898. Luebke's article was written as a rebuttal to David F. Trask, "Note on the Politics of Populism," *Nebraska History* (June 1965): 157-161, who had suggested that with the depression of 1893 many small-town merchants found it possible to unite with the farmers against "Wall Street." Luebke concludes, "The Populist fever thus seems to have fixed the attachment of Main Street for the Republican party."

67. Precinct returns were obtained from the county clerk's office in each of the counties studied or from the files of the county newspapers.

CHAPTER 6: The Populists in County and State Politics

1. *Kearney County Democrat*, July 13, October 5, November 6, 1886; *Minden Gazette,* August 20, 27, 1891.

2. See chapter 5 for the organization of the Alliance. Throughout this chapter, I use the term Populist to describe those people who joined the Independent party. The Independents later changed the name of their party to the People's party.

3. See Omar M. Kem, "Memoirs," I, 90-91, owned by Claud J. Kem, Cottage Grove, Oregon.

4. Dale P. Stough, ed., *History of Hamilton and Clay Counties, Nebraska* (Chicago, 1921), I, 422.

5. *Kearney County Democrat*, November 16, 1886.

6. *Omaha World Herald*, May 21, 1890.

7. John D. Hicks, *The Populist Revolt* (Lincoln, 1960), 156; *Omaha World Herald*, October 14, 1890.

8. Kem, "Memoirs," I, 91-92.

9. *Omaha Bee*, March 14, 1889, November 2, October 27, 1890; *Hayes County Republican*, July 10, 1890. See also Dale J. Hart, "Edward Rosewater and the Omaha Bee in Nebraska" (Master's thesis, University of Nebraska, 1938), 52.

10. Kem, "Memoirs," I, 91-93.

11. Ibid., 95-96.

12. *Aurora Sun*, June 21, 1890, February 21, 1891.

13. Ibid., August 2, June 21, 1890.

14. Hicks, *The Populist Revolt*, 156.

15. Ibid., 157; *Farmers' Alliance*, June 21, 1890; *Omaha World Herald*, July 5, 30, 1890. The convention included all reform groups and thus was not solely an Alliance convention.

16. James L. Sellers and Marie V. Harmer, "Charles H. Van Wyck—Soldier and Statesman," *Nebraska History* 12 (1931): 371.

17. *Omaha World Herald*, April 16, 1890.

18. Ibid., April 6, 1890, quoted from the *Scotia Herald.* See also *Omaha World Herald*, April 23, 1890.

19. Ibid., April 15, 1890, quoted from the *Platte City Argus.*

20. Sellers and Harmer, "Van Wyck," 353. See also *Omaha World Herald*, October 20, 1890, for a Van Wyck countercharge.

21. See John D. Barnhart, "The History of the Farmers' Alliance and of the People's Party in Nebraska" (Ph.D. diss., Harvard University, 1929), 33; *Western Rural*, October 22, 1887; Roy V. Scott, "Milton George and the Farmer's Alliance Movement," *Mississippi Valley Historical Review* 45 (June 1958): 90-109.

22. *Omaha World Herald*, July 30, 1890.

23. Ibid., October 10, 1890; Sellers and Harmer, "Van Wyck," 351; *Farmers' Alliance*, October 18, 1891; Arthur F. Mullen, *Western Democrat* (New York, 1940), 95.

24. *Omaha World Herald*, April 16, 1890; Sellers and Harmer, "Van Wyck," 355.

25. *Omaha World Herald*, January 5, 1891, July 1, 1892; *Hamilton County Register*, February 25, 1893; *Aurora Sun*, February 14, 1891.

26. *Omaha World Herald*, September 17, 1890, July 21, 1891; Sellers and Harmer, "Van Wyck," 360; A. E. Sheldon, "Nebraskans I Have Known," *Nebraska History* 19: 336, 338. See also William F. Zimmerman, "The Legislative History of Nebraska Populism" (Master's thesis, University of Nebraska, 1952), 72.

27. N. C. Abbot, "Silas A. Holcomb," *Nebraska History* 24: 187-191.

28. Sheldon, "Nebraskans I Have Known," 194.

29. *Omaha World Herald*, August 19, 1891; Sheldon, "Nebraskans I Have Known," 331-339.

30. Ibid.

31. See Kem, "Memoirs," I; "Honorable O. M. Kem," *Publications of the Nebraska State Historical Society* 9: 517; *Kearney County Democrat*, October 19, 1886; *Gering Courier*, October 7, 1892; *Aurora Sun*, August 2, 1890.

32. *Aurora Sun*, September 13, 1890; *Hamilton County Register*, February 28, 1891.

33. Stough, *History of Hamilton County*, 420-426.

34. Nebraska, *Journal of the House of Representatives of the State of Nebraska* (Lincoln, 1891), 1-5. These men had never been mentioned in the *St. Paul Phonograph.*

35. *Kearney County Gazette*, July 31, 1890, August 20, 1891. At one time, the editor of the *Gazette* complained that the "Pops pay no attention to Minden people." *Kearney County Workman*, September 2, 1891; *Minden Gazette,* August 20, 1891.

36. *Hayes Herald*, September 20, 1888, March 21, 1889.

37. *Hayes County Republican*, December 19, 1889, June 26, November 6, 1890.

38. Ibid., June 26, August 7, November 6, 1890.

39. *Gering Courier*, January 10, 1889.

40. Ibid., July 18, August 1, 1890, August 7, 1891, September 2, 1892.

41. *Cuming County Advertiser*, June 17, 1890.

42. See election graph for Cuming County in chapter 6 (Figure 9).

43. See Ernest Clifford Bowman, "The Populist Press in Nebraska" (Master's thesis, University of Nebraska, 1927).

44. *Omaha World Herald*, April 21, 1891.

45. Stough, *History of Hamilton County*, I, 402.

46. *Hamilton County Register*, June 13, 1891.

47. *Gering Courier*, September 4, 1896.

48. Ibid., July 15, 1892.

49. *Minden Gazette*, January 14, 1892.

50. Many of the reforms attributed to the Populists received great support among members of all parties. The struggle for the Australian ballot, for example, received support from many staunch Republican and Democratic newspapers. The Republican state platform in 1890 advocated restrictions of monopolies, the Australian ballot, reduction of railroad rates, union organizations, industrial accident laws, public-owned grain elevators, and even tariff reduction. See Dale J. Hart, "Edward Rosewater and the Omaha Bee in Nebraska Politics" (Master's thesis, University of Nebraska, 1938), 48. For some of the politics of the convention, see *Omaha World Herald*, July 28, 1890.

51. *Omaha World Herald*, July 29, October 13, 1890; see also George T. Hunt, "The Regulation of the Liquor Traffic in Nebraska" (Master's thesis, University of Nebraska, 1932), 144; *Hamilton County Register*, April 11, 1891.

52. See the files of the *Omaha Bee* and *Omaha World Herald*. The prohibitory amendment failed by an enormous margin in Omaha—23,918 to 1,555. Morton's hostility toward the Miller faction of the party continued. See Charles Brown to Morton, August 13, 15, 1890, Morton Letters, State Historical Society of Nebraska Library, Lincoln.

53. See Figure 10 for statewide election figures.

54. James C. Olson, *J. Sterling Morton* (Lincoln, 1955). Sellers and Harmer, "Van Wyck," 353.

55. See Paula E. Coletta, "William Jennings Bryan's Nebraska Years," *Nebraska History* 23 (1952): 71–94.

56. McIntyre, "Morton and Bryan," 14; *Omaha World Herald*, April 15, 1892; Olson, *Morton*, 338. See also Jesse E. Boell, "William Jennings Bryan Before 1896" (Master's thesis, University of Nebraska, 1929), 86.

57. Robert F. Patterson, "Gilbert Monnell Hitchcock, 1859–1934," manuscript, 23, State Historical Society of Nebraska Library.

58. *Omaha World Herald*, April 15, 1892; Olson, *Morton*, 338; J. Sterling Morton and Albert Watkins, *History of Nebraska* (Lincoln, 1918), II, 240.

59. Olson, *Morton*, 340; Sellers and Harmer, "Van Wyck," 363; Morton and Watkins, *History of Nebraska*, III, 342.

60. Patterson, "Hitchcock," chap. 4, 24.

61. Ibid., 31. Morton to David Brown, September 3, 1894, Morton Letters, State Historical Society of Nebraska Library.

62. Boell, "Bryan," 164.

63. *Grand Island Daily Independent*, September 27, 1894; *Omaha World Herald*, April 15, 1892; Patterson, "Hitchcock," chap. 4, 28; McIntyre, *Morton and Bryan*, 14; Sheldon, "Nebraskans I Have Known," 335.

64. Sheldon, "Nebraskans I Have Known," 335-336. Johannes M. Klotsche, "The Political Career of Samuel Maxwell" (Master's thesis, University of Nebraska, 1928), 36-37, confirms Rosewater's general hostility toward the Populists. Rosewater just disliked Majors more.

65. See correlation matrix in appendix.

66. See John K. Lewis, "Differences in Voting of Rural and Urban Groups in the Nebraska Legislature" (Master's thesis, University of Nebraska, 1937), for a discussion of rural power during the 1920s.

CHAPTER 7: Cultural Conflict During the Populist Era

1. *Hamilton County Register*, June 13, 1891. See also the *Workman*, August 24, 1892, for a similar idea.

2. *Omaha World Herald*, June 8, 1891. Although Democrats used the nativist issue against the Populist candidate, Joseph Edgerton, I could find no evidence of his involvement with the APA.

3. See chap. 8 for a statistical treatment of the Populist movement.

4. For the effect of drought, see John D. Barnhart, "Rainfall and the Populist Party in Nebraska," *American Political Science Review* 19 (August 1925). Frederick C. Luebke, *Immigrants and Politics: The Germans of Nebraska, 1880-1890* (Lincoln, 1969), covers German settlement in great detail.

5. Luebke, *Immigrants and Politics*, 191.

6. U.S. Department of Interior, Bureau of the Census, *Eleventh Decennial Census, 1890*, I, 641-644. These adjusted figures are used throughout the remainder of this chapter.

7. For a further discussion of this problem, see George A. Boeck, "A Historical Note on the Uses of Census Returns," *Mid-America* 44 (January 1962): 46-50.

8. *Eleventh Decennial Census*, 1890, xvi, xxi. Colfax County precincts were used in the statistical portion of this study, but the county was not used in those portions of this paper concerned with a more subjective description of local power relationships.

9. Ibid., I, 641-644.

10. *Omaha World Herald*, July 7, 1890. See also C. J. Kubicek, "The Czechs in Butler County, 1870-1940" (Master's thesis, University of Nebraska, 1958), 116.

11. Victor Rosewater, "The Life and Times of Edward Rosewater," manuscript, 200, State Historical Society of Nebraska Library, Lincoln.

12. *Cuming County Advertiser*, April 24, 1889.

13. Ibid., May 6, 1890.

14. *Omaha World Herald*, October 6, 1891.

15. Ibid., September 29, 1890; Rosewater, "Life and Times of Edward Rosewater," 196; Kubicek, "Czechs in Butler County," 108.

16. *Cuming County Advertiser*, April 24, 1889.

17. Ibid., October 15, 1889.

18. See Ruth J. Stough, "The American Protective Association" (Master's thesis, University of Nebraska, 1931), 1-10, 13-14.

19. *Omaha World Herald*, January 1, 1891.

20. *Hamilton County Register*, April 4, 1889.

21. *Gering Courier*, July 16, 1892.

22. From an interview with Mrs. Fred DeWeiss, January 16, 1962, a childhood resident of Omaha during the early 1890s.

23. *American*, August 13, 1891.

24. Ibid., May 4, 1894.

25. Ibid., June 29, 1894.

26. All three major Populist papers in this study, the *Hamilton County Register*, the *St. Paul Phonograph*, and the *Minden Gazette* had definite prohibitory leanings; however, so did the Republican papers in those counties.

27. *American*, August 31, 1894.

28. Stough, "The American Protective Association," 73; *Hamilton County Register*, January 28, 1893.

29. *Omaha World Herald*, November 8, 1891.

30. Stough, "The American Protective Association," 64; *American*, September 7, 1894.

31. *Gering Courier*, September 13, 1895.

32. *American*, February 10, 1893.

33. *Granger*, August 10, 1894.

34. See the files of the *American*, 1891-1896.

35. E. F. Morearty, Sr., *Omaha Memories* (Omaha, 1917), 44.

36. *American*, August 10, 1894.

37. *Omaha World Herald*, November 8, 1891.

38. Ibid.

39. Ibid., November 3, 1891.

40. Stough, "The American Protective Association," 59, lists the solid APA vote in Omaha at about 4,000; *Omaha World Herald*, January 16, 1892.

41. Stough, "The American Protective Association," 59.

42. *Omaha Bee,* April 2, 1885.

43. *American,* November 4, 1892.

44. Ibid., August 31, 1894.

45. Morearty, *Omaha Memories*, 55.

46. *American*, August 24, 1894.

47. *Cuming County Advertiser*, November 20, 1894; *Granger*, August 10, 1894; *American*, August 24, 1894.

48. See page 89 for a graph illustrating German voting behavior.

49. Nebraska, *Laws, Joint Resolutions and Memorials of the State of Nebraska, 16th Session* (Omaha, 1881), 270-281.

50. See Helen E. Storms, "The Nebraska Election of 1890" (Master's thesis, University of Nebraska, 1924), 84; *Omaha World Herald*, April 10, 11, November 1, 1890.

51. Storms, "The Nebraska Election of 1890," 81-82.

52. See Julia P. Watson, "The Evolution of the Temperance Movement in Nebraska" (Master's thesis, University of Nebraska, 1926), pp. 1-20, for this point of view.

53. *Omaha World Herald*, September 24, 1890. For an analysis of prohibitionist thought, see Joseph R. Gusfield, *Symbolic Crusade* (Urbana, 1963). Like Paul Kleppner, *Cross of Culture* (New York, 1970), Gusfield argues for a cultural basis for politics in the late nineteenth century.

54. *Omaha World Herald*, May 18, 1890.

55. Ibid., September 24, 1890.

56. Ibid., July 6, 1891. Gougar, a national leader, often spoke in Nebraska.

57. Ibid., May 20, 1890.

58. L. E. Fuller, letter to the editor, *Omaha World Herald*, September 21, 1890.

59. *Hayes County Republican*, October 9, 1890.

60. *Kearney County Gazette*, August 7, 1890.

61. *Hayes County Herald*, September 13, 1888; *Kearney County Gazette*, August 7, 1890.

62. *Hayes County Herald*, September 13, 1888.

63. *Gering Courier*, November 14, 1890.

64. *Cuming County Advertiser*, September 2, 1890.

65. Ibid., September 7, 1882.

66. *Cuming County Advertiser*, September 2, 1890.

67. *Gering Courier*, October 25, 1888.

68. Ibid., September 8, 1888.

69. *Omaha Daily Republican*, November 14, 1882.

70. *Schuyler Sun*, November 10, 1887. The *Omaha World Herald* reported on May 21, 1890, that prohibition was the most important issue for the German voters of Cedar County. The Germans also were reported to be holding back from the Alliance because their priests compared it with the Masons.

71. *Omaha World Herald*, October 30, 1890.

72. Ibid., September 17, 1890, July 7, 1891; *Gering Courier*, September 8, 1898.

73. Rev. B. Sproll, letter to the editor, *Hamilton County Register*, January 24, 1891.

74. Roy T. Bang, *Heroes Without Medals* (Minden, 1952), 127.

75. *Kearney County Gazette*, April 13, 1886; John D. Barnhart, "The History of the Farmers' Alliance and of the People's Party in Nebraska" (Ph.D. diss., Harvard University, 1929), 234. Barnhart did not feel that the prohibition movement had a significant effect on Nebraska politics outside of the "larger cities of the state."

76. *Gering Courier*, September 8, 1888, shows how the city fathers put up with the saloon because of financial reasons. See also *Hamilton County Register*, March 21, 1891.

77. *Aurora Sun*, March 21, April 11, 1891.

78. *Gering Courier*, September 8, 1888.

79. *Minden Gazette*, May 15, 1890.

80. *Hayes County Herald*, April 18, 1889; *Hayes County Republican*, October 11, 1890. The antiprohibition *Omaha World Herald*, July 23, 1890, quoted Hayes Center banker C. H. Eubank as saying that Hayes County would vote two-thirds against prohibition.

81. *Aurora Sun*, March 11, 1891.

82. *Omaha World Herald*, April 2, 1890. In Norfolk, the issue concerned the amount of money required for a license. The saloon owners wanted a lower fee than the five hundred dollars previously voted by the city council. See also ibid., March 31, 1890.

83. Ibid., September 31, 1890.

84. *West Point Republican*, October 30, 1891.

85. *Kearney County Gazette*, March 19, 1890.

86. *Omaha World Herald*, July 6, 1890.

87. *Central City Courier*, reprinted in *Omaha World Herald*, May 3, 1891.

88. *Gering Courier*, May 30, 1890.

89. *Omaha World Herald*, September 16, 1890.

90. *Kearney County Gazette*, March 19, 1890.

91. *Omaha World Herald*, January 6, 1891.

92. Both Gene Clanton, *Kansas Populism* (Lawrence, 1969), 100-101, 139, and Walter T. K. Nugent, *The Tolerant Populists* (Chicago, 1963), 130, 147, chronicle the troubles Kansas Populists experienced with the prohibition issue. See the graphs showing election returns for Cuming and Douglas counties.

93. Ethnic composition at the precinct level is available in the manuscript, "Schedules of the Nebraska State Census of 1885," State Historical Society of Nebraska, Lincoln. Precincts of known or suspected large foreign-born population were located and counted.

94. Nebraska politics after 1890 differed considerably from that of Ohio, Wisconsin, and Michigan as described by Paul Kleppner in *The Cross of Culture* (New York, 1970). In those states, Kleppner shows that the pietism associated with Bryan's crusades alienated immigrant voters and directed them into McKinley's "Party of Prosperity," where they established a new Republican majority that ruled for the next decade and a half. This study, together with that of Luebke, *Immigrants and Politics*, has shown that German and other immigrant voters in Nebraska peaked for the Democracy in 1890. Thereafter they vacillated between the parties, but probably maintained a marked Democratic orientation. Luebke points out that the Germans vacillated. Writing from another point of view, this study emphasizes that even after 1896 the German counties constituted the core of Democratic strength in the state.

CHAPTER 8: The Nebraska Populists—A Statistical Breakdown

1. Economic and cultural data were obtained from the U.S., Department of Interior, Bureau of the Census, *Eleventh Decennial Census of the United States, 1890*. Election statistics by counties are found in *The Nebraska Blue Book and Historical Register, 1918* (Lincoln, 1918). Election returns by precinct were obtained from the county press and from the offices of the county clerk in several counties.

2. John D. Barnhart, "The History of the Farmers' Alliance and of the People's Party in Nebraska" (Ph.D. diss., Harvard University, 1929), gives a complete description of the campaign of 1890.

3. John D. Hicks, *The Populist Revolt* (Nebraska, 1960), 58-59.

4. James C. Malin, "Notes on the Literature of Populism," *Kansas Historical Quarterly* 1 (February 1932).

5. Louis B. Schmidt, "The Internal Grain Trade of the United States, 1850-1890," *Iowa Journal of History and Politics* 19 (April 1921): 196-245.

6. Michael P. Rogin and John L. Shover, *Political Change in California: Critical Elections and Social Movements, 1890-1966* (Westport, Conn., 1969), 10-16; Sheldon Hackney, *Populism to Progressivism in Alabama* (Princeton, 1969), 27.

7. William Diamond, "Urban and Rural Voting in 1896," *American Historical Review* 46 (January 1941): 281-305.

8. I did not use the rural–urban categories used by the United States Census Bureau. The 1890 census lists population by precinct and includes the population of any village within the precinct. Since the Census Bureau's classification lists those living in small villages as rural residents, I compiled a statistical breakdown that rigidly separated farmers from any villagers.

9. The program for the Pierson product–moment correlation analysis used in this portion of the study was developed at Stanford University and published by Norman H. Nie, Dale H. Bent, and C. Hadlai Hull, *Statistical Package for the Social Sciences* (New York, 1970).

10. The roll calls were secured from Nebraska, *House Journal of the Legislature of the State of Nebraska* for the respective legislatures. In order to get a scale, the legislature must be divided. Consequently all roll calls in which the house split 80 percent to 20 percent or above were recorded.

11. The basic methodological work consulted for this paper was L. F. Anderson, M. W. Watts, and A. R. Wilcox, *Legislative Roll-Call Analysis* (Evanston, 1966). Most of the statistical measures presented in this chapter are explained in this work. The computer programs used for an analysis of categoric groups and agreement scores are listed in the appendix. They were adapted for use on the IBM 360-30 by the computer center at UMKC. A brief description of some of these statistical measures seems in order.

Index of disagreement measures the degree of dissimilarity between two opposing categorical groups. It is the reverse of the index of likeness presented in Anderson. It is computed in the following manner:

Populist   Yeas, 14; Nays 50

Rep./Dem.   Yeas, 20; Nays 13

Percent Populists in affirmative = 14/64 × 100 = 22

Percent D/R in affirmative = 20/33 × 100 = 61

Index of disagreement = 61 − 22 = 39

Any index, of course, should simplify a concept the researcher is trying to present. In this case, presenting the figure for the index of disagreement seems the clearest way of expressing disagreement, better, for example, than repeatedly expressing the percentage of yeas and nays for a series of measures. The use of the index of disagreement rather than the more common index of likeness was suggested by Allan G. Bogue, "Bloc and Party in the United States Senate: 1861-1863," *Civil War History* (1967).

The *Rice index of cohesion* was used in the preliminary analysis, but is not included in the tables presented in this chapter. It measures solidarity within *one* group, not conflict between two groups as does the index of disagreement.

The Rice index for the above vote would be:
    Populist   Yeas, 22%, Nays 78%
    Rep./Dem.   Yeas, 61%, Nays 39%
          Rice index – Populists   78-22 = 56
                  Dem./Rep. 61-39 = 22

Agreement scores, as explained in the text, are the percentage of times two legislators agree. They are explained in Anderson, *Roll-Call Analysis*, chap. 4.

The *Guttman scale* techniques used in this chapter are similar to those outlined in Anderson. After each contested roll call was recorded, all bills in discernible issue areas were grouped together and tested for scalability. I have employed Guttman scaling as a tool to characterize the voting behavior of categoric groups in the house. Thus, in the course of testing items for scalability, I set the tests for admission of items into the scales at the highest practical levels to insure that roll calls reflecting crosspressures or ambivalent responses were excluded and that the resultant scales characterized as accurately as possible behavior within a given issue area.

To do this I emphasize the statistical correlations between the responses on each roll call, as well as the more traditional measure of scalability, the coefficient of reproducibility, CR, which is a measure of the errors or unscalable votes scattered throughout the scale. The statistical measure which combines reproducibility and correlation is $\emptyset/\emptyset$ max. This is explained in David M. Wood, "Majority vs. Opposition in the French National Assembly, 1956-1965: A Guttman Scale Analysis," *The American Political Science Review* 72 (March 1968): 88-109, and James W. Hilty and Gary M. Fink, "The U.S. Senate, 1933-1944: A Quantitative Analysis" (Columbia, Mo., forthcoming).

$\emptyset/\emptyset$ max as a test for scalability provides for a comparison between cells *b* and *c* of the normal fourfold table employed in the pairwise method of scale-finding, which the more often used Yules' *Q* does not. Moreover, when $\emptyset/\emptyset$ max was pegged at the 0.70 level it was found that no pair of items was admitted to a scale less than the 0.94 level for *cr* and 0.92 level for Yules' *Q*.

Although the use of $\emptyset/\emptyset$ max will make use of the coefficient of reproducibility less important in Guttman scaling, the CR was computed for the scales used in this paper. They are:

Scale I	0.96
II	0.90
III	1.00
IV	1.00
V	0.98
VI	1.00
VII	1.00
VIII	0.98

12. This was an attempt at systems analysis defining a legislator's behavior by his role in the legislature. To do this, I constructed an index by giving a legislator one point for every bill, resolution, etc., that he authored, and one point for each committee assignment. Three points were given for being a committee chairman. "Actives" were those above average in activity; "passives" were below average. Unfortunately, this idea produced no discernible results, and I left this category out of most tables and scalograms.

13. The biographical data used to establish the categorical groupings can be found in the Nebraska House journals for respective years.

14. The average disagreement score is the average disagreement of all categoric groups on one issue. Although a rather crude device, it does seem to reflect the relative contentiousness among the different issue areas.

15. This point of view can be found in David F. Trask, "A Note on the Politics of Populism," *Nebraska History* (July 1965).

16. "Scaling" means that votes on one bill are closely related to votes on another—thus they measure on the same scale.

17. Similar conclusions about the Kansas Populist legislatures in the 1890s are found in Henry Fillmore Hartsell's "Kansas Populists: Agrarian Reformers" (Master's thesis, University of Missouri, Kansas City, 1971).

Appendix

PIERSON PRODUCT–MOMENT CORRELATION COEFFICIENTS: POPULIST PERCENTAGE OF GUBERNATORIAL VOTES, 1890–1896 AND SELECTED VARIABLES

	Gubernatorial vote 1890	Gubernatorial vote 1892	Gubernatorial vote 1896	Percent wheat	Cattle per farm	Prohibition vote	Percent Protestant	Population incr., 1885–1890	Distance from Chicago	Mortgage as per-cent of income	Tenant farm increase	Population incr., 1880–1890	Value of farm product
Gubernatorial vote 1890	—												
Gubernatorial vote 1892	0.64												
Gubernatorial vote 1896	-0.02	0.00											
Percent land in wheat	0.34	0.29	-0.05										
Cattle per farm	-0.24	-0.28	0.07	-0.18									
Prohibition vote, 1890	0.36	0.32	0.05	0.15	-0.21								
Percent Protestant	0.06	-0.10	-0.04	0.11	-0.42	0.32							
Population incr., 1885–1890	0.10	0.13	-0.14	0.21	-0.25	-0.01	0.19						
Distance from Chicago	0.24	0.49	0.01	0.19	-0.22	0.29	-0.05	0.24					
Mortgage payment as percent of income	0.24	0.37	-0.01	0.11	0.02	0.30	-0.00	0.17	0.73				
Tenant farm increase	0.17	0.35	-0.03	0.19	-0.19	0.29	-0.21	0.18	0.68	0.56			
Population incr., 1880–1890	0.25	0.18	-0.06	0.20	-0.07	-0.07	0.08	0.25	-0.03	-0.06	0.05		
Value farm products	-0.17	-0.44	0.07	-0.07	0.18	-0.22	0.06	-0.25	-0.86	-0.72	-0.62	0.13	

Bibliography

PRIMARY SOURCES

Federal Government

U.S. Department of Interior. Bureau of the Census. *Eleventh Decennial Census of the United States, 1890.* Washington: Government Printing Office, 1895.

    Report on the Statistics of Agriculture in the United States at the Eleventh Census: 1890, Washington, 1895. *Report on the Population of the United States at the Eleventh Census: 1890,* Part I, Washington, 1895. *Report on Real Estate Mortgages in the United States at the Eleventh Census: 1890,* Washington, 1895.

——. *Twelfth Decennial Census of the United States, 1900,* Washington: Government Printing Office, 1902.

    Twelfth Census of the United States, Taken in the Year 1900, Volume V, *Agriculture,* Part I. Washington, 1902.

State of Nebraska

Board of Agriculture. *Annual Report,* 1893–1896. Lincoln: Jacob North and Company, 1894–1896.
Board of Transportation. *Annual Report,* 1887–1890. Lincoln, 1887–1890.
House. *Journal, Seventeenth Session.* Lincoln, 1881.
——. *Journal, Nineteenth Session.* Lincoln, 1885.
——. *Journal, Twentieth Session.* Lincoln, 1887.
——. *Journal, Twenty-first Session.* Lincoln, 1889.

——. *Journal, Twenty-second Session.* Omaha, 1891.
——. *Journal, Twenty-third Session.* York, 1893.
——. *Journal, Twenty-fourth Session.* York, 1895.
Senate. *Journal, Nineteenth Session.* Lincoln, 1885.
——. *Journal, Twentieth Session.* Lincoln, 1887.
——. *Journal, Twenty-first Session.* Lincoln, 1889.
——. *Journal, Twenty-second Session.* Omaha, 1891.
——. *Journal, Twenty-third Session.* York, 1893.
——. *Journal, Twenty-fourth Session.* York, 1895.
Nebraska Blue Book and Historical Register. Nebraska Legislature Reference
    Bureau, Lincoln, 1889.
Nebraska Blue Book and Historical Register. Nebraska Legislature Reference
    Bureau, Lincoln, 1891.
Nebraska Blue Book and Historical Register. Nebraska Legislature Reference
    Bureau, Lincoln, 1893.
Nebraska Blue Book and Historical Register. Nebraska Legislature Reference
    Bureau, Lincoln, 1918.
Official State Atlas of Nebraska, 1885. Philadelphia: Evarts and Kirks, 1885.

Collections of Letters and Records

Maxwell, Samuel. Correspondence. State Historical Society of Nebraska Li-
    brary, Lincoln.
Morton, J. Sterling. Correspondence. State Historical Society of Nebraska
    Library, Lincoln.
Nebraska State Farmers' Alliance Records. State Historical Society of Ne-
    braska Library, Lincoln.
Weller, Luhman Hamlin. Correspondence: 1880–1900; Waller Papers, 1828–
    1912; Wisconsin State Historical Society Library, Madison.

Manuscripts

Harvey, Robert. "Howard County," MSS. State Historical Society of Ne-
    braska Library, Lincoln.
Kem, Omar M. Typed MSS. Owned by Claud J. Kem, Cottage Grove, Oregon.
Patterson, Robert F. "Gilbert Monell Hitchcock, 1858–1934." Typed MSS
    from University of Colorado Studies, XXVI, no. 3, November 1940,
    Boulder, Colorado.

Porter, W. F. "Populism and What It Stood For." MSS. State Historical Society of Nebraska Library, Lincoln.
Rosewater, Victor. "The Life and Times of Edward Rosewater." Typed MSS. State Historical Society of Nebraska Library, Lincoln.
"Schedules of the Nebraska State Census of 1885," MSS, on microfilm. State Historical Society of Nebraska Library, Lincoln.

Interviews

Mrs. Fred DeWeiss. January 16, 1962.
Col. F. D. Eager. January 3, 1959.

Scrapbooks

Bryan Scrapbooks. State Historical Society of Nebraska Library, Lincoln.
Morton Scrapbooks. State Historical Society of Nebraska Library, Lincoln.
Van Wyck Scrapbooks. State Historical Society of Nebraska Library, Lincoln.
Thurston Scrapbooks. State Historical Society of Nebraska Library, Lincoln.

Newspapers

Lancaster County (Lincoln)
   The Alliance, 1889.
   Farmers' Alliance, 1889–1892.
   Nebraska State Journal, 1886–1892.
Douglas County (Omaha)
   Omaha Bee, 1880–1892.
   Omaha Herald, 1886–1889.
   Omaha World Herald, 1889–1895.
   Omaha Republican, 1885–1890.
   The American, 1890–1896.
Colfax County
   Schuyler Sun, 1885–1895.
Cuming County
   West Point Republican, 1886–1895.
   Cuming County Advertiser, 1889–1895.
   Cuming County Progress, 1882, 1886.
   Boamer Times, 1889–1892.

Hamilton County
  Hamilton County Register, 1890–1891.
  Hamilton County Republican, 1886–1895.
  The Aurora Sun, 1889–1891.
Hayes County
  Hayes County Herald, 1888–1889.
  Hayes County Republican, 1889–1890, 1892–1896.
  Hayes County News, 1885–1886.
Howard County
  St. Paul Press, 1890–1896.
  St. Paul Republican, 1891–1896.
  St. Paul Phonograph, 1889–1896.
Kearney County
  Kearney County Democrat, 1886–1893.
  Kearney County Gazette, 1886, 1890, 1892–1894.
  Minden Gazette, 1890–1891.
  Workman, 1890–1893.
Scotts Bluff County
  Gering Courier, 1888–1895.
Other Nebraska Newspapers
  Grand Island Daily Independent, 1894.
  Nemaha County Granger, 1891.
  The Conservative, 1899.
Out of State
  Council Bluffs Non-Pareil, 1885–1892.
  Western Rural, 1887–1888.

SECONDARY SOURCES

Dissertations and Theses

Barnhart, John D. "The Farmers' Alliance and the Peoples' Party in Nebraska." Ph.D. dissertation, Harvard University, 1927.

Beal, Anabel Lucille. "The Populist Party in Custer County, Nebraska: Its Role in Local, State, and National Politics, 1889–1906." Ph.D. dissertation, University of Nebraska, 1965.

Bellardo, Lewis J. "Local Aspects of the Trans-Mississippi Agrarian Crusade." B.A. thesis, Rutgers University, 1965.

Boell, Jesse E. "William Jennings Bryan Before 1896." Master's thesis, University of Nebraska, 1929.

Bowman, Ernest Clifford. "The Populist Press in Nebraska." Master's thesis, University of Nebraska, 1936.

Curtis, Earl Guy. "Biography of John Milton Thayer." Master's thesis, University of Nebraska, 1933.

Dethloff, Henry C. "Populism and Reform in Louisiana." Ph.D. dissertation, University of Missouri, 1964.

Durisch, Laurence Logan. "The Organization and Personnel of the Nebraska Railway Commission." Ph.D. dissertation, University of Nebraska, 1932.

Farmer, Floyd M. "The Land Boom in Southwest Nebraska." Master's thesis, University of Nebraska, 1936.

Fiore, Alphonse T. "History of Italian Immigration in Nebraska." Master's thesis, University of Nebraska, 1938.

Fosbury, Eve May. "Biography of John Millen Thurston." Master's thesis, University of Nebraska, 1920.

Glynn, H. L. "The Urban Real Estate Boom in Nebraska During the 80's." Master's thesis, University of Nebraska, 1927.

Hahn, Harlan Dean. "One Partyism and State Politics: The Structure of Political Power in Iowa." Ph.D. dissertation, Harvard University, 1964.

Hart, Dale J. "Edward Rosewater and the Omaha Bee in Nebraska Politics." Master's thesis, University of Nebraska, 1938.

Hart, Roger Louis. "Bourbonism and Populism in Tennessee, 1875–1896." Ph.D. dissertation, Princeton University, 1970.

Hartsell, Henry Fillmore. "Kansas Populists: Agrarian Reformers." Master's thesis, University of Missouri–Kansas City, 1971.

Hunt, George T. "The Control of the Liquor Traffic in Nebraska." Master's thesis, University of Nebraska, 1932.

Johnson, H. T. "History of Beet Sugar Industry in Nebraska." Master's thesis, University of Nebraska, 1934.

Keuster, Frieda C. "The Farmers' Alliance in Nebraska." Master's thesis, University of Nebraska, 1927.

Klotsche, Johannes M. "The Political Career of Samuel Maxwell." Master's thesis, University of Nebraska, 1928.

Knibbs, J. E. "The Political Map of Nebraska, 1900–1934." Master's thesis, University of Nebraska, 1935.

Knollenberg, Helen Claudine. "The Political Career of Church Howe in Nebraska." Master's thesis, University of Nebraska, 1933.

Knudsen, Rudolph Alvin. "Regulation of Nebraska Railroad Rates, 1867–1906." Master's thesis, University of Nebraska, 1937.

Krause, Robert K. "History of West Point, Nebraska, to 1900." Master's thesis, University of Nebraska, 1935.

Kubicek, C. J. "The Czechs in Butler County, 1870–1940." Master's thesis, University of Nebraska, 1958.

McGinnis, Mabel Margaret. "Doctor George L. Miller." Master's thesis, University of Nebraska, 1934.

Miller, Raymond C. "The Populist Party in Kansas." Ph.D. dissertation, University of Chicago, 1928.

Nugent, Walter T. K. "Populism and Nativism in Kansas, 1888–1900." Ph.D. dissertation, University of Chicago, 1961.

Raymond, B. M. "A Study of Political and Economic Conditions in Nebraska in the Early Nineties." Master's thesis, University of Nebraska, 1923.

Scott, Mittie Y. "The Life and Political Career of William Van Allen." Master's thesis, University of Nebraska, 1924.

Smith, Carl A. "Party Alignments in Nebraska, 1908–1916." Master's thesis, University of Nebraska, 1950.

Storms, Helen E. "A Study of the Nebraska State Election of 1890." Master's thesis, University of Nebraska, 1924.

Stough, Ruth Knox. "The American Protective Association." Master's thesis, University of Nebraska, 1931.

Trask, David Stephens. "Anti-Populism in Nebraska." Master's thesis, University of Nebraska, 1968.

——. "The Nebraska Populist Party: A Social and Political Analysis." Ph.D. dissertation, University of Nebraska, 1971.

Watson, Julie Permelia. "The Evolution of the Temperance Movement in Nebraska." Master's thesis, University of Nebraska, 1926.

Zimmerman, William F. "The Legislative History of Nebraska Populism, 1890–1895." Master's thesis, University of Nebraska, Lincoln, 1925.

Books

Alexander, Thomas B. *Sectional Stress and Party Strength*. Nashville: Vanderbilt University Press, 1967.

Anderson, Lee F., Watts, Meredith W., Jr., and Wilcox, Allen R. *Legislative Roll Call Analysis*. Evanston: Northwestern University Press, 1966.

Atherton, Lewis. *Main Street on the Middle Border*. Bloomington: University of Indiana Press, 1954.

Baker, Gordon E. *Rural versus Urban Political Power*. New York: Random House, 1955.

Bang, Roy T. *Heroes without Medals*. Minden, Nebraska: Warp Publishing Company, 1952.

Bell, Daniel, ed. *The New American Right.* New York: Criterion Books, 1955.

Benson, Lee. *Merchants, Farmers and Railroads.* Cambridge: Harvard University Press, 1955.

——. *The Concept of Jacksonian Democracy.* Princeton: Princeton University Press, 1961.

Bentley, Arthur R. *The Conditions of the Western Farmer as Illustrated by the Economic History of a Nebraska Township*, Johns Hopkins University Studies in Historical and Political Science (July–August, 1893).

Berge, George W. *The Free Pass Bribery System.* Lincoln: Independent Publishing Company, 1905.

Berkhoffer, Robert F., Jr. *A Behavioral Approach to Historical Analysis.* New York: The Free Press, 1969.

Biographical and Historical Memoirs of Adams, Clay, Hull and Hamilton Counties, Nebraska. Chicago: The Goodspeed Publishing Company, 1890.

Bogue, Allan G. *From Prairie to Cornbelt.* Chicago: Quadrangle Books, 1963.

——. *Money at Interest.* Ithaca, New York: Cornell University Press, 1955.

Brown, Andrew T. *Frontier Community.* Columbia: University of Missouri Press, 1963.

Bryan, William Jennings. *The First Battle.* Chicago: W. B. Conkey Co., 1896.

Buck, Solon J. *The Granger Movement, 1870–1880.* Cambridge: Harvard Historical Studies, 1913

Burner, David. *The Politics of Provincialism: The Democratic Party in Transition, 1918–1932.* New York: Alfred A. Knopf, 1968.

Burr, George L., and O. O. Buck, ed. *History of Hamilton and Clay Counties.* Chicago: S. J. Clarke Publishing Company, 1921. 2 vols.

Cather, Willa. *My Antonia.* Lincoln: University of Nebraska Press, 1960.

Clanton, O. Gene. *Kansas Populism, Men and Ideas.* Lawrence: University of Kansas Press, 1969.

Coletta, Paola E. *William Jennings Bryan: Political Evangelist, 1860–1908.* Lincoln: University of Nebraska Press, 1964.

Cowing, Cedric C. *Populists, Plungers, and Progressives.* Princeton: Princeton University Press, 1965.

Curti, Merle. *The Making of an American Community: A Case Study of Democracy in a Frontier County.* Stanford: Stanford University Press, 1959.

Dahl, Robert A. *Pluralist Democracy in the United States: Conflict and Consent.* Chicago: Rand McNally, 1967.

——. *Who Governs?* New Haven: Yale University Press, 1961.

Destler, Chester McArthur. *American Radicalism 1865–1901: Essays and Documents.* New London, 1946.

Dick, Everett. *Sod House Frontier, 1854–1890.* New York: D. Appleton-Century Company, 1938.

Durden, Robert F. *The Climax of Populism: The Election of 1896.* Lexington: University of Kentucky Press, 1965.

Dykstra, Robert R. *The Cattle Towns.* New York: Alfred A. Knopf, 1968.

Fite, Gilbert C. *The Farmers Frontier, 1865–1900.* New York: Holt, Rinehart and Winston, 1966.

Fogel, William Robert. *Railroads and American Economic Growth: Essays in Econometric History.* Baltimore: The Johns Hopkins Press, 1964.

Glad, Paul W. *The Trumpet Soundeth: William Jennings Bryan and His Democracy.* Lincoln: University of Nebraska Press, 1960.

Goldman, Eric. *Rendezvous with Destiny.* New York: Random House, 1956.

Green, Thomas L., ed. *Scottsbluff and the North Platte Valley.* Scottsbluff: The Scottsbluff Centennial Committee, 1950.

Griswold, A. Whitney. *Farming and Democracy.* New York: Harcourt, Brace and Co., 1948.

Gusfield, Joseph R. *Symbolic Crusade: Status Politics and the American Temperance Movement.* Urbana: University of Illinois Press, 1963.

Hackney, Sheldon. *Populism to Progressivism in Alabama.* Princeton: Princeton University Press, 1969.

Hays, Samuel P. *The Response to Industrialism: 1885–1915.* Chicago: University of Chicago Press, 1957.

Hibben, Paxton. *The Peerless Leader, William Jennings Bryan.* New York: Farrar and Rinehart, Inc., 1929.

Hicks, John D. *The Populist Revolt: A History of The Farmer's Alliance and People's Party.* Lincoln: University of Nebraska Press, 1961.

Higham, John. *Strangers in the Land: Patterns of American Nativism, 1860–1925.* New Brunswick, New Jersey: Rutgers University Press, 1955.

Hofstadter, Richard. *The Age of Reform, From Bryan to F.D.R.* New York: Alfred A. Knopf, 1955.

Howard, Perry H. *Political Tendencies in Louisiana, 1812–1952.* Baton Rouge: Louisiana State University, 1957.

Hunter, Floyd. *Community Power Structure.* Chapel Hill: University of North Carolina Press, 1953.

Inventory of the County Archives of Nebraska, No. 47, Howard County. St. Paul: The Nebraska Historical Records Survey, WPA, 1941.

Jensen, Richard. *The Winning of the Midwest: Social and Political Conflict, 1888–1896.* Chicago: University of Chicago Press, 1971.

Jones, Stanley L. *The Presidential Election of 1896.* Madison: University of Wisconsin Press, 1964.

Key, V. O., Jr. *Southern Politics.* New York: Vintage Books, 1949.

Kirkland, Edward C. *Industry Comes of Age: Business, Labor and Public Policy, 1860-1879.* New York: Holt, Rinehart and Winston, 1961.

Kirwan, Albert D. *Revolt of the Rednecks.* New York: Harper Torchbooks, 1951.

Kleppner, Paul. *The Cross of Culture: A Social Analysis of Midwestern Politics, 1850-1900.* New York: The Free Press, 1970.

Larsen, Lawrence H., and Glaab, Charles N. *Neenan-Menasha, Wisconsin: A Study in Urbanization and Industrialization.* Madison: University of Wisconsin Press, 1969.

Levin, Murray B. *The Alienated Voter.* New York: Holt, Rinehart and Winston, 1961.

Lipset, Seymour Martin. *Agrarian Socialism: The Cooperative Commonwealth Federation in Saskatchewan.* Berkeley: University of California Press, 1950.

Lowitt, Richard. *George W. Norris: The Making of a Progressive, 1861-1912.* New York: Syracuse University Press, 1963.

Lubell, Samuel. *The Future of American Politics.* Garden City, New York: Doubleday Anchor Books, 1955.

Luebke, Frederick C. *Immigrants and Politics: The Germans of Nebraska, 1880-1900.* Lincoln: University of Nebraska Press, 1965.

Macrae, Duncan, Jr. *Issues and Parties in Legislative Voting.* New York: Harper and Row, 1970.

Martin, Sister M. Aguinta. *The Catholic Church on the Nebraska Frontier, 1854-1885,* Studies in American Church History, XXVI. Washington, D.C.: The Catholic University Press of America, 1937.

Martin, Roscoe C. *The People's Party in Texas: A Study in Third Party Politics.* The University of Texas Bulletin, No. 3308. Austin: University of Texas, 1933.

Morearty, Edward F., Sr. *Omaha Memories.* Omaha: Swartz Printing Company, 1971.

Morton, J. Sterling, and Watkins, Albert. *History of Nebraska.* Lincoln: Western Publishing and Engraving Company, 1918.

Mullen, Arthur F. *Western Democrat.* New York: Wildred Funk, Inc., 1940.

National Cyclopedia of American Biography. New York: John T. White and Company, 1904.

Newell, LeRoy Sims. *A Hoosier Village: A Sociological Study with Special Reference to Social Causation.* Studies in History, Economic, and Public Law, Columbia University, 1912. New York: AMS Press, 1968.

North, Douglas C. *Growth and Welfare in the American Past.* Englewood Cliffs: Prentice-Hall, 1966.

Nugent, Walter T. K. *The Tolerant Populists: Kansas Populism and Nativism.* Chicago: University of Chicago Press, 1963.

Nye, Russel B. *Midwestern Progressive Politics: A Historical Study of Its Origins and Development, 1870–1950.* East Lansing: Michigan State College Press, 1951.

Hon. O. M. Kem, Publications of the Nebraska State Historical Society, IX.

Olson, James C. *History of Nebraska*. Lincoln: University of Nebraska Press, 1955.

——. *J. Sterling Morton*. Lincoln: University of Nebraska Press, 1942.

Pollack, Norman, ed. *The Populist Mind*. Indianapolis: Bobbs-Merrill, Inc., 1967.

——. *The Populist Response to Industrial America.* Cambridge: Harvard University Press, 1962.

Polsby, Nelson W. *Community Power and Political Theory.* New Haven: Yale University Press, 1963.

Ridge, Martin. *Ignatius Donnelly: The Portrait of a Politician.* Chicago: University of Chicago Press, 1962.

Rogin, Michael Paul. *The Intellectuals and McCarthy: The Radical Specter.* Cambridge, Massachusetts: The M.I.T. Press, 1967.

——, and Shorer, John L. *Political Change in California.* Westport, Connecticut: Greenwood Publishing Corporation, 1970.

Rosicky, Rose. *A History of Czechs in Nebraska.* Omaha: Czech Historical Society of Nebraska, 1929.

Rothman, David J. *Politics and Power: The United States Senate, 1869–1901.* New York: Atheneum, 1969.

Saloutos, Theodore. *Farmer Movements in the South, 1865–1933.* University of California Publications in History, LXIV. Berkeley and Los Angeles: University of California Press, 1960.

Scott, Roy V. *The Agrarian Movement in Illinois.* Urbana: University of Illinois Press, 1962.

Shannon, Fred A. *The Farmer's Last Frontier: Agriculture, 1860–1897.* New York: Farrar and Rinehart, Inc., 1945.

Sheldon, Addison E. *Nebraska: The Land and the People.* Chicago: Lewis Publishing Company, 1931. 3 vols.

Shils, Edward A. *The Torment of Secrecy.* Glencoe: The Free Press, 1956.

Shugg, Roger W. *Origins of Class Struggle in Louisiana.* Baton Rouge: Louisiana State University Press, 1939.

Smith, Page. *As a City upon a Hill.* New York: Alfred A. Knopf, 1966.

Sorenson, Alfred. *The Story of Omaha.* Omaha, 1923.

Stough, Dale P., comp. *History of Hamilton and Clay Counties, Nebraska.* Chicago: The S. J. Clark Publishing Company, 1921. 2 vols.

Taylor, Carl C. *The Farmers' Movement, 1620-1920.* New York: American Book Company, 1953.

Thompson, J. M. "Farmers' Alliance in Nebraska." *Proceedings of the Nebraska State Historical Society* (Lincoln, 1902), V.

Tilly, Charles. *The Vendée.* Cambridge: Harvard University Press, 1964.

Veblen, Thorstein. *Imperial Germany and the Industrial Revolution.* New York: Viking Press, 1939.

Wade, Richard. *The Urban Frontier: The Rise of Western Cities, 1790-1830.* Cambridge: Harvard University Press, 1959.

Watkins, Albert. *History of Nebraska.* Lincoln: Western Publishing and Engraving Company, 1913. 3 vols.

Wiebe, Robert H. *The Search for Order, 1877-1920.* New York: Hill and Wang, 1967.

Wittke, Carl. *We Who Built America: The Saga of the Immigrant.* Rev. ed. Cleveland: Press of Western Reserve University, 1964.

Wood, Asa Butler. *Fifty Years of Yesterdays.* Gering, Nebraska: Courier Press, 1959.

Woodward, C. Vann. *Tom Watson, Agrarian Rebel.* New York: The Macmillan Company, 1938.

Wylie, Laurence. *Village in the Vaucluse.* Cambridge: Harvard University Press, 1957.

Journals

Ander, O. Fritof. "The Swedish American Press and the Election of 1892." *Mississippi Valley Historical Review* 23 (March 1937): 533-554.

Argersinger, Peter H. "The Divines and the Destitute." *Nebraska History* 51 (Fall 1970): 303-318.

Atherton, Lewis E. "The Midwestern Country Town—Myth and Reality." *Agricultural History* 26 (July 1952).

Barnhart, John D. "Rainfall and the Populist Party in Nebraska." *American Political Science Review* 19 (August 1925): 527-541.

Burnet, Jean. "Town Country Relations and the Problem of Rural Leadership." *The Canadian Journal of Economics and Political Science* (August 1947): 395-397.

Coletta, Paola E. "A Tempest in a Teapot? Governor Poynter's Appointment of William V. Allen to the United States Senate." *Nebraska History* 38 (1957): 155-163.

——. "William Jennings Bryan's First Nebraska Years." *Nebraska History* 33 (1952): 111-121.

——. "Bryan's First Congressional Campaign." *Nebraska History* 37 (1956): 103-119.

——. "W. J. Bryan and the Nebraska Senatorial Election of 1893." *Nebraska History* 31 (1950): 183-203.

Derge, David R. "Metropolitan and Outstate Alignments in Illinois and Missouri Legislative Delegations." *The American Political Science Review* 52 (December 1958).

Diamond, William. "Urban and Rural Voting in 1896." *American Historical Review* 46 (January 1941): 281-305.

Dixon, Frank H. "Railroad Control in Nebraska." *Political Science Quarterly* 13 (December 1898): 617-647.

Dykstra, Robert R. "Last Days of Texas Abilene: A Study on Community Conflict on the Farmer's Frontier." *Agricultural History* 34 (1960): 107-119.

——. "Town-Country Conflict: A Hidden Dimension in American Social History." *Agricultural History* 38 (October 1964): 195-204.

Farmer, Hallie. "The Economic Background of Frontier Populism." *Mississippi Valley Historical Review* 10 (March 1924): 406-427.

Ferkiss, Victor C. "Populist Influences on American Fascism." *The Western Political Quarterly* 10 (June 1957): 350-373.

Glaab, Charles N. "Jessup W. Scott and a West of Cities." *Ohio History* 83 (Winter 1964).

——. "The Historian and the American Urban Tradition." *Wisconsin Magazine of History* 47 (Autumn 1963).

Grob, Gerald N. "The Knights of Labor, Politics and Populism." *Mid America* 29 (January 1958): 3-21.

Handlin, Oscar. "American Views of the Jew at the Opening of the Twentieth Century." *Publications of the American Jewish Historical Society* 40 (June 1951): 323-344.

Heberle, Rudolph. "On Political Ecology." *Social Forces* 29 (October 1952): 1-9.

Hicks, John D. "The Political Career of Ignatius Donnelly." *Mississippi Valley Historical Review* 8 (June 1921): 80-132.

Higgs, Robert. "Railroad Rates and the Populist Uprising." *Agricultural History* 44 (July 1970): 291-297.

Higham, John. "Another Look at Nativism." *American Catholic Historical Review* 44 (July 1958): 147-158.

——. "Anti-Semitism in the Gilded Age: A Reinterpretation." *Mississippi Valley Historical Review* 43 (March 1957): 559-578.

Jeffrey, Mary L. "Young Radicals of the Nineties." *Nebraska History* 38 (1957): 25-41.

Komarovsky, Mirra, ed. *Common Frontiers in the Social Sciences.* Glencoe, Illinois: The Free Press and Falcon Wing's Press, 1957.

Lankford, John. "Culture and Business: The Founding of the Fourth State Normal School at River Falls." *Wisconsin Magazine of History* 47 (Autumn 1963): 26-34.

Lowitt, Richard. "Populism and Politics: The Start of George W. Norris' Political Career." *Nebraska History* 42 (June 1961): 76.

Luebke, Frederick C. "Mainstreet and the Countryside: Patterns of Voting in Nebraska During the Populist Era." *Nebraska History* (Fall 1969): 257-275.

Lundberg, George. "The Demographic and Economic Basis of Political Radicalism and Conservatism." *American Journal of Sociology* 32 (March 1927): 719-732.

Malin, James C. "Notes on the Literature of Populism." *Kansas Historical Quarterly* (February 1932): 718-720.

Mercer, Samuel David. "A Republican Estimate of Party Problems in 1892," letter edited by John Higham, *Nebraska History* 33 (1952): 54-57.

Miller, Raymond C. "The Background of Populism in Kansas." *Mississippi Valley Historical Review* 11 (March 1925): 469-489.

Nixon, Herman C. "The Cleavage within the Farmers' Alliance Movement." *Mississippi Valley Historical Review* 15 (June 1928): 22-33.

———. "The Populist Movement in Iowa." *The Iowa Journal of History and Politics* 24 (1926): 3-107.

Nugent, Walter T. K. "Some Parameters of Populism." *Agricultural History* 40 (October 1966): 255-270.

Pollack, Norman. "Handlin on Anti-Semitism: A Critique of American Views of the Jew." *Journal of American History* 51 (December 1964): 391-403.

———. "Hofstadter on Populism: A Critique of the 'Age of Reform.'" *The Journal of Southern History* 26 (November 1960): 478-506.

Rosewater, Victor. "W. J. Bryan and Edward Rosewater." *Nebraska History* 13 (1932): 113-115.

Rothstein, Morton. "America in the International Rivalry for the British Wheat Market, 1860-1914." *Mississippi Valley Historical Review* 47 (December 1960).

Schmidt, Louis B. "The Internal Grain Trade of the United States, 1860-1890." *Iowa Journal of History and Politics* 19 (April 1921): 196-245.

Sellers, James L., and Harmer, Marie V. "Charles H. Van Wyck—Soldier and Statesman." *Nebraska History* 12 (1931): 81-128, 190-246, 322-373; 13 (1932): 3-36.

Sheldon, Addison E. "Nebraskans I Have Known." *Nebraska History* 19 (1938). 191-206, 331-339.

——. "Populist Recollections." *Nebraska History* 19 (1938): 45.

Shulze, Robert O., and Blumberg, Leonard U. "The Determination of Local Power Elites." *American Journal of Sociology* 63 (November 1957): 290-296.

Trask, David F. "A Note on the Politics of Populism." *Nebraska History* 46 (January 1965).

Trask, David S. "Formation and Failure: The Populist Party in Seward County, 1890-1892." *Nebraska History* 51 (Fall 1970): 281-301.

Truesdell, Leon E. "The Development of the Rural-Urban Classification in the United States: 1874-1949." *Current Population Reports*, Series P-23, no. 1.

Index

Abbott, M. J., 38, 43, 46, 53
Abrahamson, Otto, 40, 51, 115
Adams, Charles Francis, 6
Adams County, the Alliance in, 77
Agee, A. W., 40, 49-50, 73
Ainsworth, Nebraska, 116
Akers, W. P., 44
Albion, Nebraska, 116
Allen, William V., 81
Alliance, Populists:
  economic activities, 62, 68-73
  factions, 77-81, 83-85, 91
  generalization about typical
  Populist, 130-131, 145, 148
  leadership, 62, 63, 76-85, 150n
    struggle between farmer and
    villager for leadership, 83-85
  legislative behavior concerning,
  74, 131-141
    cultural issues, 136, 139, 141
    education issues, 137, 141
    interest issues, 137-138
    medical care issues, 138-139
    militia issues, 139
    railroad issues, 134, 135, 140
    state institutions, 137-138
    sugar beet promotion, 137-138
  newspapers, 71-73, 107
  organization and growth, 62
    in Cuming County, 64
    in Hamilton County, 62-63
    in Hayes County, 63

    in Kearney County, 63
    in Scotts Bluff County, 63
  political activity, 76
    in Cuming County, 83, 89
    in Custer County, 77, 78
    in Douglas County, 96
    in Hamilton County, 77, 78,
    81-85, 87, 91, 93
    in Hayes County, 82
    in Howard County, 82, 84, 95
    in Kearney County, 77, 82
    in Scotts Bluff, 83, 85, 97
  programs, 64-65
  relations with villagers, 64-75, 84
  rhetoric, 66-67. *See also* Cultural
  conflict; Politics; Reform; Rural-
  urban conflict; Structure of
  power
American, The, 104-109
American Protective Association, 12,
102, 104-111
Anti-Monopoly party, 10, 25-26, 76
Anti-Semitism, xvi, 101-102, 105,
149n
Arbor Day, 15
Auburn, Nebraska, 8-9, 116
Aurora, Nebraska:
  development by old-timers, 40
  growth of the Alliance in, 62
  interest rates in, 29
  liquor license fees, 115
  newspapers, 71

obtaining a normal school, 73-74
political structure, 49, 50
Populist editors at, 73
Populist party in, 81-82
prohibition in, 112, 116
visions of grandeur, 37
Aurora Normal Bill, 74
Aurora Sun, part in county political
structure, 49, 54-55
commenting on the Alliance,
69-70
farmers' opinions expressed in,
57-58
Avoca, Nebraska, 116
Axtell, Nebraska, 115

Bates, General Delevan, 38, 40, 42,
49-50
Bauman, Otto, 57
Beatrice, Nebraska, 25, 116
Berry, C. F., 83
Blaine, James G., 7
Bogue, Allan G., xiii, 155n26-27,
162n
Boyd, James E., 17, 84-85, 109,
113
Bromfield, Nebraska, 62
Bruner, Uriah and John, 39-40, 44,
57
Bryan, William Jennings, xv, 90-93
Burlington Railroad Company, 7,
15-16, 23, 51
Burnett, A. H., 51
Burr, George L., 71, 84
Burrows, Jay, 77-81
Butler County, Bohemian immi-
grants in, 103-104
Buzzell, J. E., 82

Cady, A. E., 52
Casper, Charles D., 55

Cedar County, 102
Central City Courier, 117
Chattel mortgages, 29
Chicago, Illinois:
shipping charges from Nebraska
to, 24-25
stockyards, favored by railroads,
24
Chicago Times, 15
Chinn, Charles, 52
Christian, Lee A., 83
Citizens Alliance, 84
Civil War, post-, in Nebraska, 3-4, 37.
See also Cultural conflict;
Politics
Cline, James A., 40
Colfax County:
Bohemian immigrants in, 103,
113
election of 1890, 118
German immigrants in, 103, 113
prohibition in, 113-114
Conspiracy, rhetoric, 65-67
Crawford, J. C., 39-40, 44, 57, 91
Creighton, John A., 113
Crete, Nebraska, 112
Crounse, Lorenzo, 90-91, 109
Cultural conflict, 101-120
anti-Semitism, xvi, 101-102, 105,
149n
immigrant adjustment, 103-104
nativists
attitudes toward immigrants,
103-105, 107
rationale, 105-106
relationship to populism, xvi,
149n
relationship to Republicans,
108-110
prohibition, 17, 56, 75, 110-119,
122, 172n, 179

relationship to populism, 52,
106-110, 125, 127, 135-136, 139,
140-141, 151n, 153n
women's suffrage, 111.
See also Politics; Voting behavior
Cuming County:
activities of "old settlers" in,
39-40
the Alliance in, 64, 69, 83
German population in, 102-103
immigrants in, 113
location, 36-37
newspapers in, 72
obtaining rail transportation, 42
political structure of, 57
prohibition in, 112-113, 116-117
Cuming County Advertiser:
on Alliance stores, 69
commenting on farmers, 46
history of, 72, 73
patriotic statements in, 104
Cuming County Progress, commenting on prohibition, 113
Curti, Merle, xvii, 150n, 160n
Custer County, the Alliance in, 77-78

Dahl, Robert A., xvi-xvii
Dannebrog, Nebraska, 52, 66
Democratic party:
cultural basis of, 14, 17, 20-21,
53, 56, 108, 113-114, 119, 151n
factions, 14-16, 19, 44, 54, 56, 57,
152n, 153n
ideology, 14-18, 54
political structure in
Cuming County, 57
Hamilton County, 54-55
Hayes County, 56
Howard County, 55-56
Kearney County, 55

Scotts Bluff County, 56
Dethlefs, John, 103-104
Doane Law, 25
Dodge County, German population
in, 102
Douglas County:
Bohemian political activity in, 104
election of 1890, 122
nativism in, 109
political trends, 1880s-1890s, 93
Driscoll, Pat H., 63, 82
Duncan, O. P., 50
Dykstra, Robert, xvii

Ebbeson, Peter, 84
Economic conditions, relationship
to populism, 123-124, 126-127, 131,
145-148, 150n, 151n, 153n, 162n,
179
Economic growth, 3, 21, 37, 41,
47, 60
Edgerton, Joseph W., 70, 81, 107
Election of:
1882, 18, 25
1884, 18, 26
1886, 110
1888, 75, 110
1890, 75, 76, 90, 108, 116,
121-122, 128, 179
1892, 90, 91, 128, 179
1894, 91, 93, 109
1896, 75, 128, 179
Elkhorn River, 43
England, Henry, 81
Ethnic groups:
Bohemian, 103, 113-114, 116-
119, 129-130, 148
Danish, 51-52, 55-56, 103, 118,
129, 130
German, 43, 102-103, 113-114,

116-119, 129, 130, 148
Irish, 103, 105-106, 113-114, 116
Polish, 51-52, 55-56, 116
Swedish, 103, 118-119, 129, 130. *See also* Cultural conflict; Politics; Voting behavior
Evans, E. L., 63

Fall, W. H., 62, 84
Farley, John J., 40, 49-50
Farmers:
    political power of, xviii, 4, 22, 35, 145-148
    unique interests of, 22, 47. *See also* Rural-urban conflict; Structure of power; Village promotion
Farmers' Alliance, 52, 80. *See also* Alliance; Village promotion
Farmers' Alliance Mutual Insurance Company, in Hamilton County, 69
Farmers' Canal Company, 44
Feltham, Lot L., 115
Floyd, L. C., 62
Frederick, J. I., 72
Fusion:
    Alliance with Democrats, 54, 56
    Anti-Monopolists and Democrats, 54
    Populists with Democrats, 83-85, 90-91, 93

Gallagher, Paxton, 71
Gardner, O. W., 42
Genoa, Nebraska, 79
Gentzke, M. O., 104
George, Milton, 80

Gere, Charles H., 7
Gering Building and Loan Association, 42
Gering Courier:
    attacking the Democrats, 113-114
    commenting on rural-village conflict, 69
    connecting the Alliance with prohibition, 117-118
    promoting agriculture, 44, 45
Gering Land Company, 44
Gering, Martin, 38, 42
Gering, Nebraska:
    the Alliance in, 63
    irrigation and beet production in, 44-45
    political structure of, 52-53
    prohibition issue in, 56, 112, 115
    real estate boom, 42
Gibbon, Nebraska, 116
Glover, A. N., William, and C. R., 40, 54, 91
Godfrey, George B., 51
Gougar, Helen, 111
Grand Army of the Republic, 4
Grand Island Independent, 109
Grand Island, Nebraska, 25, 45, 74-75
Grand Island Sugar Beet Company, 74-75
Grange, xv, 8, 15, 25, 76
Granger, 107
Greeley County, 103
Greenback party, xv, 76
Grosvenor, J. H., 84
Gulf of Mexico, proposed railroad to, 43, 51
Gumaer, Alfred W., 52
Guttman scaling, 132, 134

Hackney, Sheldon, xvi
Hainer, Edward J., 40, 44, 49-50, 116
Hall County, German population in, 102
Hamilton County:
    Alliance economic activity in, 69
    attracting settlers, 42
    creameries, 44
    Democratic party in, 54-55
    farmers' frustrations in, 57-58
    growth of the Alliance, 62, 78
    location of, 36-37
    mortgages in, 28
    obtaining a normal school, 73-74
    political structure, 48-50
    political trends, 1870s-1890s, 93
    Populist party in, 76-79, 81-82, 83-85, 129
    promotional activities, 38, 40
Hamilton County News, 47
Hamilton County Register:
    acceptance by Populists, 84
    attacking beet refineries, 74
    on immigrants, 105
    on Jews, 101
    origins, 71
    Populist rhetoric in, 66-67
    on prohibition, 114-115
Hamilton County Republican, 40, 48-50, 70
Hamilton, J. M., 72
Hampton, Nebraska, 50, 62
Hannibal, Rasmus, 52
Hart, W. D., 43
Harvey, Robert, 52
Hastings, L. W., 40, 49
Hastings, Nebraska, 25
Hawes, I. W., 55

Hayes Center, Nebraska:
    place in county political structure, 53
    prohibition in, 56, 112, 116
    promotional activities, 44
    railroad, 42-43
Hayes County:
    the Alliance in, 29, 63, 68-69, 82-83
    fusion in, 56-57
    location, 35-37
    mortgages in, 27-28
    political structure, 40-41, 53
    prohibition in, 56, 116
    promotional activities, 38
Hayes County Herald, 47
Hayes County Republican, 38, 53, 64, 66
Hecox, T. E., 82
Hicks, John D., xvi, 122, 147, 149n, 150n
Hildebrand, J. O. P., 55-56
Hines, Pat A., 55
Historiography:
    liberal-progressive interpretation of populism, xvi, xvii, 145-148, 149n, 150n, 156n
    revisionist interpretations, xvi, 149n, 150n, 151n
Hitchcock, Gilbert M., 90-91
Hofstadter, Richard, xvi, 147
Holcomb, Silas A., 81, 91-93
Holdrege, C. M., 23
Holt County, 103
Homestead Act, 27
Horn, Valentine, 62, 82
Howard County:
    the Alliance in, 82
    Democratic party in, 55-56

founding of, 38-39
fusion in, 56-57
immigrants in, 103, 113
locations, 36-37
newspapers, 72, 84
People's party in, 66
political structure, 51-52
political trends, 1880s-1890s, 93, 118
prohibition in, 113, 116
Howard, F. M., 79
Howe, Church, 6, 8-10
Hughes, M. J., 57
Hull, Joel, 38, 40, 43, 50-51, 115
Hurlbut, E. W., 54

Ingersoll, E. P., 25
Ingersolls, Bob, 111
Interest rates, 9, 28-30, 60, 67-69, 124, 126, 127, 155n26-27, 153n.
    See also Bogue, Allan G.
Iowa, prohibition in, 112
Iowa Maximum Rate Law of 1874, 26
Ivey, J. W., 63

Jefferson, Thomas, 146
Jensen, Richard J., xxii, 151n
Jews, and the Populists, 101-102.
    See also Cultural conflict

Kearney County:
    the Alliance in, 63, 69, 82, 118
    Democratic party in, 55
    founding of, 38-39
    fusion in, 56-57
    immigrant groups in, 103
    location, 36-37
    newspapers, 72, 84
    People's party in, 76-77

political structure, 50-51
power structure, 40
prohibition in, 118
the railroad and, 43
Kearney County Democrat, 55
Kearney County Gazette:
    place in county political struc-
    ture, 50-51
    political stance, 72
    on prohibition, 112, 117
    the railroads and, 43
Kearney, Nebraska, 25, 37, 41
Keith County, 29
Kellie, J. T., 63, 82
Kelly, W. C., 104
Kem, Omar M., 28, 65-66, 77, 78-79, 81
Kent, Lewis A., 40, 51
King, Judge J. M., 83
Kleppner, Paul, 151n, 153n, 173n
Knights of Labor, 107, 139
Koontz, Jasper, 63, 82
Kountz, Herman, 112
Krick, Edward, 63, 82

Lease, Mary Elizabeth, xv
Lincoln, Nebraska, xv, 7, 42, 45, 48, 136, 137
Lubell, Samuel, 119
Luebke, Frederick C., 150n, 153n, 165n, 173n

Madison County, 102
Majors, Thomas J., 91-93, 109-110
Malin, James, 123
Manderson, Charles F., 26, 45
Marquette, Nebraska, 50
Martin, Roscoe, 130
Maximum Freight Act, 62

Maycock, Joseph, 84-85
McCarty, T. F., 82
McCook, Nebraska, 41, 45
McFarlane, Peter, 42
McKeighan, William A., 81
McPheeley, James L., 43, 51
McShane, John A., 113
Methodology:
    correlation analysis, 121-122,
    174n
    criteria for selection of sample
    counties, 35-37
    determination of leadership and
    structure of power, 150n, 157n,
    158n, 160n, 161n
    general statement, xvii, xviii,
    150n
    legislative roll call analysis,
    131-132, 174-176n
    rural-urban classification, 156n,
    157n
Miller, Dr. George L., 14, 16-17, 112
Minden Gazette, 67, 72
Minden, Nebraska:
    Democratic party in, 55
    founding of, 38-39
    political structure, 50-51
    power structure, 40
    prohibition in, 11, 115-116
Missouri Pacific Railway Company,
6, 9-10
Morearty, A. B., 108
Morton, J. Sterling, 7, 14-18, 85,
90-91, 109

Nance County, 58-59
Nebraska asylum, 11
Nebraska Institution for the Feeble
Minded, 138
Nebraska, railroad rates, 23-27.
    See also Railroads, and rates

Nebraska State Journal, 7
Nebraska Volksblatt, 104
Neligh, John D., 37, 39-40, 42, 44,
57
Newberry, Fred, 62, 71, 74, 81
Newberry Maximum Rate Bill, 84
New Deal, xv-xvi
Norfolk, Nebraska, 45, 104, 116
North Platte, Nebraska, 116
North Platte Valley, 44-45
Northwestern Railroad, 43
Nugent, Walter T. K., xvi, 150n

Oak, Nebraska, 71
Oakes, Henry, 83
"Old settlers," 39, 49-50
Omaha Bee, 5, 10-11, 53
Omaha, Nebraska:
    immigrant groups in, 103-104
    John Thurston and, 5-7
    legislators, 136-137
    nativism in, 12, 105-106
    political activity, 48, 104, 108-
    109
    prohibition in, 111-112, 117
    shipping complaints, 24-25
    visions of grandeur, 37
Omaha Republican, 7
Omaha World Herald:
    and Bryan, 91
    on Church Howe, 10
    on county debt, 30
    on immigrant groups, 105
    on Populist "calamity howling,"
    67-68
Ord, Nebraska, 116
Orleans, Nebraska, 116
Osceola, Nebraska, 116
O'Sullivan, P. F., 57
Otoe County, 6
Oxnard, Henry T., 45, 74-75

Parker, Henry C., 82
Paul brothers, 38-39, 52
People's party. *See* Alliance
Peru Normal School, 11
Phelps County, 103
Phillips, Nebraska, 50, 62
Piasecki, x, 55-56
Pierce County, 102
Pietists. *See* Cultural conflict;
Voting behavior
Plainview, Nebraska, 116
Platte County, 102
Politics:
    cultural basis of, 4, 14, 17, 18-21,
    113-114, 119, 127-128, 151n,
    153n, 172n
    economic basis of, 4, 5, 14, 18,
    21, 57, 93, 131, 153n
    factional basis of, 5, 7, 11
    ideological basis of, 6, 7, 54
    pluralistic nature of, 4, 3-21
    role of Civil War, 4, 21.
    See also Alliance; Democratic
    party; Republican party; Rural-
    urban conflict; Village promotion
Poppleton, Andrew Jackson, 6
Populism. *See* Alliance
Populist Revolt, The, xvi, 122, 147,
149n, 150n
Powers, John B.:
    election of 1894, 91-93
    mollifying urbanites, 70
    nativism and, 106
    political career, 77-81
    prohibition and, 102, 118
Poynter, William A., 81
Prices, 24, 27, 30-31, 60-61, 154n
Progressive movement, xvi, 75

Railroads, and:
    economic growth, 8, 23

    passes, 8
    political power, 10, 25
    rates, 22-27, 43, 60, 154n, 179
    regulation, 8-10, 15, 25-27, 55,
    133-135, 164n
Real estate boom, 41
Reform:
    prior to Populism, 54-55, 64-65,
    76-78, 109, 140-141
    village advocacy of, 9, 39, 46,
    53, 147-148, 164n, 168n
        concurrent with populism,
        136-141, 147, 148, 161n,
        162n
    village fear of Populist reforms,
    53-54
    village middle class, pro-
    motion of
        agriculture, 137-138
        cultural pluralism, 136,
        139-141
        education, 137, 141
        medical care, 138 139
        state institutions, 137-138
    See also Alliance; Republican
    party, factions; Rosewater,
    Edward; Village promotion
Republican Advocate, 52
Republican party:
    factions, 5, 12, 17, 78-79, 109, 152n
    party structure in
        Hamilton County, 48-50
        Hayes County, 53
        Howard County, 51-52
        Kearney County, 50-51
        Scotts Bluff County, 52-53
Rice Index of Cohesion, 132
Richards, Lucius D., 46, 85, 113,
116
Ritualists. *See* Cultural conflict;
Voting behavior

Rosewater, Edward:
    the Alliance and, 78-79, 152n
    The American and, 109
    conflict with villagers, 53-54
    election of 1892, 90
    election of 1894, 91-93
    feud with Church Howe, 9
    feud with John Thurston, 6-7
    political career, 10-12
    prohibition and, 112
    the railroads and, 5
Rural-urban conflict:
    "calamity howling," 67-68, 163n
    difference of interests between
        farmers and villagers, 22, 31, 35,
        46-47
    discussion of, 145-148
    farmer criticism of village in-
        terests, 21, 56-58, 65, 68-69,
        164-165n
    method of rural-urban classifica-
        tion, 156n-157n.
    villager criticism of farmers,
        xviii, 67-68, 73-74. *See also*
        Reform; Structure of power;
        Village promotion; Voting be-
        havior

St. Clair, Robert, 55
St. Paul, Nebraska:
    founding of, 38-39
    political structure, 51-52
    prohibition in, 112
    "ring," 52, 56
    village role in political structure,
        55-56
Saint Paul Phonograph, 52, 64, 72
St. Raynor, Henry, 44, 113
Saline County, 103
Sarpy County, 102

Saunders County, 103
Sayre, Edward W., 42
Schoville, D. A., 49-50
Schuyler Sun, 114
Scotts Bluff County:
    the Alliance in, 63, 69
    irrigation and beet production
        in, 44-45
    location, 35-36
    political structure, 52-53
    power structure, 40-41
    promotional activities, 38
    the railroads and, 43
    real estate boom, 42
Severy, M. H., 79
Sidney, Nebraska, 44-45
Slocumb High License Bill, 110,
    113, 115, 117
Spanogle, A. J., 40
Springfield, Nebraska, 116
Sproll, Reverend B., 114-115
Standard Oil Company, 70-71
Stanley, N. F., 49-50
Stanton County, 102
Stark, W. L., 84
State Agricultural Society, 15, 31,
    131n
State Board of Transportation, 26
Structure of power:
    economic leaders, 37-39, 41-42,
        48, 53
    methodology, xvii, xviii, 150n
    "rings," 50-53, 56-59
    village domination of politics,
        31, 41, 48-49, 50-52, 57-59,
        133, 145-148; variations, 40, 51.
        See also Democratic party; Re-
        publican party; Rural-urban
        conflict; Village promotion
Sutton Advertiser, 67

Sutton, Nebraska, 116
Swedish Farmers' Mutual Fire Insurance Company of Cuming and Burt counties, 69

Talmadge, Nebraska, 116
Tariff, 9, 16-18, 54
Taxes, 60
Tecumseh, Nebraska, 116
Thayer, John M., 4
Thompson, John C., 104
Thurston, John M., 5-7, 12, 109
Trask, David S., xii, 151n
Turner Thesis, 122
    equality of office holding, 52
    leadership, 37-39, 160n
    relationship to populism, xvi, 146-148
    settlement process, 37-39.
    See also Curti, Merle; Rural-urban conflict; Structure of power; Village promotion

Union Labor party, 56, 77, 83
Union Pacific Railroad Company, 6, 16, 23
University of Nebraska, 45

Valentine, E. K., 44, 57
Van Wyck, Charles H.:
    the Alliance and, 78-81
    election of 1892, 91
    election of 1894, 91-93
    nativism and, 107, 109
    Rosewater and, 10-12
Village promotion, 37-47, 145, 159n
    as a characteristic of the era, 37
    in Cuming County, 37, 39, 42-44
    in Hamilton County, 38, 40, 42, 44

    in Hayes County, 38, 40, 42, 44
    in Kearney County, 38, 40
    in Scotts Bluff County, 38, 40, 42-44
    primacy of, 26
    profits from, 42
    promotion of
        agriculture, 15, 31, 44-45, 74-75, 153n
        irrigation, 44
        manufacturing, 37, 43, 44
        railroads, 8, 42, 44
        state institutions, 6, 7, 46, 73-74, 137-141
Vorhes, J. T., 81-82
Voting behavior:
    Bohemian, 20, 118-119, 129-130
    Catholic, 14, 18, 20-21, 107, 110, 129
    Danish, 51-52, 55, 118, 129
    Democratic, 14, 18-21, 55, 92
    German, 20, 107, 118-119, 128, 130, 171n
    Irish, 20
    Polish, 51-52, 55
    Populist, 85-87, 90, 92-93, 110, 129
    Republican, 12-14, 18, 88, 92-93
    rural-urban, 75, 129-130
    statistical analysis of, 121-131
    Swedish, 118-119, 129

Wayne County, 102
Wayne, Nebraska, 116
Weaver, James B., 130
Westervelt, James, 42
West Point Building and Loan, 42
West Point, Nebraska:
    development, 39-40, 43-44
    German immigrants in, 104
    political structure, 57